POVERTY IN BRITAIN, 1900–1965

Social History in Perspective
General Editor: Jeremy Black

Social History in Perspective is a series of in-depth studies of
the many topics in social, cultural and religious history.

PUBLISHED

John Belchem   *Popular Radicalism in Nineteenth-Century Britain*
Sue Bruley   *Women in Britain Since 1900*
Anthony Brundage   *The English Poor Laws, 1700–1930*
Simon Denith   *Society and Cultural Forms in Nineteenth-Century England*
Joyce M. Ellis   *The Georgian Town, 1680–1840*
Peter Fleming   *Family and Household in Medieval England*
Ian Gazeley   *Poverty in Britain, 1900–1965*
Kathryn Gleadle   *British Women in the Nineteenth Century*
Harry Goulbourne   *Race Relations in Britain since 1945*
Anne Hardy   *Health and Medicine in Britain since 1860*
Tim Hitchcock   *English Sexualities, 1700–1800*
Sybil M. Jack   *Towns in Tudor and Stuart Britain*
Helen M. Jewell   *Education in Early Modern England*
Alan Kidd   *State, Society and the Poor in Nineteenth-Century England*
Arthur J. McIvor   *A History of Work in Britain, 1880–1950*
Hugh McLeod   *Religion and Society in England, 1850–1914*
Donald M. MacRaild   *Irish Migrants in Modern Britain, 1750–1922*
Donald M. MacRaild and David E. Martin   *Labour in Britain, 1830–1914*
Christopher Marsh   *Popular Religion in the Sixteenth Century*
Michael A. Mullett   *Catholics in Britain and Ireland, 1558–1829*
Richard Rex   *The Lollards*
George Robb   *British Culture and the First World War*
R. Malcolm Smuts   *Culture and Power in England, 1585–1685*
John Spurr   *English Puritanism, 1603–1689*
W.B. Stephens   *Education in Britain, 1750–1914*
Heather Swanson   *Medieval British Towns*
David Taylor   *Crime, Policing and Punishment in England, 1750–1914*
N.L. Tranter   *British Population in the Twentieth Century*
Ian D. Whyte   *Migration and Society in Britain, 1550–1830*
Ian D. Whyte   *Scotland's Society and Economy in Transition, c.1500–c.1760*
Andy Wood   *Riot, Rebellion and Popular Politics in Early Modern England*

Please note that a sister series, *British History in Perspective*, is available,
covering key topics in British political history.

Social History in Perspective
Series Standing Order
ISBN 0–333–71694–9 hardcover
ISBN 0–333–69336–1 paperback
(*outside North America only*)

You can receive future titles in this series as they are published by placing
a standing order. Please contact your bookseller or, in case of difficulty,
write to us at the address below with your name and address, the title
of the series and the ISBN quoted above.
Customer Services Department, Macmillan Distribution Ltd
Houndmills, Basingstoke, Hampshire RG21 6XS, England

Poverty in Britain, 1900–1965

Ian Gazeley

First published 2003 by
PALGRAVE MACMILLAN
Houndmills, Basingstoke, Hampshire RG21 6XS and
175 Fifth Avenue, New York, N.Y. 10010
Companies and representatives throughout the world

PALGRAVE MACMILLAN is the global academic imprint of the Palgrave
Macmillan division of St. Martin's Press, LLC and of Palgrave Macmillan Ltd.
Macmillan® is a registered trademark in the United States, United Kingdom
and other countries. Palgrave is a registered trademark in the European
Union and other countries.

ISBN 0–333–71618–3 hardback
ISBN 0–333–71619–1 paperback

This book is printed on paper suitable for recycling and made from fully
managed and sustained forest sources.

A catalogue record for this book is available from the British Library.

Library of Congress Cataloging in Publication Data
Gazeley, Ian.
    Poverty in Britain, 1900–1965 / Ian Gazeley.
        p.   cm. — (Social history in perspective)
    Includes bibliographical references and index.
    ISBN 0–333–71618–3 (cloth)
    1. Poverty—Great Britain—History—20th century.   2. Poor—Great
    Britain—History—20th century.   I. Title.   II. Social history in
    perspective (Palgrave (Firm))

HC260.P6 G39 2003
339.4'6'094109041—dc21

                                                                    2002035693

10   9   8   7   6   5   4   3   2   1
12   11   10   09   08   07   06   05   04   03

Printed in China

For Karen

CONTENTS

LIST OF TABLES

ACKNOWLEDGEMENTS

This book grew out of work undertaken with two separate co-authors, Andy Newell and Pat Thane. Both also provided invaluable advice on particular aspects of poverty addressed in this book. Several colleagues at Sussex were also very supportive, Carol Dyhouse and Alun Howkins in particular. I also owe a debt to two long-term mentors, Nick Crafts and Tim Hatton. Part of the material on wages and earnings is taken from the results of a project funded by the ESRC and I gratefully acknowledge the research support provided by ESRC grant R000221394. I would also like to acknowledge the trustees of the Mass-Observation Archive, University of Sussex. Of course, all errors are mine alone.

INTRODUCTION

'Do not trouble your head with social problems; what is wrong with the poor is poverty,' or so wrote George Bernard Shaw.[1] It has also been observed that 'there is no "true" measure of poverty', so it is important to be clear what is being addressed in this book.[2] It is concerned with the material conditions of poor people in Britain in the first 60 years of the twentieth century. It focuses on the period of British history when investigations of poverty were carried out on the basis of determining people's ability to meet a set of defined basic needs. Often, these surveys and their most famous proponents, Booth, Rowntree and Bowley, are seen as trying to measure something called 'absolute poverty'. But this is not the case.[3] The standards of basic needs used to define the poverty-line income are not absolute in any scientific sense. Only the food necessary to avoid starvation, and ultimately death, can be determined in this way.[4] Not only is the food component of these poverty lines above starvation levels, but they also incorporate allowances for non-food consumption for which there are no extrinsic minimum standards.[5]

The extent to which the food component of a poverty line is above starvation level and the allowance that is made for non-food items determines the extent of social participation implied in the investigators' definition of poverty. This allowance might be very small, in which case the poverty line could be described as a 'subsistence' measure. These usually have a food allowance that will cheaply satisfy some desired extrinsic consumption standard in terms of energy and nutrient intakes plus a sum to cover expenditure on other basic needs, such as housing, clothing, fuel and light. The most famous example of this approach, and the starting point of our analysis, is Rowntree's *Poverty: A Study of Town Life*, first published in 1901. Clearly, the 'minimum' sum necessary to cover these basic needs is socially determined and will change over time in response to changing expectations of poverty. Even the 'minimum'

1

food component is liable to change over time in relation to improvements in nutritional knowledge. Subsistence definitions of poverty are, therefore, relative measures. As Townsend and Wedderburn wrote, 'when Galbraith himself described an affluent society as one in which "wants are increasingly created by the process by which they are satisfied", such an interest was already heralded. Definitions of "needs" cannot fail to be influenced by current standards of wants.'[6]

Alternatively, the poverty-line measure might include a more generous allowance for housing, clothing, fuel and light and be based on a varied diet that easily satisfied contemporaneous dietary standards. It might also include an allowance for travel, leisure activities, a holiday and the occasional alcoholic drink. Under these circumstances, the poverty line includes an allowance that is designed to meet the needs of social participation.[7] This is most clearly a social construction and provides testimony, if any were needed, to the relative nature of the concept. Rowntree's second social survey, *Poverty and Progress*, which was first published in 1941, was based on a revised 'Human Needs' standard that explicitly included an allowance for social participation. Exactly when a poverty line stops being a subsistence measure and starts being a social participation measure is unanswerable objectively, of course.[8] In consequence, perhaps, the relationship between Rowntree's subsistence and social participatory standards, and what this conceptual change means for the measurement of poverty, has generated a fair amount of disagreement. However, one way of evaluating different relative poverty measures is to consider their relationship to per capita income, and how this has changed over time.[9]

Nearly all textbooks on the economic and social history of Britain during the twentieth century refer to the results of Rowntree's 1899 survey of York, and his subsequent inquiries. There are, however, a great number of poverty surveys carried out prior to the Second World War. Most of these rely upon the methodology devised by Arthur Bowley. While Bowley himself was clearly influenced by Rowntree's first survey of York, it was Bowley's poverty line that was adopted (with some modification) in London, Merseyside, Sheffield, Southampton and Bristol during the 1930s. Collectively, these regional surveys form a substantial body of inquiry, the results of which are less frequently reported.

During the 1960s, these 'minimum needs' poverty lines (whether subsistence or social participatory) became unfashionable. This seems partly because they were wrongly interpreted as an attempt to specify an absolute standard, but also for ideological reasons.[10] As Bradshaw *et al.*

argue, 'Townsend and Abel-Smith condemned the value judgements they saw clothed in objective criteria of the primary poverty definition developed by Rowntree and employed by Beveridge.'[11] Townsend was to go on to develop a distinct conceptual approach based on indicators of relative deprivation.[12] But in the 1960s, the alternative to the minimum needs poverty line was an approach based on comparison of income with the contemporaneous level of state benefit, as exemplified in Abel-Smith and Townsend's *The Poor and the Poorest* in 1965. This marks the end of the period in which the minimum needs poverty-line approach dominated the empirical investigation of poverty in Britain. It is also where this book ends.

The minimum needs methodology was important in this period for another reason. In 1942 Beveridge recommended a series of reforms to existing social policies, including reform to the benefit paid for unemployment, sickness and during retirement. Both Rowntree and Bowley advised the Beveridge Committee, and Beveridge's recommendations follow a minimum needs conception of poverty (whether these were sufficient for subsistence or enough to allow for social participation is a disputed issue). The Beveridge Report forms the basis of the post-war reform to the welfare state and although National Assistance benefits are not identical to those recommended in the report, they were clearly initially based on a minimum needs conception of poverty. And it is this standard, increased partly to reflect changes in prices and partly government social policy objectives, that forms the benchmark in *The Poor and the Poorest*.

Twentieth-century minimum needs investigations need to be interpreted carefully within the context of the prevailing ideology, but it is the implicit argument of this book that it would be wrong to dismiss the results of these surveys for they do illuminate both the extent and causes of poverty in Britain at this time. As Sen writes, 'To ignore such information as hunger and hardship is not just abstinence from "pseudo-scientific accuracy", but is blindness to important parameters of the common understanding of poverty.'[13] Bradshaw *et al.* recently cite a number of different uses of minimum needs standards: (1) they can provide standard of living norms for a given family type, (2) they can be used to make comparisons of living standards over time, (3) they can be used to make comparisons of living standards between regions. The material collected for minimum needs investigations, such as records of household expenditure, can also be used to derive 'standardised comparisons of living standards' for different family types (in other words, equivalence

scales between different household types).[14] In fact, one of the features
of minimum needs poverty-line investigation that often gets overlooked
is that the investigator defines the comparison of living standards for
different family types by imposing an equivalence scale. Empirically, which
equivalence scale is used can make a substantial difference to judgements
about the extent of poverty and, by implication, its causes.

The disadvantages of the minimum needs poverty-line approach are
also well known, though the observation that 'they are not objective'
is not one of them. Nearly all of the investigations carried out in Britain
between 1901 and 1965 were simple headcount measures of poverty.[15]
That is, in such and such a town, x per cent of people were without the
income to provide minimum needs. As Sen points out, this tells us nothing
about the extent of the shortfall in income of those below the poverty
line and has the perverse characteristic of being insensitive to a transfer
of income from poor to rich.[16] Somewhat surprisingly perhaps, at least
one survey of poverty in interwar Britain also provides information on
the distribution of incomes above and below the poverty line.[17] Such
considerations are also important in the context of twentieth-century
social policy because Beveridge believed that it was possible to have
a universal system of insurance, based on income transfers within the
working class, which would reduce 'want'.[18]

There is another type of investigation, related to the minimum needs
poverty-line approach, which provides information on the material
conditions of the poor during the first half of the twentieth century.
The direct investigation of the nutritional adequacy of diets provides
evidence on the extent of malnutrition, often carried out using the same
extrinsic dietary standards used in poverty-line inquiries. Detailed data
on nutritional attainment and some anthropometrical data were collected
in small-scale studies both before and immediately after the First World
War. The largest survey carried out towards the end of the interwar
period, by Boyd-Orr, suggested that nearly half the population had
diets that were inadequate with respect to one or more nutrients, and
a smaller proportion had a diet that was seriously deficient.[19] From 1940
the Ministry of Food initiated its own surveys of the nation's diet and the
information collected by the National Food Survey reveals significant
changes in the incidence and pattern of malnutrition across the Second
World War. Of course, between 1900 and the end of the 1950s, the
dietary standards applied changed considerably too, as the importance
of vitamins and minerals was discovered and then the detrimental affect
of high-fat diets was observed.

These surveys share one of the difficulties of headcount, income-based, poverty-line measures when applied to families, however, since both assume that the distribution of resources is optimal within households. These should be seen as two alternative conceptions of poverty, according to Sen. The difference between them is that the direct method identifies those who fail to attain a prescribed consumption standard (in this case a dietary one). The income method identifies those who do not have the ability to meet this standard.[20]

The investigation of working-class diet was in its heyday either side of the First World War. During this period, there were a number of dietary inquiries that owed much to the methods developed by Dr J. C. Paton. Most of these surveys relied upon an understanding of nutritional science that was itself in its infancy. In consequence, many of the conclusions drawn by Paton and his co-researchers, regarding the inadequacy of working-class diets, would not now be sustainable. Taking a longer perspective, the Second World war was the great watershed in the history of nutritional inequality in Britain. Prior to this conflict there was a pronounced class gradient in the adequacy of diets. During the war, and in the years of peace that followed, most Britons' diets satisfied contemporaneous recommended dietary standards. This was partly a result of wartime social policy (rationing), but also due to increased incomes and continuous employment for most working people after 1940.

Data on morbidity and mortality have been used to infer changes in the health of particular groups over time and between regions. For the first half of the century, historians have argued over how to interpret movements in mortality levels, especially infant and maternal mortality indices, but possibly the most difficult question has been to try to establish whether mass unemployment in interwar Britain led to a deterioration in health. Attempting to establish a causal link between unemployment and ill health is problematic, because ill health is also associated with poverty and unemployment and poverty are highly correlated.[21] In addition, much of the official data on morbidity have been shown to be unreliable prior to the Second World War. There are also good reasons, relating to the administration of benefit, why people would want to be classified as sick rather than unemployed – though the reverse may also have been true for individuals with dependants.[22]

This book is organised chronologically. The first two chapters are concerned with the period between the turn of the twentieth century and the end of the First World War. The following two address the interwar period and the final two chapters consider the period between the beginning of the Second World War and the early 1960s. For each of these three sub-periods, the analysis and description of poverty investigation are contextualised within a broad framework that examines changes in real incomes, employment and occupation. Important changes in social policy are also discussed, not least because of their obvious likely impact on poverty.[23]

Most of the material discussed in this book relates to the material condition of poor working-class families. It is unashamedly a 'materialist' thesis. It is not concerned with cultural changes and the way in which these have undoubtedly affected people's standards of living during the century or the political dimension to changes in living standards.[24]

1

VICTORIAN LEGACY

Introduction

At the beginning of the twentieth century Britain was easily still the richest country in Europe, as measured by per capita income, and wage earners' income had been rising steadily for at least a generation.[25] Although historians have debated the impact of industrialisation on the well-being of the population at length during the eighteenth and first half of the nineteenth century, there has been relatively little disagreement about working-class living standards in the period between 1870 and 1914. It is tempting to believe that the explanation for the general consensus of opinion is simply that the quantitative indicators of workers' living standards, and specifically the real wage series, suggest that there was unquestionable improvement in the standard of life for most people.

But set against the background of real wage amelioration, there is a considerable body of contemporary evidence that indicates that the poorest sections of Victorian society were experiencing serious impoverishment and destitution. The results of pioneer social investigators' research are rehearsed in all textbooks, yet the impression given by Booth or Rowntree's findings that a constant 30 per cent of the population of London and York were in poverty, rests uneasily juxtaposed with the evidence on the behaviour of average real wages, as Ashworth was to note:

'The great Victorian Boom', 'the good years', and even more gilded labels have been attached to the third quarter of the nineteenth century. But then even a summary account has to move forward only

7

a very few years, recognise that a falling cost of living was easing the condition of the masses, and yet draw attention to 'the submerged tenth' (or larger fraction) and refer to the hundreds of thousands living 'below the poverty line', i.e. without the means to buy enough neces-sities to keep themselves physically healthy.[26]

The aim of this chapter is to consider the extent to which progress did, in fact, encompass groups at the bottom of the earnings distribution: specifically, urban labourers and agricultural workers. There were a number of investigations of poverty carried out in Britain prior to the Great War, although Rowntree's is far the best known. His investigation of poverty in York at the turn of the century is central to this narrative for two reasons. First, Rowntree's application of a poverty line, which he used to determine the numbers in York without the income necessary to purchase basic needs, had a dramatic influence on most subsequent empirical investigation of poverty for over half a century. Bowley modi-fied Rowntree's poverty line measure, and nearly all investigations of poverty in the interwar period apply Bowley's standard, with little or no further modification, but it was Rowntree who was responsible for devising the method. Second, any attempt to resolve the apparent paradox noted by Ashworth requires a critical evaluation of the findings of pre-war poverty surveys. These investigations also reveal important facts about the nature and causes of poverty in Britain, which will be considered in Chapter 2.

1.1   Occupational Class

Before we examine the behaviour of real incomes, it is necessary to consider the extent of class stratification in Britain before the First World War. At the time of the 1911 population census, there were just over 12.9 million men and 5.4 million women 'economically active'. As Table 1.1 shows, based on the Goldthorpe class classification, the vast majority of these men and women were in manual occupations: 73.6 per cent of all 'economically active' men and 76.7 per cent of all 'economically active' women were so defined.[27] While there is good reason to believe that the original census returns that Goldthorpe based his classification upon underestimate female employment in 1911, these figures serve as a rough guide to the relative size of the working class in Britain in the period before the First World War. They indicate that the

Table 1.1   Distribution of economically active population in 1911

	Males	Females
Self-employed and higher-grade professionals	1.5	1.0
Employers and proprietors	7.7	4.3
Administrators and managers	3.9	2.3
Lower-grade salaried professionals and technicians	1.4	5.8
Inspectors, supervisors and foremen	1.8	0.2
Clerical workers	5.1	3.3
Sales personnel and shop assistants	5.0	6.4
Skilled manual workers	33.0	24.6
Semi-skilled manual workers	29.1	47.0
Unskilled manual workers	11.5	5.1
Total	100	100

Source: A. H. Halsey, *Change in British Society*, 4th edn (1995), Table 2.1, pp. 40–1.

manual working class was about 75 per cent of the economically active population.[28] From Table 1.1, it can be seen that 11.5 per cent of economically active men and about 5.1 per cent of women were in unskilled manual occupations. A further 29.1 per cent of economically active men, and 47 per cent of women, were in semi-skilled manual work, and about one-third of all men and one-quarter of economically active women were employed in skilled manual work. The vast majority of manual workers, therefore, worked in an occupation requiring the application of a skill of one sort or another.

Depending on family size, the condition of the local labour market and life cycle stage, some of the families with adults in these occupational classes would have been regarded by contemporaries as being in 'poverty'. Exactly what they might have meant by this description, we will come to in a moment, but at this stage it is also important to remember that there were other groups of people, who were not 'economically active', who might also have been regarded as being in 'poverty' by contemporaries. The most obvious would be found among the elderly, many of whom would no longer be part of the formal labour market as enumerated by census returns. About 5 per cent of the population of England and Wales were over 65 years old, the majority of which were female. According to the Hamilton Committee's findings in 1900, the proportion of old people in rural areas was typically greater than in urban areas. Relatives or friends maintained fewer than one in five old people. Two out of five men and nearly one-half of all old women claimed to have an income of less than 10 shillings per week, and just over 15 per cent of men and a little more than 27 per cent of women were, or had been, in receipt of poor relief.[29] In total, there were nearly 0.89 million people receiving poor relief in 1911, either in workhouses or in the form of outdoor relief from their parish, a significant proportion of whom were elderly.[30]

1.2   State Provision

As a last resort, it was possible to seek assistance from the parish under the poor law, but help from an official agency was testimony to desperation. Citizens were expected to make provision for their own needs and those that were unable to do so survived with help from families and neighbours or from charity afforded by the better off. According to Fraser, the social philosophy of Victorian Britain was based upon 'four great tenets: work, thrift, respectability and above all self-help'.[31] Although philanthropy and voluntarism were increasingly important for providing assistance to the Victorian poor, preventing many from experiencing the degradation of the workhouse, for most philanthropists the real purpose of charity was to try and engineer the moral improvement of the poor. The Charity Organisation Society (COS), which was founded in 1869, is a good example. Although the COS tried to assist those that could become independent, and pioneered casework methods, its early leaders were 'rigorously traditional' and the COS was 'one of the staunchest defenders of the self-help individualist ethic'.[32] As much as this type of philanthropic activity was important in purely monetary terms, it would be wrong to think of transfers as being entirely from rich to poor. The poor also helped each other, on the basis that they might themselves rely upon similar help. The part played by working-class self-help organisations, such as friendly societies and the Co-operative movement, were important in this context. By the 1870s, friendly societies had 4 million members, with benefits that varied from provision of a decent burial to more ambitious medical and unemployment insurance schemes.[33]

The poor law had been reformed by the 1834 Poor Law Amendment Act to tackle the 'problem of pauperism', which was regarded as the result of personal failing. Following the principle of 'less eligibility', the parish was to provide relief that was inferior to the standard of living that a labourer could obtain without assistance. The 'workhouse test', which was introduced in 1874, was supposed to act as a deterrent and conditions were such within workhouses that any person who was prepared to accept the 'offer of the house' was given relief.

The 1905 Royal Commission on the Poor Laws undertook an immensely detailed study of poverty and poor relief and reported in 1909. The Commissioners were unable to agree on a unanimous report and presented both a majority and minority report, although there was much common ground between them. Both reports condemned the existing system as being too locally various and unsystematically administered. The minority report severely criticised the continuance of the general mixed workhouse and noted that workhouses were 'everywhere abhorred by the respectable poor' and that they had 'positively injurious effect on the character of all classes of inmates, tending to unfit them for the life of respectable and independent citizenship'.[34] The majority report placed more emphasis on the moral causes of poverty and person failing, while the minority report accepted that poverty could result from moral lapses (gambling and drinking in particular), but placed more emphasis on economic causes of destitution.[35]

The nature and type of poor relief offered in England and Wales changed in the closing decades of the nineteenth century. The 40 years or so before the First World War was characterised by what Williams refers to as a 'crusade against out relief' and an 'indoor strategy of classification and treatment'.[36] After the introduction of the workhouse test, the granting of outdoor relief to able-bodied males became legally constrained, though it remained possible to give unconditional out relief to all other classes of pauper.[37] Most people who received outdoor relief were elderly, widows and children, and even among these groups, efforts were made to assist the able-bodied to find work – if necessary, by removing dependent children to the workhouse. Gradually, as the nineteenth century drew to a close, the administration of poor relief became less punitive.[38] As Table 1.2 shows, the proportion of people receiving poor relief was roughly 25 per 1000 population in the decade prior to the First World War and about two-thirds of these received relief outside the workhouse. The extent to which outdoor relief was granted, and to whom, varied from region to region, but evidence of intemperance or improvidence was often sufficient grounds to deny outdoor relief to the infirm, widows and the elderly.

For certain categories of pauper, particularly the elderly, those that were sick and children, conditions within workhouses started to improve at the end of the nineteenth century. It was recommended that guardians

Table 1.2 Numbers of people receiving poor relief prior to the First World War

	Indoor relief		Outdoor relief		Total		Unemployment
	Mean numbers (000s)	Rates per 1000 estimated population	Mean numbers (000s)	Rates per 1000 estimated population	Mean numbers (000s)	Rates per 1000 estimated population	Trade union per cent
1900	188	5.9	500	15.7	767	25.0	2.3
1901	186	5.8	489	15.2	781	24.3	3.5
1902	213	6.5	502	15.4	797	24.4	4.2
1903	221	6.7	511	15.5	818	24.8	5.0
1904	229	6.9	516	15.5	832	25.0	6.3
1905	240	7.1	547	16.3	879	26.1	7.1
1906	248	7.3	550	16.2	892	26.2	4.5
1907	251	7.3	542	15.8	887	35.8	4.4
1908	256	7.4	540	15.6	893	25.7	5.6
1909	267	7.6	551	15.7	916	26.1	9.1
1910	275	7.8	540	15.2	916	25.9	6.6
1911	275	7.7	508	14.2	886	24.8	5.0
1912	267	7.4	408	11.3	780	21.6	3.1
1913	265	7.3	412	11.3	784	21.5	2.3

Source: Karel Williams, *From Pauperism to Poverty* (1981), Table 4.5, p. 161 and Table 4.11, p. 183.[39]

provided 'adequate' scales of out relief, but that they should 'passively adjust the kind of relief offered according to the past and present behaviour of the claimant'.[40] This is reflected in an increased number and proportion of paupers receiving indoor relief from the turn of the century until the First World War.

Most of the social surveys carried out in the first 30 years of the twentieth century only investigate poverty outside of the workhouse, but, as Bowley reminds us, to these totals it is necessary to add the numbers living within poor law institutions.[41] Several social surveys note the number of families in receipt of poor relief.[42] Only one study, however, specifically investigated the conditions of people in receipt of poor relief. In *How the Destitute Live*, the Liberal Christian League examined outdoor relief in Norwich during January and February 1912, among 895 cases of non-able-bodied – 'children, sick and infirm people, and aged folk past work'. The largest number were families of widows, or where the man was an invalid and unable to work. The remainder were old people. The number of cases where the relief was judged as insufficient was 471, or just under half. The amount of relief granted varied, but old people normally received between 3s 6d and 4s 6d per week, rarely 5s; married couples 6–7s per week and 2s for every child not earning. Widows typically only received allowances for children, not themselves, while the sick and infirm received relief of up to 5s per week. In eight cases, detailed budgets for one week are recorded and expenditure per head per day varied between 1d and 4¾d. Not surprisingly, children were often living on a diet consisting solely of white bread, jam and tea.[43] Most were living below Rowntree's poverty line and the survey concluded that the children were 'chronically hungry, stunted, and undernourished, ill-clad and ill-shod, and notably below the physical average of other children'.[44] The committee also reported its astonishment with the 'hardships many people would undergo rather than enter the workhouse'.[45]

In the years immediately preceding the First World War, new welfare legislation was introduced that coexisted with the poor law. The most important legislation was the 1908 Old Age Pensions Act and the 1911 National Insurance Act. Both reports of the Royal Commission on the Poor Laws were similar in their analysis of unemployment.[46] The majority and minority reports recognised that the principles of the 1834 Poor Law Amendment Act were outdated. They pointed to the importance of cyclical fluctuations in employment and the problems posed by seasonal underemployment. Both reports recommended labour exchanges, education and training for young people, the regularisation of employment by local and public authorities and unemployment insurance.[47] The 1911 Insurance Act had two parts, one relating to health insurance and the other to unemployment. Unlike pensions, these were contributory schemes, based on actuarial principles, which offered limited duration benefits for the insured risk. Employees, employers and the state made contributions, but at a fixed rate, which introduced a regressive element into the schemes.[48] Dependants were not covered by either scheme, though gradually an allowance for dependants was introduced during the interwar period. Unemployment insurance was compulsory, but only in defined industries, amounting to 2.3 m. people by 1914.[49]

When the 1908 Old Age Pension Act introduced non-contributory old age pensions for people over the age of 70, half a million people, the majority women, qualified. Most importantly, this scheme was administered by the Post Office, not the parish. From January 1909, an old age pension of 5s per week was introduced. This was 2s less than the poverty-line income for a single person estimated by Rowntree and was seen as an inducement for younger workers to save for their old age. It was not designed to provide subsistence benefit in old age. As Thane points out, those who survived into their sixties generally ceased to be able to support themselves by work; those without savings or relatives who were able to support them, were liable to spend the closing years of their lives in acute poverty.[50]

1.3   Real Wages

How much did workers earn and how had it changed compared with their parents? These are obviously central questions to any understanding of what is meant by the term 'standard of living', though for most people, real income would be only one of a number of factors that influenced such an assessment – albeit an important one. Until fairly recently, most estimates of changes in money and real wages relied on the extensive works of Arthur Bowley and George Wood.[51] Bowley, who was Professor of Statistics at the London School of Economics, collected and analysed a wealth of data relating to late nineteenth- and twentieth-century living standards and poverty. His work is the starting point for most general accounts of changes in living standards in Britain during this period. Bowley found that while money wages were rising between 1882 and 1899, prices were falling. This produced increases in average real wages of over 2 per cent per annum in the last two decades of the nineteenth century. From then on, however, average real wage growth declined a little until the First World War and this was due to prices increasing faster than money wage rates.[52]

A number of writers have critically reviewed Bowley and Wood's evidence.[53] Feinstein has reworked their estimates and his conclusions suggest that, although the extent of average real wage growth in the period 1882–1913 was much as Bowley himself suggested, the time path of change was substantially different. His results are set out in Table 1.3 along with Bowley's for comparison. Where possible, Feinstein used earnings rather than wage-rate data and he extended the coverage of Bowley's series to include examples of occupations in other sectors, particularly the tertiary sector, where the movement of wages was often very different from that in highly unionised manufacturing industries. This turns out to be important, because most of the revisions to the behaviour of money wages are the result of extending the coverage of the series. Revisions to the cost of living index, in particular making the weights more appropriate for average working-class expenditure patterns and including items such as alcohol and tobacco that Bowley had omitted, were empirically less important.[54] Taken together, Feinstein's revisions suggest a more moderate growth in average real wages until 1899 – about $1\frac{1}{2}$ per cent per annum, but then modest growth, rather than decline, from the turn of the century to the First World War.

These figures relate to average working-class wage earners. Feinstein's conclusions suggest that there is little evidence for a decline in average working-class real incomes prior to the First World War. Nevertheless, while Feinstein's revisions to Bowley's calculations fundamentally alter our perception of the Edwardian period, they could also be consistent with significant variance in the growth of real wages by sector or by skill.

Table 1.3 Estimates of the growth in nominal wages, prices and real wages (annual percentage growth rates), 1882–1913

	Real wages		Money wages		Cost of living	
	Bowley	Feinstein	Bowley	Feinstein	Bowley	Feinstein
1882–99	2.03	1.58	1.01	0.92	−1.01	−0.66
1899–1913	−0.46	0.13	0.76	1.26	1.23	0.97

Source: Charles Feinstein, 'What Really Happened to Real Wages?: Trends in Wages, Prices, and Productivity in the United Kingdom, 1880–1913', *Economic History Review* (1990), Table 1, p. 330 and Table 4, p. 344.

Table 1.4   Real earnings of general labourers and agricultural labourers, 1900–13

Year	General labourers	Agricultural labourers
1900	100.0	100.0
1901	110.7	100.6
1902	99.8	100.5
1903	100.0	101.1
1904	100.3	101.4
1905	100.4	102.0
1906	102.1	102.3
1907	100.2	100.4
1908	99.2	99.8
1909	99.4	100.2
1910	97.8	99.0
1911	98.3	99.6
1912	99.2	98.5
1913	101.4	101.6

Source: Author's calculations from Charles Feinstein, 'New Estimates of Average Earnings in the United Kingdom, 1880–1913', *Economic History Review* (1990), Table 4, p. 608 and 'A New Look at the Cost of Living', in James Foreman-Peck (ed.), *New Perspectives on the Victorian Economy* (Cambridge, 1991), Table 6.4, pp. 170–1.

The detailed evidence on the behaviour of the real earnings of 'general labourers' and 'agricultural labourers' is set out in Table 1.4. This shows Feinstein's new earnings series for these two groups deflated by his revised cost of living index. From this table, it is clear that these two groups at the bottom of the wage distribution made little appreciable gain in real earnings between the turn of the century and the First World War, which is consistent with Feinstein's estimate of 0.13 per cent per annum growth in average real wages during this period. Of course, this is a crude exercise and takes no account of regional differences in pay, which are likely to have been important in this period.[55]

Were skilled workers faring any better? What happened to the pay differential between skilled and unskilled workers is a disputed issue in this period. Phelps-Brown points to the general stability in pay differentials for manual workers in building, shipbuilding, engineering and railways between 1880 and 1910.[56] In contrast, Williamson suggests that there was some *narrowing* in urban pay inequality between 1901 and 1911 and between agricultural and unskilled urban workers, although the changes he found are modest for this decade.[57] Overall, therefore, it appears unlikely that the poor were becoming relatively poorer in the years immediately preceding the First World War.

Evidence on the distribution of wage earners' incomes is also heavily dependent on Bowley's work. He estimated male income distribution for 1914, using the 1906 wage census in conjunction with data on changes in wage rates.[58] From the perspective of investigating poverty it might be desirable to consider household, rather than individual incomes, but this is not possible to estimate reliably for this period. Bowley's estimates of the changes in male earnings distribution, along with his description of the group represented in 1914, are reported in Table 1.5.

Bowley's figures indicate that an income of about a £1 per week would correspond to the bottom 10 per cent of male earnings immediately prior to the First World War. Bowley also suggests that in 1911, 12 per cent of male earners, about one million in total of 8 million, were earning less than a pound per week and 32 per cent, or about 2.5 million men, were earning less than 25s per week.[59] Bowley's estimate of the frequency distribution of male earnings is reported in Table 1.6. Notice that only 6 per cent of male earners had incomes greater than 45s per week in 1911.

Bowley reckons that women workers' average full-time earnings in 1906 were about 11.8s per week, but he does not provide estimates of the distribution of women's earnings.[60] There was a significant disparity in average earnings between men and women. Women were primarily segregated into low-wage work such as agriculture, textile manufacture and domestic service. There relatively low wages reflected the dominance of ideas based on male breadwinning, where men were paid a 'family wage', to support their dependants.

Table 1.5 Distribution of men's earnings for full normal week, 1906 and 1914

	1906	*1914*	*1914 representation*
Lowest deciles	19s 6d	21s 0d	Bottom of the unskilled
Lower quartile	23s 4d	25s 2d	Top of unskilled
Median	29s 4d	31s 6d	Top of semi-skilled
Upper quartile	37s 2d	39s 4d	Skilled
Highest quartile	46s 0d	47s 0d	

Source: A. L. Bowley, *Wages and Incomes since 1860* (1937, pp. 42 and 46). 1906 figures from earnings and hours census, excluding mining and agriculture. 1914 figures estimated by Bowley, including agriculture and mining.

Table 1.6   Frequency distribution of male earnings, 1911

Weekly wage	Number of men (million)	Per cent of total
Under 15s	0.32	4
15–20s	0.64	8
20–25s	1.60	20
25–30s	1.68	21
30–35s	1.68	21
35–40s	1.04	13
40–45s	0.56	7
Over 45s	0.48	6

Source: Attributed to Arthur Bowley, May 1911 in P. Snowden, *The Living Wage*, p. 28.

Nevertheless, according to Cadbury *et al.*'s detailed investigation into women's wages in Birmingham in 1905, married women were paid higher wages than single women, because they were generally more skilled (by virtue of longer service), or, because according to employers they were 'steadier', and generally on piecework.[61] Married women and widows made up about 23 per cent of women wage earners in Birmingham, just over one in four of which were widows, which made it 'compulsory for them to work'.[62] As Table 1.7 shows, of these working women, about one-third had partners who were earning less than 25s. Among those women not in full-time paid employment, about the same proportion

Table 1.7   Women's labour force participation in Birmingham, 1905

	Per cent women occupied in factories, laundries or as charwomen	Per cent women not occupied with paid work
Partner earning 25s and over	26.26	50.0
Partner earning less than 25s	32.20	35.79
Partner's wage not stated	15.43	10.17
Widows	25.52	3.77
Unmarried women keeping house for fathers	0.59	0.27
Total	100	100

Source: E. Cadbury, Cecile M. Matheson and G. Shann, *Women's Work and Wages*, 2nd edn (1908), p. 214.

had partners earning less than 25s per week, significantly less than the proportion with partners earning more than this amount. There was little difference between the number and ages of children between these groups.[63]

It may not be possible to generalise from results of this Birmingham investigation, of course. Patterns of female labour force participation varied enormously between towns in relatively close proximity. In 1911, 6.9 per cent of married women and widows were in full-time employment in Barrow, compared with 11 per cent in Lancaster and 35 per cent in Preston. The last was a textile town, and the mills were large employers of women workers.[64] It is clear, however, that a sizeable proportion of men were working for a wage that was insufficient to maintain a family above contemporaneous ideas of the poverty line. Under these circumstances, women's earnings would help prevent poverty in families with more than one member in paid work. For households headed by women workers, the lower pay of women, in circumstances in which male earnings often could not satisfy basic needs, frequently resulted in dire destitution.[65] At this time, women headed a fairly large number of households, usually because of death of a male partner, desertion or because they were supporting aged relatives.[66]

In some areas, it was common for married women to work, but for many women, *full-time* paid employment would cease with marriage, or birth of first child, though this was by no means always the case as Roberts has shown.[67] At the time of the 1911 population census female labour force participation rates were about one in three women over the age of 10 (32 per cent), or just under one in three of the entire female population (29 per cent). These proportions represent 5.4 million 'occupied' women, according to the 1911 census. In addition, an unknown number of women would not have been enumerated as 'occupied', even though they worked for wages. Included in this category would be women who did outwork or 'homeworked'. Howarth and Wilson's study of West Ham reveals the extent to which women were engaged in 'homework', many of whom worked to 'meet some definite part of family expenditure, such as children's clothes or boots'.[68] Much of this work was itself casual and probably not subject to accurate census enumeration as waged work was regarded as work undertaken outside the home. In addition, an unknown number of women would not have been recorded as employed because they did seasonal jobs, such as harvest workers, which occurred outside the census period.[69]

In 1911, 13.7 per cent of married women in England and Wales were recorded as being in full-time paid employment, compared with 54.5 per cent of unmarried women. Moreover, these relative proportions varied between rural and urban districts, with a greater proportion of married women working full-time in urban areas.[70] It would be incorrect, however, to infer from this that these women did not continue to make a contribution to family income. Contemporary poverty and wage surveys reveal the extent to which women would combine casual dressmaking, childminding, charring and laundering and taking in lodgers, with responsibility for household domestic tasks.[71] According to Roberts's oral historical evidence, about 40 per cent of women in north-west England 'earned money on a part-time basis at some point in their married life'.[72]

The contribution that children made to the family economy is also difficult to estimate precisely for this period. It is clear that many working-class children would have been required to work as soon as they were old enough to bring in a wage. In some cases, this could be very young indeed. The 1870 Education Act provided elementary education for children up to the age of ten and school attendance became compulsory in 1880, though for many children schooling was patchy, especially in rural areas. In 1900, free education was available to all children in England and Wales until at least the age of 11. According to Thane, 'In 1902 perhaps 50,000 children in England and Wales were working more than 20 hours a week (some of them between 30 and 50 hours) in addition to 27.5 hours at school.'[73] In large families especially, these children made a significant contribution to the everyday struggle against poverty.

1.4   Family Expenditure

If household income is difficult to estimate reliably, there is a wealth of evidence on household expenditure patterns available for the period from Board of Trade reports and social investigators' inquiries. As Table 1.8 shows, in 1914 an *average* household in the lowest deciles of the income distribution would have spent about 62 per cent of their expenditure on food.[74] This compares with Bowley's estimate of 60 per cent for average working-class food expenditure and about 33 per cent for average consumer expenditure on food. The source for Bowley's figure for food expenditure was an inquiry by the Board of Trade. In 1904 they collected nearly 2000 urban working-class family budgets, and the average expenditure on food varied from about 57 per cent of family income in

Table 1.8   Patterns of household expenditure, 1904–14

	Bowley 1904, average working-class expenditure	Mackenzie 1914, lowest deciles expenditure	Average consumer expenditure, 1900–4
Food	60	61.7	33.1
Rent	16	17.1	11.3
Clothing	12	7.3	9.4
Fuel/light	8	4.9	4.4
Other	4	9.0	42.0

Source: I. Gazeley, 'The Cost of Living for Urban Workers', *Economic History Review* (1989), p. 210 and calculated from Mackenzie, *Economica*, p. 227.

the north of England to nearly 65 per cent in Scotland.[75] In rural areas, the Board of Trade estimated that food expenditure accounted for about 73 per cent of agricultural labourers' average earnings in 1902.[76]

In *How the Casual Labourer Lives*, Eleanor Rathbone concluded that her study of Liverpool working-class family expenditure 'yielded no absolutely new facts of importance and perhaps suggested no really novel conclusions'.[77] This is unduly modest. Rathbone and her co-investigators collected 40 household budgets between 1907 and 1908. The budgets were kept for significantly different lengths of time, ranging from one to 62 weeks. Those kept for longer periods provide some of the best evidence of working-class expenditure on durable items, particularly clothing, which is liable to be understated in weekly inquiries.[78] In 16 of the 40 families, the wives of casual labourers were also working (charring, washing, sewing or hawking), and some of the others kept lodgers.[79] Rathbone's expenditure survey is important for it provides an insight into how poor families survived from week to week, using credit to cover a shortfall in one week or 'lumpy' expenditure such as clothes or shoes.

More than any other item, the cost of accommodation varied from region to region and, of course, this would affect income available for other categories of expenditure. According to the Board of Trade investigation, relative to London prices, the cost of accommodation varied significantly in the 73 towns surveyed in 1905. The variance in non-rent prices was, by comparison, fairly negligible. When rents and prices were combined, the cheapest prices were found in Lancashire and Cheshire and Midland towns, which were about 15 per cent cheaper than London and about 8 per cent cheaper than southern counties' towns.[80] The importance of regional differences in the cost of accommodation was confirmed in the more extensive 1912 Board of Trade survey.[81]

1.5   Social Surveys and Poverty

The genesis of the social survey certainly pre-dates the nineteenth century, but towards the end of Victorian period the investigation of socio-economic questions using social survey techniques became widespread.[82] Bulmer *et al.* attribute this increased interest in social investigation to middle- and upper-class concern about the impact of urbanisation and industrialisation on urban and rural workers.[83] As the nineteenth century progressed, there was an increased desire for 'scientific' as opposed to purely impressionistic study, although important empirical and impressionistic investigations were carried out in the middle of the nineteenth century.[84] Charles Booth's investigation, *The Life and Labour of the People in London*, which was published between 1889 and 1903, is seen as 'the first great empirical study in the social survey tradition', which when first published, according to Bulmer *et al.*, 'created a sensation'.[85] Booth was motivated by a desire to consider the factual basis for the impressionistic accounts of poverty in the metropolis given in *The Bitter Cry of Outcast London*, which was published in the *Pall Mall Gazette*.[86] Booth's London survey primarily addressed two questions: how many were poor and why they were poor.[87] The short answers to these questions were about 30 per cent and mainly due to irregular wages and the workings of the casual labour market.[88] It is worth noting Hennock's caution, however, that Booth regarded the poor as 'lacking comfort, but as neither ill nourished nor-ill-clad' and only considered the 'very poor' to be 'in want', which he thought accounted for just over 8 per cent of the population of London.[89]

But it is Rowntree's study of York, *Poverty: A Study in Town Life*, carried out in 1899 and published in 1901, that is seen as refining the operation of empirical poverty research. In the years before the First World War, Rowntree's survey was followed by a number of other studies that attempted to apply his methodology to other areas, either loosely or precisely. Most of the regional social surveys carried out before the First World War attempt, at some point, to estimate the number of people in their area that fell below Rowntree's poverty line. Rowntree also investigated the state of deprivation existing among the rural poor just before the outbreak of war in *How the Labourer Lives*, and made two follow-up surveys of poverty in York: *Poverty and Progress*, carried out in 1936 and *Poverty and the Welfare State* in 1950. Both the second and third social surveys of York were made using a different poverty line than the one he used in 1899, however.

Social investigations of poverty should not be divorced from the prevailing intellectual climate in which they were carried out. The nineteenth-century Benthamite analysis of the cause of destitution, based on individual failing, was gradually giving way to an analysis of the causes of poverty that accepted that it could be the result of structural failure, largely outside the control of individuals. This was especially true of explanation that pointed to irregular or low wages. Two intellectual developments are usually seen as important in this context, as Jose Harris has written:

> On the one hand, violent mass demonstrations in the mid-1880s sharply reinforced earlier fears about the parasitic menace of a feckless and degenerate urban 'residuum'; on the other hand, it became more and more apparent that mass unemployment was afflicting not merely the residuum but large numbers of regular, organised and often highly skilled workers whose industries were vulnerable to international fluctuations of trade.[90]

There was a growing pressure, based on moral argument that sought more collective solutions to social problems, which found political expression in both 'New Liberalism' and Fabianism.[91] As important was a growing campaign for 'national efficiency', as evidence increased of the narrowing of the gap between the economies of Britain and its rivals, particularly Germany and the United States.[92] Indeed, there is a clear similarity between the language used by Rowntree to describe the income necessary for 'merely physical efficiency' and that needed to maintain 'national efficiency'.[93] These social imperialistic concerns, of the early twentieth-century ruling elite, were fuelled by the revelation that of the 20,000 volunteers for the South African War (1899–1902), 'only 14,000 were considered fit to join'.[94]

More generally, among conservative groups, there was a growing realisation that economic and military superiority was incompatible with a feeble, malnourished and impoverished workforce. This 'hardening of feeling against industrial inefficiency and social inadequacy' was reinforced by the recommendations of the 1904 Interdepartmental Committee on Physical Deterioration.[95] This committee, composed of civil servants, concluded that, while deterioration remained unproven, standards of working-class nutrition and hygiene gave grave cause for concern. While most of the committee's recommendations were firmly grounded in socio-environmental explanations of poverty, they also made an infamous recommendation of transportation to labour colonies for the 'waste elements in society'.[96]

But it would be wrong to see the gradual acceptance of the idea that poverty had a socioeconomic explanation as being completely incompatible with an analysis that also located some responsibility with individual moral failing. Most of the new empirical school shared established views on the importance of thrift and the dangers of drink and gambling. Rowntree, as Williams reminds us, edited a collection of essays on gambling and his father produced 'the standard Edwardian manual on temperance'.[97] While Snowden lamented the 'submerged two million' in poverty in 1912, his views were typical of most middle-class Edwardian commentators in apportioning blame:

> It must be admitted, of course, that considerable numbers of working-class families greatly aggravate their poverty by the wasteful and unwise expenditure of some part of their insufficient means. 'The poverty of the poor is their destruction.' The appalling expenditure upon drink, while not the cause of low wages, deprives many families of the enjoyment of a higher standard of living.[98]

1.6   Rowntree's Concept(s) of Poverty

York was Rowntree's home city. Briggs notes in his biography that it also had the benefit of being comparatively small and 'for all its "representative" qualities could be guaranteed to capture public attention'.[99] Moreover, it is a walled, ancient city with a Minster that was familiar to people who knew nothing of working-class slums:

> If Rowntree could show convincingly that there was a thick layer of poverty in an ancient city like York, it would be a far more impressive demonstration of the extent of Britain's social problem than an investigation of industrial Manchester or Birmingham. It would provide an answer also to those critics of Charles Booth who believed that he had uncovered a special 'metropolitan problem' of quite exceptional character.[100]

Rowntree devised a measure of poverty that was based on an assessment of the circumstances of families, as revealed by direct interview. His house-to-house survey of *all* working-class households in York also allowed him (or one of his team of volunteer investigators) to collect socio-economic data. In total, 11,560 working-class families comprising 46,754 people were studied from a total population of York of 75,812, as Rowntree excluded what he referred to as the 'servant keeping classes'.[101] Material gained from interviews was cross-checked with information supplied by employers, other agencies and neighbours. The inclusion of information provided by this last group helped the investigators form an opinion as to the 'character' of the family. In reality, this involved investigators making impressionistic assessments based on evidence of 'obvious want and squalor', intemperance and thriftlessness.

He found that 27.84 per cent of the population of York were in *total poverty*. This is an impressionistic estimate that is not income based and, as Williams indicates, it confuses moral judgements with empirical investigation.[102] Those that were unable to meet the minimum need for the maintenance of 'merely physical efficiency', some 9.91 per cent of the population of York, Rowntree labelled as being in *primary poverty*. Rowntree estimated the number of people in primary poverty by defining a set of minimum needs and then comparing household income to the cost of these needs. Those families who had total earnings 'sufficient for the maintenance of merely physical efficiency were it not that some portion was absorbed by other expenditure, either useful or wasteful', Rowntree defined as being in *secondary poverty*: some 17.73 per cent of the population of York.[103] This figure was not independently ascertained, but was deduced by subtraction (*total poverty* minus *primary poverty*). Notice that these figures refer to individuals, not households, and to the percentage of the population of York in poverty, not the percentage of working-class people. Among the wage-earning classes, 43.4 per cent were in total poverty, of which 15.46 per cent were in primary poverty.[104]

The nature of Rowntree's investigations and the interpretation that should be placed on his findings have received considerable attention since their time of publication.[105] As Veit-Wilson notes, great confusion surrounds the subsequent reporting of Rowntree's method and results.[106] In recent appraisal of Rowntree's contribution to social investigation, Hennock argues that Rowntree was a major innovator in his *methods* of investigation. In particular, he points to the systematic investigation of household income and the distinction between secondary and primary poverty. At the same time Hennock argues that Rowntree was conservative in his *aims*, since his primary aim was to replicate Booth's survey of London.[107]

Rowntree, unlike Booth, was able to classify all his households by income. This allowed him to compare household income with household 'needs' in a more sophisticated way than had Booth, 12 years earlier. Rowntree's poverty-line approach is an enduring feature of his first social survey of York that conditioned the methodology of most subsequent empirical investigation of poverty for half a century. However, Hennock's claim that one way in which Rowntree was innovative was due to him finding a way of determining 'how many were really poor and how many just wasteful', seems difficult to accept for the reasons given by Williams.[108] Although Rowntree found a mechanism for answering this question, it is not clear that his answer should be accorded the status common in historical text, although according to Veit-Wilson, Rowntree's secondary poverty category should be seen as an attempt to illuminate the nature of poverty.[109] Unlike his poverty-line approach, however, Rowntree's efforts to ascertain the extent of 'obvious want and squalor' was not repeated by near contemporaneous or by subsequent investigations. Despite the fact that only one-third of people Rowntree found to be in poverty were in primary poverty, it was this measure of poverty that was replicated in subsequent inquiries.

Rowntree's method for estimating those unable to meet the minimum needs of 'merely physical efficiency' varied according to the nature of need.[110] Food needs were calculated by translating contemporaneous recommended dietary allowances into a diet that would satisfy them. Rowntree's diet included no butcher's meat and was devised from the diets recommended for workhouse paupers in 1897, at York unit prices.[111] It is sometimes argued that Rowntree viewed this as 'scientifically absolute', but as Veit-Wilson writes, 'Rowntree realised that even his primary poverty line was relative.'[112] Dietary standards themselves cannot be treated as extrinsic minimum standards of consumption because they change over time in accordance with developments in nutritional thinking and as such, should be seen as being socially determined. Moreover, if 'absolute' or scientific' identification of need is interpreted as meaning without recourse to value judgement, Rowntree's food component of his primary poverty-line measure required him to translate recommended dietary allowances into a diet that would satisfy them. This obviously involved the exercise of judgement on the palatability or 'reasonableness' of the proposed diets.[113] For as Townsend succinctly observed,' . . . estimates of need, even nutritional needs, cannot be absolute; they must be relative to the kind of society in which a man is living'.[114] Rowntree's diets were undoubtedly meagre and uninteresting, but they were not 'least-cost', in the arithmetic sense.[115]

For rent and expenditure on clothing, fuel and other sundry items, Rowntree had no readily available standard of minimum needs. His poverty-line measure for these items varied. The figure for minimum expenditure on accommodation was based on the observed minimum working-class rent expenditure, while 'minimum' sums for clothing and fuel and sundry items were ascertained by interviewing the poor and asking them what they thought was a reasonable minimum expenditure on items. The cost of items under these expenditure headings, for a reference family of a man, wife and three children, were combined to arrive at Rowntree's poverty-line income of 21s 8d. As Williams points out, this poverty-line measure was a combination of the application of a 'minimum' standard of consumption in conjunction with behaviouristic and expectations-based components.[116] In consequence, his primary poverty-line measure should be seen as a specific type of relative measure, rather than an absolute measure of minimum needs.[117]

This observation is not intended to imply that because it is not 'absolute' it should be ignored or discarded. Veit-Wilson claims that Rowntree used a 'physical subsistence' minimum as a heuristic device to guard against contemporary critics who might otherwise think it too generous.[118] Rowntree's biographer tells us that his book was 'read by socialists and non-socialists alike' and that his conclusions were 'taken seriously by people of quite different religious and political persuasions'.[119] Even so, Helen Bosanquet, social investigator of some repute, disputed Rowntree's findings because she 'accused him of adopting the "highest possible estimate" of food requirements'.[120] As we shall see, despite the meagre nature of Rowntree's dietary standard, there is some force to Bosanquet's general criticism, when Rowntree's standard is compared with either Booth's or Bowley's.

One aspect of Rowntree's primary poverty measure that has been largely ignored is the way he treated the needs of adults relative to those of children. In his description of the poverty line, Rowntree notes that '. . . the quantity of food necessary for an individual varies with age and sex of that individual, and with the severity of the muscular work performed'.[121] Based on the recommendations of Atwater, an American nutritionist, Rowntree expresses the food needs of women and children as proportions of the needs of a man performing moderate muscular work (Table 1.9).

Table 1.9   Rowntree's food equivalence scale,
based on Atwater

Man	1.0
Woman	0.8
Boy 14–16 years old	0.8
Girl 14–16 years old	0.7
Child 10–13 years	0.6
Child 6–9 years	0.5
Child 2–5 years	0.4
Child under 2 years	0.3

Source: Rowntree, *Poverty: a Study of Town Life*, p. 91.

Rowntree needed to use an equivalence scale so that 'the food consumed by any given family can be readily expressed in terms of a common unit; viz. the food consumed "per man per day". Thus the nutrient required for families of varying sizes can be easily compared.'[122] This practice was not completely new, but was extremely influential in determining the approach of most subsequent social investigations of poverty or dietary adequacy. However, Rowntree was not the first social investigator to recognise that the needs of adults and children were not the same. In Booth's 1889 survey of poverty in London, he used 'equivalent male adults' in order to analyse the average expenditure of families in each of his occupational classes, but the details of Booth's equivalence scale are scant.[123]

Although in the discussion of his primary poverty line, Rowntree is aware of the importance of the concept, and he carefully costs a diet that would satisfy his adopted minimum nutritional standards for men, women and children of various ages, he ignores these calculations in his calculation of primary poverty.[124] Rather, he adopts a figure for primary poverty food costs of 3s per week for adults (both males and females) and 2s 3d each per week for children, no matter of what age.[125] The use of this equivalence scale, as opposed to Atwater's, had important consequences for the measurement of primary poverty in York, as Gazeley and Newell have shown. Maintaining all of Rowntree's other assumptions, but correcting the error in the equivalence scale he *actually used*, reduces the implied level of primary poverty in York significantly.[126]

Rowntree's minimum rent expenditures were based upon observed rents paid for various classes of accommodation, the cost of which generally increased with the number of rooms.[127] For clothing, Rowntree used

Table 1.10   Rowntree's primary poverty-line weekly expenditures

Family type	Food	Rent	Household sundries	Rowntree total	Gazeley and Newell total
1 man	3s	1s 6d	2s 6d	7s	
1 woman	3s	1s 6d	2s 6d	7s	
1 man, 1 woman	6s	2s 6d	3s 2d	11s 8d	11s 8d
1 man, 1 woman, 1 child	8s 3d	2s 6d	3s 9d	14s 6d	13s 11d
1 man, 1 woman, 2 children	10s 6d	4s	4s 4d	18s 10d	16s 11d
1 man, 1 woman, 3 children	12s 9d	4s	4s 11d	21s 8d	19s 6d
1 man, 1 woman, 4 children	15s	5s 6d	5s 6d	26s	21s 6d
1 man, 1 woman, 5 children	17s 3d	5s 6d	6s 1d	28s 10d	23s
1 man, 1 woman, 6 children	19s 6d	5s 6d	6s 8d	31s 8d	24s 2d

Sources: Rowntree, *Poverty: a Study in Town Life* (1901), p. 110 and Ian Gazeley and Andrew Newell, 'Rowntree Revisited: Poverty in Britain, 1900', *Explorations in Economic History*, 37 (2000), Table 1, p. 178 and Table 4, p. 185.

an identical standard for men and women and used an average proportional figure for the needs of children.[128] Rowntree argued that fuel requirements were a fixed cost, independent of family size, and the cost of other sundry items in his primary poverty-line measure was included on a per capita basis.[129] Rowntree's table of minimum necessary expenditure per week of families of various sizes is reproduced as Table 1.10, but the total expenditures are too high for families with children. This is because Rowntree overestimated children's food needs if comparison is made with either the estimates of children's needs derived from household expenditure data, or the equivalence scales adopted roughly contemporaneously by Booth or Bowley.

What impact did Rowntree's choice of equivalence scale have on the measurement of poverty in York? For Rowntree's chosen reference family, of a man, woman and three children, taking account of the reduced needs of children relative to adults reduces the poverty line from 21s 8d to about 19s 6d per week. The error was greater for families with more children. Had Rowntree taken account of the reduced needs of children, he would have found significantly fewer families in York with incomes below his primary poverty-line measure.[130] *Exactly* how many is impossible to say from Rowntree's published work, but using the fragments of information presented in *Poverty*, Gazeley and Newell estimate an incidence of primary poverty of about 6 per cent rather than about 10 per cent. Of course, since those families living in total poverty were ascertained impressionistically, and those in secondary poverty were derived by subtraction, the conclusion that Rowntree overestimated primary poverty, necessarily means that he underestimated secondary poverty by an exactly offsetting amount.[131]

1.7   Bowley's 'New Standard'

Bowley refined Rowntree's primary poverty-line measure in his investigations of poverty in northern industrial and mining towns prior to the First World War. In *Livelihood and Poverty* (1915) Bowley and Burnett-Hurst took a random sample equivalent to about 1 : 20 working-class houses in Northampton, Warrington and Stanley in the summer and autumn of 1913 and in Reading in the autumn of 1912.[132] As Hennock has recently pointed out, Bowley was not interested in replicating Rowntree's impressionistic study of total poverty; only the income-based primary poverty measure.[133]

Bowley and Burnett-Hurst interpreted their measure of primary poverty as the minimum standard necessary for physical health and summed up the results of their inquiry, thus:

> ...quite apart from the secondary poverty of those whose income is injudiciously spent and quite apart from accidents – or rather certainties – such as temporary sickness and unemployment, permanent, as distinct from occasional, poverty exists in certain places on a scale which is really appalling.[134]

The statistics behind this statement are reproduced in Table 1.11. There is significant variance in the proportions of households or individuals below Bowley's poverty line between these four towns, ranging from just over one in 20 in Stanley to just over one in five in Reading. Because Bowley's earnings figures relate to a 'normal' week, and made no allowance for losses caused by short time, unemployment or illness, these proportions are liable to underestimate the numbers in primary poverty.[135]

In addition to making allowances for alterations in relative prices, Bowley formulated his 'new standard' by modifying Rowntree's primary poverty measure in a number of other ways. First, he included an allowance for meat in his minimum needs diet.[136] Second, he treated accommodation needs in a more sophisticated fashion. Bowley's rent component in his 'new standard' was '...the "cheapest house" which would give one room per "equivalent adult"'.[137] Third, Bowley modified

Table 1.11   Percentage in poverty in northern towns in 1912–13

	Working-class households below 'new standard' poverty line	All households below 'new standard' poverty line	Working-class individuals below 'new standard' poverty line	All individuals below 'new standard' poverty line
Northampton	7.6	5.9	9	7
Warrington	11.6	10.9	15	12
Stanley	5.4	–	6	4.5
Reading	20.4	15.1	29	19

Source: A. L. Bowley and A. R. Burnett-Hurst, *Livelihood and Poverty* (1915), pp. 38–9 and 42–3.

Rowntree's food minimum needs equivalent scale to make 'greater allowance for adults and less for young children'. Because, as we have already seen, Rowntree had in practice treated the needs of all children under 16, irrespective of their age, as identical.[138] Bowley's 'new standard' expenditure equivalent scales are given in Table 1.12. As family size increases, Bowley's 'new standard' gives fewer equivalent adults than Rowntree's primary poverty measure, but looks remarkably similar to Booth's estimates of 'equivalent male adults'. Other things being equal, therefore, for the same income and demographic structure, Bowley's 'new standard' would produce fewer families in primary poverty than would Rowntree's.

Table 1.12   'Minimum needs' equivalence scales compared

	Booth 1887 food equivalence scale	Rowntree 1899 primary poverty schoolchildren	Bowley 1912 'new standard' all children
Couple	1.00	1.00	1.00
Couple and 1 child	1.21	1.24	1.21
Couple and 2 children	1.38	1.61	1.42
Couple and 3 children	1.62	1.86	1.66
Couple and 4 children	1.86	2.23	1.89
Couple and 5 children	2.17	2.47	2.15
Couple and 6 children	2.35	2.71	2.37

Source: Ian Gazeley and Andrew Newell, 'Rowntree Revisited: Poverty in Britain, 1900', *Explorations in Economic History*, 37 (2000), Table 2, p. 179.

Summary

At the beginning of this chapter, we noted the 'paradox' of rising real incomes and a constant proportion of the population identified in poverty by Booth and Rowntree in 1899 and 1901. Feinstein's estimates of average real wage growth indicate a somewhat slower growth of real wages prior to 1900 and then rather faster growth thereafter until the beginning of the First World War, than indicated by Bowley's figures. For poor urban labourers and agricultural workers, Feinstein's data suggest that the real wages of these two groups remained fairly constant in the decade or so before the onset of war. At the same time, while the total proportion of the population in receipt of poor relief was not subject to great change, the number and proportion receiving indoor relief were increasing.

Rowntree had more than one conception of poverty. His primary poverty measure, that was income based, overestimated the needs of children. This imparted a considerable upward bias to his estimate of the numbers experiencing primary poverty. Probably a figure of about 6 per cent of the total population of York was in primary poverty, as Rowntree attempted to measure it, rather than the near 10 per cent he reports. Comparison with the results of Bowley's first northern town survey is not straightforward because Bowley modified Rowntree's poverty-line measure in a number of ways. Bowley noticed that Rowntree's primary poverty-line calculations overestimated the needs of schoolchildren and he made adjustments accordingly. The results of his investigation using his 'new standard' are roughly comparable with the revised estimate of primary poverty in York. Taken together, it is clear that the incidence of primary poverty in northern towns varied greatly at the beginning of the century. Bowley's figures range from about 6 per cent of the population of Northampton to 15 per cent in Reading. A revised figure of about 6 per cent of the population in York seems consistent with the relative prosperity of York at the top of the trade cycle. It also suggests that rather than regarding primary poverty as being widespread and of roughly similar incidence, we should seek to explore the reasons for the variation in the numbers in primary poverty between towns and local regions.

The precise extent to which it is possible to generalise the findings of Rowntree or Bowley to other towns remains unclear. Bowley and Burnett-Hurst were certain that the four towns they surveyed, three of which had populations of about 70,000–90,000 in 1911, were 'probably not unrepresentative of the large number of towns ranging in population from 40,000 to 150,000'.[139] But they were clear that their evidence could not be regarded as typical of larger metropolitan cities, such as London, Birmingham, Liverpool, Manchester or Glasgow. Although there were no poverty-line studies of these metropolitan areas in the period immediately before the First World War, there were social surveys carried out in many of these cities that examined both the quantitative dimension of poverty as revealed by comparisons of household expenditure, and families' experiences of life on extremely low incomes, which confirm many of Rowntree's and Bowley's findings concerning the nature of poverty.

One further caution is necessary, however. As was discussed in the introduction to this book, all headcount measures of poverty suffer from the disadvantage of treating equally those who only just fail to have the means to meet minimum needs and those who are significantly below the minimum needs standard. For Rowntree's survey we do not know how far, on average, people were below the poverty line or how this may have been subject to change in the years leading up to the First World War.

2

THE NATURE AND CAUSES
OF POVERTY, 1900–18

Introduction

Having established the parameters of empirical poverty investigation
and the behaviour of real incomes, it is now appropriate to consider the
causes of poverty as revealed by contemporary social investigation.
Most surveys thought that poverty was due to a variety of reasons,
including low or irregular wages, large family size, illness or incapacity,
old age and unemployment. A large number of dietary surveys were also
undertaken during this period. These analysed the nutritional content
of household diet and compared the outcome with the values in
contemporary dietary standards. Although conceptually distinct, in
many respects, this approach shares much in common with the poverty-
line primary poverty measure (see Introduction, pp. 1–2). Both require
estimates of dietary consumption and comparison with an extrinsic
standard and both rely upon the use of equivalence scales.

In the period before the First World War, contemporary investigations revealed significant differences between the dietary intakes of poor
urban and rural workers. There are also well-documented differences
in proxy indicators of health between the town and countryside, in
particular the incidence of infant mortality. The link between poor diet
and relatively low levels of health concerned contemporaries and has
been the subject of much heated debate ever since. This is one aspect of
the investigation of trends in poverty and ill health during this period
that has a clear resonance with the debate about living standards during
the Industrial Revolution.

Arthur Bowley thought that the First World War was responsible for a substantial reduction in the incidence of poverty. This was primarily due to reductions in family size and growth in real wages. Notwithstanding Bowley's optimism, the debate about the impact of the war on the health of Britons remains highly charged. One thing is clear, however. The First World War represented a discrete break with the Victorian analysis of the causes of poverty. After the war, it would be irregular work rather than low wages that was identified as the principal explanation of poverty.

2.1 The Causes of Urban Poverty prior to the First World War

Before the war, Bowley found that the principal cause of primary poverty in the northern towns (except Stanley) was low wages. As Bowley comments, 'In no town does permanent unemployment or irregularity of work of a capable man rank as an important cause.'[140] In two towns, Northampton and Reading, the proportion of adult males earning less than £1 per week (20s) was greater than in York in 1899.[141] Stanley was a coal town and, as such, male earnings were relatively high. As Table 2.1 reveals, the next most important causes of primary poverty were death of the principal wage earner, illness and old age.

Stanley is exceptional in one other important respect. Exclusive male breadwinning was the most prevalent form of household structure. In over two-thirds of all working-class households, the man was the sole

Table 2.1 Pre-war causes of primary poverty (%)

	Northampton	Warrington	Stanley	Reading	York
Chief wage earner dead	21	6	25	14	27
Chief wage earner, ill or old	14	1	50	11	10
Chief wage earner unemployed	–	3	–	2	3
Chief wage earner irregularly employed	–	3	–	4	3
Wages insufficient	65	87	25	69	57

Source: Derived from Bowley and Burnett-Hurst, *Livelihood and Poverty*, Table IX, p. 40.[142]

earner (69 per cent). In the other towns the situation was very different. In nearly half of all working-class households joint breadwinning was the norm. In Reading, 41 per cent of women or children provided contributions to household income, while in Warrington and Northampton the proportions were higher (45 and 51 per cent, respectively).[143]

Variation in the pattern of household breadwinning in Victorian Britain was identified by Horrell and Oxley, who analysed the 1024 household expenditure records collected by the United States Commissioner of Labour in 1890–1. These budgets reveal that the pattern of family breadwinning varied between textile industries, in which men contributed about two-thirds of household income, and the other industries, such as iron and steel, where they contributed about 80 per cent on average.[144] In textiles, both women and children had higher earnings relative to other industries. Coal mining was a hybrid in this context, with high earnings for (male) children, but limited opportunities for female earnings. Moreover, Horrell and Oxley show how the pattern of female and child earnings changes over the lifetime and were often responsible for 'keeping families from hardship in the most demanding phases of the life-cycle'.[145]

One of Rowntree's enduring analytical insights into the nature of poverty was the realisation that it varied over the life cycle.[146] Rowntree thought poverty was likely during childhood, early middle age and old age. Nearly 40 years later, in *Men without Work*, the Pilgrim Trust refers to the 'cycle of working-class economic life'. They describe how unskilled workers were able to earn their maximum wage fairly early in adult life, then married and remained comparatively prosperous until the birth of the first child. As the young family grew, they were 'probably living well below the poverty line'. As the children grew older and started earning, it made a 'great difference to the family budget', even though young people's wages were not high. Eventually the couple were alone, as children left home, and remained in reasonable comfort 'provided the husband remain[ed] in employment', until they reached pensionable age. After the age of 65, there was every chance of the couple experiencing poverty, unless living with their children.[147]

The Dundee Social Union's *Report on Housing and Industrial Conditions* (1905), provides rare and detailed evidence on family structure, labour market participation and earnings in the period immediately before the First World War. 'Lady Inspectors' found that of the 3029 cases visited, 769, a mere 25.4 per cent, were entirely dependent on male earnings. Almost as many, some 684, about 22.6 per cent, were female-headed households. A further 433, about 14.3 per cent, were dependent on the wages of both male and female partners, and another 656, about 21.7 per cent, were other types of two-wage households (such as mother and older child). The remainder, some 487 families, or about 16 per cent of this total, was composed of households of three wage earners or more.[148]

Where the adult male partner was the sole wage earner, about half were earning less than £1 per week, and about half of those had families with three or more dependants. All contemporary investigators would place these families below a 'poverty line', and earnings of 'about a pound per week' for a family of two adults and three children are sometimes seen as typifying the family structure of families most likely to be in poverty. But this is far from true. Of the 684 households who were solely dependent on the earnings of the female breadwinner in the Norwich survey, in only three cases did the women earn more than £1 per week, though relatively few of these families that were living on less than £1 per week had large families. This was undoubtedly fortunate, because 655 of these female breadwinner families had earnings of less than 15s per week and 197 had earnings of less than 10s per week. Not surprisingly, therefore, in joint breadwinning households, where both partners were working, about 30 per cent of households had combined incomes below 25s per week.[149]

Further evidence concerning the tenuous existence of families reliant upon the earnings of regularly employed men is provided in Lady Florence Bell's *At the Works: A Study of a Manufacturing Town*. This study, published in 1907, is representative of studies based on the 'voluntary visiting of the poor', though Bell was not motivated by the desire for social reform.[150] Florence was the wife of a successful ironmaster, Sir Hugh Bell, and her study of the life of Middlesborough ironworkers is credited as being highly influenced by Charles Booth's *Life and Labour of the People of London*.[151] It also clearly owes much to Rowntree's *Poverty*, as Bell analyses family expenditure in the context of a 'poverty line' and life-cycle poverty and she also places great emphasis on the importance of women as 'competent managers' of the family budget. But that is where the similarity ends, for as John points out, *At the Works* eschews the Victorian desire for 'scientific' rigour and description of investigators' method.[152]

Middlesborough was a prosperous iron and steel town with a population of 91,302 in 1901.[153] Bell herself warns that few of the working-class families met would be expected to be in 'absolute poverty' since she only visited those employed at the ironworks in receipt of a regular wage.[154]

Of the '900 houses carefully investigated, 125, in round numbers, were found to be absolutely poor'.[155] These were people who 'never have enough to spend on food to keep themselves sufficiently nourished, enough to spend on clothes to be able to protect their bodies adequately, enough to spend on their houses, to acquire a moderate degree of comfort'. Bell also drew attention to the vulnerability of working-class families to poverty at particular life-cycle stages, 'The time when existence seems to press most hard is during the first twelve or fourteen years after marriage, when there is usually a family of young children, who have to be provided for and who cannot earn.'[156] She also describes 175 households who were 'so near the poverty line that they are constantly passing over it'.[157] And here, like Rowntree, Bell thought a lack of thrift or 'skilful management' were likely causes of poverty.[158]

There were exceptions to the view that equated responsibility for 'secondary poverty' with poor management or thriftlessness. Magdalene Stuart, who wrote under the pseudonym Maud Pember Reeves, and who was a member of the Fabian Women's Group, recorded the daily lives of poor families in Lambeth who lived on *Round About a Pound a Week* between 1909 and 1913. Pember Reeves's inquiry was notable for its concentration on the role of mothers, both as manager and providers, but her views on drinking were also quite different from Rowntree, or indeed, most other early twentieth-century social investigators.[159] Reeves was at pains to defend most working-class families: 'married men in full work who keep their job on such a wage do not and cannot drink'.[160] In the period immediately prior to the First World War, the annual volume of beer drunk had declined to about 28 gallons per head from the peak levels of about 34 gallons per head in 1875–6.[161] It seems unlikely that abstinence was practised by all regularly employed men, and while it is clear that heavy drinking would have reduced the household income available to satisfy basic needs, it would have also provided a source of energy (albeit a relatively expensive one).

Incapacitating illness, childbirth and death of a family member were likely to have long-lasting and serious consequences for the household economy. Illness would prevent work and require expenditure on medicine and nourishing food and, in the event a doctor was consulted, the payment of doctor's fees would necessarily have required families to incur debt. These debts would have to be repaid and this would act as a continual drain on resources until they were cleared. The same is true of 'confinement', and investigators regularly note that the expenses associated with childbirth were an important cause of indebtedness.

Most serious of all was illness resulting in death. If of the main breadwin-ner, this would be little short of disaster, but the death of a child was a calamitous psychological event that could also transform the position of the family from that of eking out a means of day-to-day survival to dire straits. Of course, if the parents had had the foresight and means to insure their child's life, there would be life assurance, but many families were so near the edge they either simply could not afford the premiums or chose to 'put food in the mouths of the living' instead. Pember Reeves challenges the common assumption of thriftlessness among the poor, by pointing out that many who could not afford it continued to make provi-sion for children's burial. She notes, in passing, that this insurance failed to benefit children:

> It is a common idea that there is no thrift among them. It would be better for the children if this were true. As a matter of fact, sums varying from 6d a week to 1s6d, 1s8d, or even 2s, go out from incomes which are so small that these sums represent, perhaps, from 2.1/2 to 10 per cent of the whole household allowance. The object of this thrift is, unfortunately, not of the slightest benefit to the children of families concerned.[162]

This ignores, however, the impact on any siblings of the cost of indebted-ness resulting from uninsured burial expenses as, 'For months afterwards the mother and remaining children will eat less in order to pay back the money borrowed.'[163] Nevertheless, the desire to give the dead 'a good send-off' was intimately bound up in notions of respectability among the working class. If insurance money was available, it also provided one of the few genuine chances poor families had to entertain. To be 'buried with ham' may have been the comic cliché that Robert Roberts describes,[164] but among the Middlesborough ironworkers Florence Bell wrote about, providing sandwiches of 'the best description' at funerals was a matter of pride for the parent, widow or widower.[165]

As Bell observed, it was not usually possible to get credit for a funeral, 'for that purpose ready-money must some how be found'.[166] Typically, in the absence of insurance, this would mean selling or pawning any items of value that the family might possess. The importance of the role of moneylenders and pawnbrokers to working-class day-to day existence is commented upon in most contemporary surveys. Rathbone writes,

> the curve of income and expenditure is to some extent smoothed by the help of the pawnbroker, or money-lender, or both.... In bad

weeks clothes and furniture are pledged and debts incurred. In good weeks the surplus is spent on getting straight again. And if anything is left it is turned into the negotiable securities of more clothing and more furniture.[167]

It is also clear that old age often meant a return to poverty, though this was by no means inevitable. Both Bell and Rowntree describe how younger family members regarded the care of older family members as entirely normal and Thane comments that, 'reciprocity between the generations, mutual support in times of need, was as notable as the dependency of aged parents'. It was typically old people without relatives who would end their days in the workhouse.[168] But it is the fragility of the position of households with a regularly employed breadwinner, and how easily their circumstances could be transformed, that is apparent in the social surveys carried out before the First World War:

> We forget how terribly near the margin of disaster the man, even the thrifty man walks, who has, in ordinary normal conditions, but just enough to keep himself on. The spectre of illness and disability is always confronting the working-man; the possibility of being from one day to the other plunged into actual want is always confronting his family.[169]

There were a number of ways that a family could be unpredictably and suddenly 'plunged into actual want'. Loss of employment of the main breadwinner was unlikely to be disastrous, however, since the family's position could be salvaged by rapid re-employment or unemployment insurance benefit from 1911 (if male and working in a trade covered by the scheme). At about the same time, Beveridge analysed the way in which seasonal and cyclical factors would affect employment in key trades. He thought that there was an 'irreducible minimum of unemployment'.[170] For engineering and compositors, he was able to make a detailed analysis of trade union unemployment statistics, for the period 1894–1903. He found that a sizeable group among unemployed compositors who were long-term unemployed (over one year), which he described as the 'chronically unemployed':

> unemployment in each year is confined to a minority which forms generally much the same proportion of total membership, varying between 18 and 26 per cent. Within this minority there is an inner ring of men who are unemployed for practically the whole year.[171]

Beveridge maintained a distinction between the chronically unemployed who 'contrive to subsist indefinitely upon charity or larceny or their wives and children's earnings' and the vast majority of applicants for relief under the Unemployed Workman's Act.[172]

It is striking that unemployment is usually fairly low down the list of 'causes of poverty' provided by investigators at this time. Rowntree and Lasker undertook a detailed investigation of unemployment in York in June 1910.[173] At the time of their study, they describe the economy of York as being 'half-way between normal trade and acute depression'.[174] The method of investigation owed much to Rowntree's more famous survey a few years earlier. A team of investigators called on every working-class house in York (population numbering about 82,000 at that time) and noted the extent of unemployment, through which means the investigator also formed an opinion as to the character of the household, which was then used to categorise the unemployed.[175] Despite the judgemental nature of this inquiry, it does provide valuable information on the characteristics of the unemployed in York, just prior to the introduction of unemployment insurance and labour exchanges in 1911.

Rowntree and Lasker found that of the 1278 people who were unemployed on 7 June 1910, the overwhelming majority were men (89.1 per cent) and they were 'not drawn principally from one or two industries, but from an astonishing variety of trades and occupations'.[176] As Table 2.2 shows, Rowntree and Lasker were able to collect details of the unemployment history of 269 workers and over four-fifths had been unemployed for longer than six weeks, roughly half of the total had been unemployed for six months or more, and nearly one in four were long-term unemployed, who had been out of work for over a year (23.1 per cent). Most were under 30 years old (53.2 per cent) and the vast majority were under 50 years old (88 per cent).[177] This is a pattern of long-term worklessness that is rather different from the interwar period, as we shall see in Chapter 4.

Of 'the vast majority', who had previously been regularly employed prior to unemployment, Rowntree and Lasker found that about one-third (74 out of a total of 217) were living below Rowntree's poverty line, the rest 'being raised above it through earnings of other members of the family'.[178] In addition, Rowntree collected detailed budgetary information from eight families whose principal wage earner was unemployed. In comparison with Atwater's standard of 3500 kcal and 125 g of protein per man per day, which was the dietary standard Rowntree had incorporated

Table 2.2   Duration of unemployment, 1910: length of time unemployed

Duration	Number	Per cent
Less than 1 week	3	1.1
Between 1 and 2 weeks	4	1.5
Between 2 and 4 weeks	21	7.8
Between 4 and 6 weeks	17	6.3
Between 6 and 8 weeks	19	7.1
Between 8 and 12 weeks	39	14.5
About 4 months	12	4.5
About 5 months	19	7.1
About 6 months	16	5.9
About 7–9 months	31	11.5
About 10–12 months	26	9.6
About 13–18 months	24	8.9
About 19–24 months	23	8.6
Over 2 years	15	5.6
Total	269	100

Source: B. S. Rowntree and B. Lasker, *Unemployment: a Social Study* (1911), p. 62.

into his poverty-line analysis of York in 1901, Rowntree and Lasker found that the energy value of unemployed families' diets ranged from 1086 to 2374 kcal per man per day and from 39 to 74 g of protein per man per day. They concluded that 'Some families are actually having to exist on less than one-third of the food necessary to keep them physically efficient and none have more than 2/3rd of that amount.'[179]

These findings were not just confined to York. Pember Reeves found that among London families who were out of work, or who work irregularly and earn less than 18s per week, food consumption of as little as 1d per day per person was not unusual, and as a result, concluded that 'The lives of the children of the poor are shortened, and the bodies of the children of the poor are stunted and starved on a low wage. And to the insufficiency of a low wage is added the horror that it is never secure.'[180] These families at the bottom of the income range within the Edwardian working class would be classified as malnourished according to any scale of recommended dietary intakes, probably grossly so. The extent to which this malnutrition was the result of unemployment per se, or to low and irregular wages, is not possible to determine with any precision, however.

2.2   Dietary Surveys

In addition to surveys of poverty there were a number of inquiries into the adequacy of working-class diets. Contemporaneous with Rowntree's investigation of York, Dr Noel Paton, Dr J. C. Dunlop and Dr Elsie Inglis undertook an investigation of the dietaries of 15 families from labouring classes in Edinburgh. The inquiry of Paton *et al.*, published in 1900, although less well known than Rowntree's, also represents an important paradigmatic poverty inquiry. Like Rowntree's survey of York that was influenced by Booth's earlier investigation of the London poor, it is possible to discern a nineteenth-century lineage to Paton *et al.*'s Edinburgh survey, most notably the dietary investigations of Edward Smith during the Lancashire cotton famine of 1862–3.[181] Paton *et al.*'s dietary survey was replicated in Glasgow in 1911–12 by Lindsay's investigation of 60 family diets and in Birmingham in 1913 by Carver's inquiry into the diets of 80 families. These three surveys, therefore, form a unique collection in which an aspect of poverty is examined using the same methodology. Later, after the First World War, Paton would be instrumental in specifying the methodology and collating the results of a number of small-scale dietary inquiries that provide the data necessary to inform judgements about the impact of the war on working-class dietaries.

The general objective of these inquiries was an investigation of the nutritional adequacy of diets due to the known association between poor diet and susceptibility to infection and disease.[182] In Birmingham, Carver was interested in the relationship between poor diet and tuberculosis, while in Glasgow Lindsay was concerned with the incidence of rickets among poor families. Her study was also noteworthy in its attempt to ascertain differences in dietary adequacy by ethnicity.[183] All three inquiries compare the food consumed by the families with a contemporaneous dietary standard, which was either Atwater's recommended dietary allowances, dating from his pioneering American research at the end of the nineteenth century, or in the case of Carver, a modified version of this standard. But unlike Rowntree and Bowley, these investigators did not seek to generalise their results beyond their immediate sample of families via a poverty-line analysis.[184] The similarity of method between the two Scottish inquiries is due to the influence of Paton who advised Lindsay during her Glasgow survey.[185]

There are a number of difficulties with this type of direct dietary analysis. Nutritionists draw the distinction between minimum nutritional intakes and recommended nutritional allowances. The former is concerned with the level of nutritional intake below which life is not possible. These levels are low and extremely controversial.[186] In contrast, a recommended dietary allowance can be viewed as 'the amount considered sufficient for the maintenance of health in nearly all people'.[187] Most recommendations incorporate a safety margin to allow for individual nutritional vari-ation.[188] These standards are not fixed over time, but change in response to scientific discoveries, such as the understanding of the physiological importance of vitamins. Carver's discussion of the way in which it was necessary to modify Atwater's dietary recommendations, demonstrates how they had changed at the beginning of the century, in response to evolving scientific opinion and socially determined ideas of 'adequacy'.[189] Because nutritional science was in its infancy at the beginning of the twentieth century, the nutritional standard is purely based upon energy needs provided by specified proportions of proteins, fats and carbohydrates.

These nutrient requirements are referenced on the needs of an adult male performing 'moderate muscular work', in which the activity level, and hence energy requirement, is a descriptor that is itself clearly ambiguous. To enable comparison of families of different composition, the dietary requirements for women and children are translated into daily male equivalents, using Atwater's equivalence scale. As we have seen, Bowley also used this equivalence scale, but although cited by Rowntree, he used a quite different equivalence scale in practice. One implication of this methodology is that the distribution of foodstuffs within the family is assumed to be nutritionally optimal. Information relating to the household distribution of food is scarce, but what little that exists suggests that this is extremely unlikely to be a reasonable assumption.

Finally, the method requires considerable accuracy. In all three dietary surveys, the investigators went to great lengths to ensure that the records of food actually consumed by the family were net of waste in preparation and consumption. The analysis of diets was based on a carefully executed questionnaire, which was usually completed for one week, followed by an interview. During the week of study, every article of food purchased by the family and eaten in the house was weighed and the price noted by the compiler. Allowances were made for waste in preparation, the stock of food present in the house at the beginning and end of the investigation period along with any consumption of food by boarders and guests.[190]

Despite this apparent precision, however, it is probable that the estimates of food consumed are biased downwards, as it is likely that some food would have been consumed outside the home and remained unrecorded. In Booth's *Life and Labour*, roughly 3 per cent of expenditure was on 'meals out' – higher than average family expenditure on sugar, potatoes, fish and vegetables.[191] In the period immediately before the First World War, fish and chip shops emerged in working-class districts, which provided a nutritious and fairly inexpensive family meal.[192] Moreover, they almost certainly under-record consumption of alcohol and hence available energy, though this would have left less income available for other items of expenditure.[193] Dingle argues that although beer was not a cost-effective source of energy, average consumption levels would generate over 5000 kcal per week.[194]

The findings of these surveys are set out in Table 2.3. These are average figures and, of course, there was variance around the mean depending on household composition and labour force participation. With the exception of the figures for the 40 Birmingham tuberculosis families, the first point to note is the striking similarity of the findings. Labourers' families were, on average, falling short of the 3500 kcal per man-day deemed necessary by contemporaries for 'healthy life'. With respect to protein and fats, contemporaries disagreed about desirable intakes, but in all cases the diets were deemed to be inadequate with respect to protein or fat intake.[195] Although these diets are inadequate when judged by these standards, the extent of malnutrition is hardly evidence to support Drummond and Wilbraham's famous claim that 'It is no exaggeration to say that the opening of the twentieth century saw malnutrition more rife in England than it had been since the dearths of medieval and Tudor times.'[196]

Mackenzie examined changes in the energy value of working-class diets between 1860 and 1914. This was an ambitious exercise that required data on income distribution, patterns of household expenditure, and

Table 2.3 Nutritional content of labourers' diets, 1900–12

	Year	kcal	Protein (g)	Fat (g)	Carbohydrate (g)
Edinburgh	1900	3328	108	88	479
Glasgow	1912	3163	110	83	473
Birmingham	1913	2860	88	88	407

Source: Author's calculations from Paton *et al.*, Carver and Lindsay.

Table 2.4   Changes in the energy value of diets, 1880–1914

	Energy 3115 kcal = 100	
	1880	1914
Lowest decile	97	89
Lowest quartile	95	100
Median	99	113
Upper quartile	105	117

Source: W. A. Mackenzie, 'Changes in the Standard of Living in the United Kingdom, 1860–1914', *Economica*, No. 3 (1921), p. 226.

retail prices at these dates.[197] Mackenzie's results are set out in Table 2.4, for a reference family of two adults and three children, based on a benchmark of 9500 kcal per reference family per week (3.87 male equivalents at 3500 per day). The figures for the lowest in 1914 are for urban workers, while those for 1880 relate to agricultural workers.

With the exception of the figures for the lowest quartile group, Mackenzie's estimates show an improvement in the energy intake of diets between 1880 and 1914. By the later date, those households above the lower quartile were satisfying their energy needs (as measured by a fairly generous standard). In 1880, this was only true of the median households and above. Her conclusions with respect to the lowest quartile are important. She also claims that a poor agricultural worker was better able to feed his family in 1880, than an urban worker was in 1914. According to Mackenzie this is explained by the former group's advantage of providing their vegetables at low cost.[198] In 1914, an urban worker's diet provided only 89 per cent of contemporaneously defined energy needs, or about 3115 kcal per man per day. Nevertheless, this intake would meet modern energy dietary recommendations.

Oddy analysed the nutritional adequacy of many of the diets recorded in budget studies and social surveys of the period (for both rural and urban families). Rather than using contemporaneous estimates of equivalence, Oddy expressed his findings in terms of nutritional intake per head. His results are reported in Table 2.5. Oddy concluded that it 'seems inescapable that families in this period with an income of less than, say, 30 shillings per week and with a family of growing children might well obtain only 2,000–2,200 calories and 50–60 grams of protein

Table 2.5 Daily nutrient intake of working-class families, 1887–1913

Weighted mean	Energy (kcal)	Protein (g)	Fat (g)	Carbohydrates (g)	Iron (mg)	Calcium (mg)
1887–1901	2099	57	58	336	10	0.31
1902–13	2398	71	65	375	12.1	0.46

Source: D. Oddy and D. S. Miller (eds), *The Making of the Modern British Diet* (1976), p. 226.

per head per day'.[199] This compares with estimates derived from food supply data, 1909–13, which suggest an average energy value close to 3000 kcal per head.[200] In relation to Mackenzie's estimates Oddy's claim seems unlikely. A poverty-line equivalent to 30s per week in 1900 is roughly equivalent to male median earnings. Mackenzie's study suggests that those at the lower quartile of the male earnings distribution and above (25s 2d per week), were satisfying a dietary standard of 3500 kcal per man-day in 1914 and it is unlikely that the situation would have been radically different in 1900.[201] Although it remains uncertain how food was typically distributed within the family, the 1904 Report of the Inter-Departmental Committee on Physical Deterioration found that a third of all schoolchildren 'went hungry' and most contemporary investigators echo Rowntree's observation that 'mother and children habitually go short'.[202]

Contemporary dietary surveys do reveal the extremely limited nature of typical labourers' family diets of the period. According to Paton *et al.*, the principal foods consumed were bread, potato, milk, eggs, vegetables, sugar, jam and meat (usually beef). In addition, small quantities of butter (or margarine), suet and dripping, cheese and fish were also eaten.[203] Lindsay was struck by how difficult it was for labourers' families to attain the 'barest necessities of life' and by their 'monotonous existence'.[204] On a day-to-day basis, the food eaten by poor families had to be easy to prepare. Cooking utensils and facilities were few, fuel cost them money, but more importantly, as Roberts writes, most women 'had little time to cook', which contributed to the low culinary standards that existed in Lancashire cotton mill towns that she examined.[205] It was for similar reasons that Pember Reeves thought that bread, margarine and jam were the diet of choice among the Lambeth poor:

> Bread, however, is their chief food. It is cheap; they like it; it comes into the house ready cooked; it is always at hand, and needs no plate

and spoon. Spread with a scraping of butter, jam, or margarine, according to the length of purse of the mother, they never tire of it as long as they are in their ordinary state of health. They receive it into their hands, and can please themselves as to where and how they eat it.[206]

Meals of tea, bread and jam are frequently recorded as the staple menu for poor families, especially for women and children. The most famous record of this type is from Rathbone's study of casual labour in Liverpool. A family of father, mother and seven children ate bread and margarine (sometimes with tea) on 13 occasions out of the 17 recorded.[207] While this example is not typical, diets that were based around bread and potatoes and a little meat or fish were the norm for many of the labouring poor, as revealed in contemporary surveys, at least.

The majority of social investigations carried out at the beginning of the twentieth century were concerned with the efficacy of expenditure revealed in working-class diets, as diseases associated with malnutrition, such as rickets, were widespread.[208] Most noted that the diets could be improved by the substitution of vegetable protein, in the form of peas, lentils and beans, for bread. Such a diet would provide a more cost-efficient means of achieving the required intake of protein as it was more cost-efficient expenditure than buying more meat.[209] Few social investigators are as open in their condemnation of the working-class diet as Paton *et al.*, who blame the prevalence of the bread, margarine and jam diet on 'the lazy habits of the labouring classes'.[210] Although widely shared, such views were far from universal, as is clear from Pember Reeves's defence of working-class Lambeth women, struggling to provide for their families with inadequate resources.[211] And as Oddy remarked, such middle-class comment 'ignored the palatability of the foods involved and their acceptability within the family'.[212]

What should we conclude from the results of these investigations? With respect to modern dietary standards, the energy values of these diets would probably be regarded as adequate.[213] Moreover, while the investigators themselves were concerned to establish a link between poor diet and ill health, lack of scientific understanding made this task a formidable one. These dietary inquiries were conducted just as the first vitamins were being discovered and it was not until the First World War that the importance of vitamins and minerals was generally recognised.[214] Moreover, there is a danger in treating all of the budget studies carried out before the First World War as equally reliable. Some were clearly carried out more carefully than others. Even for the better surveys, the evidence is often fragmentary, with relatively few budgetary records. And those that were recorded were usually kept for one week only.

Moreover, as Roberts points out, 'it is doubtful if the working classes were quite as poor as one may logically conclude from the statistics about wages, poverty lines and larger than average families'.[215] On the basis of oral evidence, Roberts questions the extent to which the description of working-class diets found in contemporary surveys is accurate, arguing that diets at the turn of the century were more varied and included significant amounts of vegetables, other than potatoes. One possible source of these foods would be allotments, and she found roughly half of families used garden or allotment produce to supplement their diets.[216] Overall, therefore, it seems likely that for urban workers, the nutritional adequacy of diets in the early part of the twentieth century had showed some advancement on those a generation earlier. Indeed, given the advance in real wages, it would be surprising if this were not so.

2.3   Rural Poor

There were a number of social surveys of the conditions of agricultural labourers and their families before the First World War, including one carried out by Rowntree. The first of these inquiries was carried out by Mann in 1903 and published in 1904. He explicitly followed the methods used by Rowntree in his survey of York to obtain evidence of life in an agricultural village, Ridgemount, in Bedfordshire, during the autumn of 1903.[217] Mann adjusted Rowntree's standard for differences in cost of rent, which produced a poverty-line income for a reference family of two adults and three children of 18s 4d per week, instead of the 21s 8d calculated by Rowntree in York.[218]

Mann found that 38.5 per cent of workers' families were in primary poverty, amounting to 41 per cent of the working-class population of the village (these proportions represented 31.5 per cent of all families and 34 per cent of all individuals in the village). Another 9 per cent of workers were in secondary poverty (equal to 7.1 per cent of the individuals in the village).[219] Mann was unhesitant in attributing most of this secondary poverty to drink. Of the 40 families in primary poverty, most were so because of old age or illness (14), then low wages (11), irregular work (6), death or desertion (5) or because of a large family (4).[220] Overall, Mann found that four-fifths of children under 16 were in poverty in the village as Table 2.6 shows, claiming that 'during childhood, poverty conditions

Table 2.6   Age distribution of villagers in primary poverty, 1903

Ages	Proportion in primary poverty
Under 16	83
16–25	12
25–55	36
Over 55	29

Source: P. H. Mann, 'Life in an Agricultural Village in England', *Sociological Papers* (1904), p. 184.

are almost inevitable'.[221] He concluded that 'the standard of life on the land is lower than in the cities; the chances of success are less and of poverty are greater; life is less interesting; and the likelihood of the workhouse as a place of residence in old age the greater'.[222]

Mann's survey was followed by Maude Davies's study of *Life in an English Village*. Between 1905 and 1907, Davies set about describing the circumstances of the people of Corsley, a parish in Wiltshire. The village consisted of 220 households, including 165 cottages inhabited by 634 people, plus more substantial dwellings, such as farmhouses. This was roughly half the population of the parish in 1831.[223] The social structure of the village can be seen from Table 2.7. Most had good gardens, which were cultivated and 'the majority add to their income by selling garden produce, even when not holding an allotment'.[224] Women-headed households

Table 2.7   The social structure and housing in Corsley, 1905–7

Occupation of householder	No. cottages	No. rooms	No. inhabitants
Small farmer, market gardeners	14	69	58
Brickmaker, shoemaker, etc.	5	20	17
Carters	13	51	66
Cowmen	7	30	31
Labourers	33	136	148
Miscellaneous agricultural	14	56	60
Miscellaneous gardeners, retired labourers	25	89	75
Artisans	20	104	85
Women householders	34	134	84
Total	165	689	624

Source: Maud F. Davies, *Life in an English Village* (1909), p. 134.

occupied about one in five cottages. Of the 37 adult agricultural labourers who were regularly employed in the village, she ascertained the cash wages of 27, which averaged 13s 11d, and after taking perquisites into account, their earnings were equivalent to 15s 3½d a week.[225] In addition there were 18 men in the parish who were not regularly employed, but worked as day labourers or woodmen at 2s 6d per day.[226]

Davies was interested to discover how many of the 220 households in Corsley were 'in a condition of poverty'.[227] Her methodology also followed Rowntree, as the income of each household is compared to a contemporaneously defined 'poverty line' and like Rowntree's survey of York, Davies's inquiry is a combination of empirical social inquiry and impressionistic description. For example, Davies found it difficult to ascertain the income of households where 'the male worker is not a wage-earner'. Under these circumstances, 'appearance of the houses and inmates, and opinion of neighbours have in these cases been taken into account and an estimate formed'.[228] Davies adopts Rowntree's 1901 poverty-line standard, omitting rent and making marginal adjustments suggested by Mann, but otherwise without modification.[229] Accordingly, Davies finds that 28 households (144 persons) were in primary poverty. She attributes the causes of rural poverty to insufficient wages or large families, the principal wage earner incapacitated by illness or old age and households without a male wage earner.[230]

Davies's construction of 'secondary poverty' is idiosyncratic, and, while clearly influenced by Rowntree, introduces the concept of 'surplus income', which is defined as 1s per head per week above the primary poverty line. She defines secondary poverty as 'all households whose income does not give '1s. per head above primary poverty, *as well as those households where the income should be sufficient, but where it is squandered and the members are obviously living in want*' (emphasis added).[231] On this basis 37 households were considered to be in 'secondary poverty'. Of the total of 70 labourers' households, she thought 16 were in primary and 13 in secondary poverty.[232] Overall, therefore, Davies's inquiry found 12.7 per cent of all households to be in primary poverty, plus a further 16.8 per cent in secondary poverty – figures comparable to Rowntree's 1901 results. Among labourers, nearly 23 per cent were in primary poverty and a further 19 per cent were in secondary poverty.

Her conclusions on the incidence of poverty in Corsley rest uneasily with the description of life in the village, as Davies's account places little emphasis on the nature or extent of rural poverty. As part of her poverty investigation, Davies collected weekly budgets from 13 households between 1905 and 1907. Davies classified the budgets according to whether there was a 'deficiency of income' or ' income sufficient', or rarely 'income ample'. In contrast with her conclusion concerning the extent of primary poverty in the village, Davies maintains that, except in the very poorest households, nearly all labourers take fresh milk, bought cheaply from local farms, and grow varied vegetables to supplement their meat and vegetable-based diets. Usually they have enough left over for sweet treats:

> The produce of the garden furnishes a large proportion of the food of the people. Potatoes, onions, greens and other vegetables figure largely in the menu of the poorest households, especially those with many children. Bacon is almost universally eaten. Meat is eaten in all but the very poorest households at least once or twice a week, and it is an article of daily consumption in the majority of cottages. . . . In some poorer families one meal takes the place of tea and supper, At tea time one sometimes finds prepared a meal of hot meat or stew, kippers and other fish, jam-tarts, etc, besides jam and cake, and in one very poor family where the mother was out working the tea appeared to consist of bread and jam and the contents of innumerable jars.[233]

Only three budgets revealed the household to be 'near the margin of primary poverty', in one case the family diet was an 'excellent one', owing to the 'cleverness' of the wife as a 'manager and cook', one other also provided a 'varied diet'. Only in one case, that of an old woman, is destitution or dependency hinted at, although we are reassured that her children provide for this woman's needs. Davies notes that 'probably a few of the very poorest old people, paupers and others, live almost entirely on bread and butter and tea'.[234]

Nineteenth-century ideas of deserving and undeserving poor also condition Davies's analysis of the character of poverty in Corsley. Respectable poor, or women-headed households, were quickly passed over, but those who had children showing some mark of deficiency (of character), such as dullness, nervousness, laziness, strangeness or peculiarities of disposition and dirtiness were subject to further inquiry.[235] Honesty, promptness in paying debt, and thrift were characteristics of respectability, irrespective of income. Evidence of criminality, drunkenness or bad language disqualified the family from 'respectability' in Davies's eyes and, unsurprisingly, she thought that 'the proportion of drunkards is greater among the people in secondary poverty'. But it is clear that the idea that poverty might have socio-economic causes, rather than being simply the result of individual moral deficiencies, also exerted a powerful influence on her investigation.

Davies concludes that among the 18 families with children at school who were in primary poverty, ten had 'deficient children', but in only four cases was this the fault of parents or home and 'These facts show emphatically that the dullness and deficiency of the children, even in a rural district where every advantage of good air and healthy surroundings is obtained, is mainly due to malnutrition.'[236] In contrast, she points to the health of children of market gardeners, who 'succeed by some means in avoiding the deadly grip of poverty'.[237] This is the conclusion she wished to place the most emphasis upon, rather than the incidence of rural poverty per se.

Rowntree and Kendall's 1913 study *How the Labourer Lives*, was concerned as much with the problem of rural depopulation as it was with the socio-economic characteristics of poverty. Unlike Mann and Davies's village-level inquiries, this is a geographically wide-ranging survey. Like Rowntree's earlier York inquiry, *How the Labourer Lives* combines a poverty-line approach with the direct analysis of household expenditure. Forty-two family budgets were collected in 1912 from eight counties in England (Oxfordshire, Essex, Berkshire, Bedfordshire, Leicestershire and the North, West and East Ridings of Yorkshire). The families included in Rowntree and Kendall's survey were not selected at random, however. They deliberately avoided very large families on the grounds that they would include children who were working.[238] The family income of the budgets collected varied between 10s and 26s 3d per week.[239]

The budgets were collected by a combination of questionnaire and interview and include details of perquisites, of which accommodation was usually the most important.[240] The average value of these payments is recorded in the 1906 Earnings and Hours of Labour Inquiry.[241] The average weekly earnings of agricultural labourers in England was 17s 6d, but if horsemen and cattlemen are included the average is 18s 4d In Wales the average for all classes of rural labour was 18s per week. These figures include an allowance for the payment in kind of accommodation and some food (milk and potatoes), which account for about 3s of the average wage in England and 4s 3d in Wales. As Rowntree and Kendall note, agricultural wages varied significantly on a county-by-county basis, from 14s 11d in Oxfordshire to 20s 10d in Derbyshire.[242] Nevertheless, the distribution of Rowntree and Kendall's family budgets were biased towards the lower end of the distribution.[243]

Using the same standard as applied in York, Rowntree and Kendall
found that a family of two adults and three children would need an
income (including perquisites) of 20s 6d. This calculation embodies the
same assumptions as Rowntree's York poverty-line analysis, with some
adjustments for changes in prices between 1901 and 1907 and for variations in living costs between urban and rural areas (principally rent). In
consequence, Rowntree and Kendall's figure is based upon the same
assumptions with respect to his equivalence scale, which were shown to
be in error for York.[244] Rowntree and Kendall note that 'with five exceptions (North Cumberland, Durham, Westmoreland, Lancashire and
Derbyshire), the average earnings in every county of England and Wales
are below it [the poverty line]'.[245] While Rowntree and Kendall were
clear that this did not mean every agricultural labourer's family was in
primary poverty, they argued that 'the wages paid by farmers ... in the
vast majority of cases, [were] insufficient to maintain a family of average
size in a state of merely physical efficient' and that rural distress and ill
health among families living below the poverty line were avoided only
through charitable gifts.[246]

Rowntree and Kendall also evaluated the nutritional content of
labourers' household diets and found that on average they only provided 90 per cent of the families' energy requirements and 76 per cent
of protein requirements, when judged against Atwater's standard of
3500 kcal and 125 g of protein equivalent per man per day.[247] Moreover,
they found that the rural diets had less variation than York urban diets.
In contrast, Lindsay noted that the energy value of British rural diets
was greater than urban diets at the beginning of the century, due to
higher carbohydrate intakes, but were lower in fat content.[248] In rural
areas, nearly all meals at breakfast and tea were of bread and margarine,
with meat and potatoes for dinner, or a meat stew with vegetables grown
in the garden or allotment. In many cases, the menus indicate that what
little meat was available was reserved for the man as the 'health of the
breadwinner must be the first consideration'.[249] Several families acknowledged to the investigator that 'the wife and children hardly ever touched
meat', or that 'meat is religiously set aside for the breadwinner'.[250]

Although the physiological necessity of maintaining the paid worker
in as good health as possible was recognised, the long-term impact on the
family economy was frequently ignored. One Leicestershire labourer's
wife acknowledged £20 for doctors' bills, including £8 for confinements,
in 18 years. Three of her eight children had died and she had herself
been 'very seriously ill', and she admitted that, 'I love meat, but I often

go without. I've not touched it now for two days. I keep it for him; he *has* to have it.'[251] Roberts records similar arrangements with respect to the distribution of resources among the urban poor: 'in apportioning of food, small girls often came off very badly indeed: mothers felt that they didn't need much – not the same as lads'.[252] And Pember Reeves reminds us that among poor Lambeth families, 'Meat [was] bought for the man.'[253] Likewise, for many of the women and children of rural England, diets would consist of bread, potatoes and margarine.

Other than small amounts of food, fuel and cleaning materials, little else was bought. It was fairly commonplace for the poorest of Rowntree and Kendall's families to have bought no new adult clothes since marriage, relying on charitable donations, and to have run up significant debts – sometimes equivalent to 10 or 20 times a week's wage. Despite Roberts's claim that the *very* poor never fell into debt, because 'nobody allowed them any credit',[254] Rowntree and Kendall record that by walking miles, it was possible for agricultural labourers to find credit.[255]

Undoubtedly, life in these rural communities was hard, with long hours of labour in the summer months and daylight hours in the winter, if work was available. Many labourers would be 'standing off' without work in the winter, hoping that extra harvest money would help see them through. An existence described by the wife of one labourer as 'You can't call it living; it's dragging of yourself along', or another, who when asked how they managed replied, 'I don't know how we manage; the thing is to get it past.'[256] In some cases it was clear to Rowntree that starvation was only prevented by produce grown in the garden or allotment.[257] For the majority of these families Rowntree and Kendall concluded that they did not have the means to meet the needs of 'physical efficiency' and they remind the reader what this meant in practice:

> It means that people have no right to keep in touch with the great world outside the village by so much as taking in a weekly newspaper. It means that a wise mother, when she is tempted to buy her children a penny-worth of cheap oranges, will devote the penny to flour instead. It means that the temptation to take the shortest journey should be strongly resisted. It means that toys and dolls and picture books, even of the cheapest quality, should never be purchased; that birthdays should be practically indistinguishable from other days. It means that every natural longing for pleasure should be ignored or set aside. It means, in short, a life without colour, space, or atmosphere that stifles and hems in the labourer's soul as in too many cases his cottage does his body.[258]

2.4   Poverty and Health

A more direct way of gauging the impact of diet on health is to examine changes in morbidity and mortality data. Most investigators agree that changes in nutrition are important in explaining variations in mortality experience. Contemporaries were also similarly convinced. Sir George Newman, Chief Medical Officer, stated in 1911 that 'defective nutrition stands in the forefront as the most important of all physical defects from which school children suffer'.[259] Other contemporaries pointed to the poor quality of the housing stock. Edwin Chadwick, for example, argued in 1903 that the poor health of schoolchildren in Aberdeen reflected their housing conditions.[260] Although mortality rates had been falling sharply since the 1870s in England and Wales, and the mortality of children aged between 1 and 4 had also begun to decline, infant mortality rates remained stubbornly high until after the turn of the century.[261] As Lewis pithily put it, 'In the 1900s it was not uncommon for women to speak in the same breath of the number of children they had raised and the number they had buried.'[262]

The 1895 Factory and Workshop Act prohibited the early return of women to work after childbirth, partly because of contemporary concerns about the impact of women's work on children's health.[263] Woolf argues that there is correlation between areas of high female employment and high rates of infant mortality in England and Wales, seemingly endorsing contemporary concerns about the impact of women's work on their children's health. Working women would not be able to breastfeed their infants and would find it hard to make adequate arrangements for the supervision of infants while they were working. Dyhouse has shown how these ideas were part of the domestic ideology that viewed the women's sphere as the home, not the workplace. They also failed to grasp the sheer economic necessity of women's work.[264] Even in households where there was a regularly employed male breadwinner, we have already seen how female earnings could be crucial in providing income for necessary expenditure, such as children's clothes and shoes. In other households, female earnings were either the sole source of income or were themselves instrumental in preventing severe destitution. Moreover, as Winter points out, significant improvements in infant mortality rates occurred during both world wars when female labour force participation rates increased sharply.[265]

According to Beaver, the explanation for the improvement in infant mortality was due to 'improvements in the safety of available infant foods'.[266] Although as Dyhouse notes, we need to exercise caution here because a large proportion of working-class mothers, possibly as many as four out of five, continued to breastfeed their infants.[267] Infant mortality did vary systematically by class, however. The starting point for this analysis is Titmuss's *Birth, Poverty and Wealth*, which, using the Registrar-General's taxonomy of class in conjunction with the 1911 population census returns, investigated how infant mortality varied in relation to economic and social status. His results are reported in Table 2.8.

There are serious defects with the 1911 classification, which did not distinguish sufficiently between various occupations in agriculture, textiles and mining to allow classification by socio-economic group.[268] Nevertheless, it is clear that infant mortality rates were inversely related to the socio-economic status of males. The infant mortality rates of unskilled male labourers were twice that of their middle- and upper-class counterparts. The reasons for the differences in infant mortality experienced by class remain the subject of dispute, and it is undoubtedly a complex question, but differences in nutritional attainment, which affect resistance to infectious diseases, are likely to have been crucially important in this period.[269] Death rates among children under four from diarrhoea and dysentery were significantly higher in 1901 and 1911 than they had been in the late nineteenth century.[270]

While the rich were clearly able to provide better medical care for their children than the poor, it is also likely that the spread of all types of epidemic diseases were checked in middle- and upper-class areas by better housing and sanitation.[271] Many working-class urban families

Table 2.8 Infant mortality per 1000 legitimate live births based on father's occupation, 1911

Class	Socio-economic group	Infant mortality (per 1000 live births)
I	Middle and upper classes	76.4
II	Intermediate I/III	106.4
III	Skilled labour	112.7
IV	Intermediate III/V	121.5
V	Unskilled workers	152.5
VI	Textile workers	148.1
VII	Miners	160.1
VIII	Agricultural workers	96.9

Source: R. Titmuss, *Birth, Poverty and Wealth* (1943), Table I, p. 23.

were living in overcrowded and filthy slums. Based on the 1901 census returns, the percentage of families occupying overcrowded tenements (defined as more than two people per room) ranged from over 30 per cent in Jarrow, Gateshead, South Shields and Newcastle to less than 1 per cent in Bedford, Northampton and Peterborough.[272] According to Bowley and Burnett-Hurst's investigation of poverty in northern towns, 50 per cent of working-class houses in Stanley, nearly 20 per cent of those in Warrington, 13.5 per cent in Reading and 8.7 per cent in Northampton were overcrowded (defined as more than one 'equivalent adult' per room).[273] Marr's study confirmed the squalid living conditions of working-class housing in Manchester and Salford in 1904. He records instances of up to six families sharing the same toilet – just under half the houses that he surveyed were damp, with just under one in five having no inside tap.[274] A similar level of deprivation existed in London. Howarth and Wilson found that 'In all, 9.27 per cent of the population of West Ham was living in an overcrowded condition in 1901,' which was nearly 25,000 people (defined as more than one person per room).[275]

Infant mortality rates among the middle and upper classes were also better because of the increased risks associated with artificial feeding in areas of high population density. At the end of the nineteenth century, *urban* areas increasingly relied upon milk brought in by rail, which was not cooled and often stood around for hours before being sold loose from the churn. From Table 2.8, it can be seen that infant mortality rates among agricultural workers in 1911 were significantly lower than their urban counterparts. After 1900, supplies of bottled and pasteurised milk gradually increased and by 1925, practically all milk sold in London had been pasteurised.[276] In addition, Beaver has argued that 'dried milk was widely accepted among the managerial, professional and artisan classes', which had the advantage over liquid milk mixtures as they 'did not import infection'.[277]

2.5   Impact of the War on Civilian Health

Traditionally, the First World War is seen as having a deleterious impact on civilian health. Drummond and Wilbraham, for example, argue that there is good evidence for a decline in health:

The most obvious sign was the lowered resistance to infection. The people could not stand up to the terrible epidemic of influenza, which swept across Europe in 1918. They died like flies; the mortality in London in some weeks was as high as 2,500. At the time it was thought that the severity of the epidemic was due to a particularly virulent strain of the infective organism. With our modern knowledge of the influence of diet on resistance to diseases, we can see that vitamin deficiencies had prepared the way.[278]

This interpretation has been challenged by Winter. He maintains that the First World War had a positive impact on health in Britain, especially among the working classes, and challenges the assertion that wartime controls were detrimental to public health.[279] Winter's argument is based on a number of different types of evidence. First, overall male life expectancy increased from 49 years in 1911 to 56 years in 1921. For working-class males, using life assurance age-specific mortality records, Winter argues that men over the age of military service had an improved chance of survival as by 1918 'working-class mortality rates had been reduced, although not enough to eliminate completely the demographic disadvantage of being a working-class man in early twentieth century Britain'.[280] Secondly, while infant mortality rates were fairly stable across the First World War in most combatant countries, in Britain infant mortality declined by about 20 per cent. In the last years of peace, infant mortality rates varied considerably from year to year, but the figures reported in Table 2.9 are indices based on an average of the rate in 1911–13.

Table 2.9 Infant mortality in England and Wales, 1905–25 (per 1000 live births, 1911–13 = 100)

1905	107
1911–13	100
1914	95
1915	99
1916	82
1917	87
1918	87
1919	80
1920	72
1921–25	68

Source: J. M. Winter, 'The Impact of the First World War on Civilian Health in Britain', *Economic History Review*, 20 (1977), Table 4, p. 495.

Winter points out that in every year other than 1915, the post neonatal mortality rate shows the most rapid improvement, though less dramatic improvements are also evident in mortality within the first month of life.[281] This is important because it reflects changes in mortality after children had been weaned and had 'lost the protection of their mothers' antibodies against infectious diseases'.[282] Moreover, these improvements were not simply restricted to certain parts of the country, although Winter acknowledges that not all indicators of health unambiguously improve during the war. Most notably there was a 6 per cent increase in tuberculosis between 1914 and 1918.

According to Winter, the explanations for the improvement in health are: better state support for infant welfare (especially antenatal and neonatal care by the Local Government Board and by the Ministry of Health from 1919),[283] rising wages, declining consumption of alcohol and improvements in food consumption. The latter, according to evidence of the Sumner Committee inquiry, which reported on working-class living standards during the war, was due to a change in working-class diets brought about by fuller employment as a consequence of wartime production:

> More milk, potatoes, bread, flour, rice, tapioca, and oatmeal were consumed per family in 1918 than in 1914. Meat was replaced by bacon and bland white bread by the more nutritious, though less aesthetically pleasing brown bread. The result may have been less appetising, starchier meals, but aside from a decline in sugar consumption, wartime diets maintained pre-war calorific levels.[284]

In this context, Winter also notes the increased consumption of condensed and dried milk, due to shortages of cows' milk. Milk substitutes may have increased infant survival rates because they 'were less likely to carry the tubercle bacillus'.[285] Not everyone is convinced, however. Bryder criticises Winter's over-reliance on aggregate mortality data, suggesting that the morbidity data provide less ground for optimism.[286] In addition, she argues that the data on maternal mortality show little wartime improvement and that, in any case, such improvement that occurs is not necessarily attributable to improved nutrition.[287] Crucially, Bryder stresses the importance of malnutrition as one possible explanation of the rise in respiratory disease during, and immediately after, the war. Moreover, Harris's analysis of the height of schoolchildren, derived from the annual reports of school medical officers, in a number of towns in England

and Wales between 1908 and 1950, suggests that the First World War did not mark a clear discontinuity. Harris argues that there were 'substantial variations in both the pace and timing of the increases that occurred'.[288] Average heights in Bradford and Croydon show clear evidence of an increase prior to 1914. In Leeds heights increase slowly after the end of the war, while in Cambridge, Rhondda and Warrington the increase began in the 1920s. In most cases Harris concludes that the evidence points to a gradual improvement in heights from the beginning of the twentieth century, which quickened in pace during the late 1920s and 1930s. Indeed, this conclusion accords with the evidence on average real wages and earnings presented in Chapter 3. Real wages and earnings increased modestly during the late 1920s, and for most of the early 1930s, due to the fall in consumer prices.

Table 2.10 sets out Feinstein's estimates of the wartime changes in retail prices, average money wages and average earnings. Feinstein's series rely heavily on the original estimates of Bowley, and the Ministry of Labour.[289] From this table, it can be seen that average weekly money wages increased steadily through the First World War and short postwar boom, so that by 1920, relative to 1913, they were about 2.5 times higher. The time path of average weekly earnings displayed a similar trend, although earnings grew slightly faster than wages during the First World War.

Feinstein's index of retail prices has been used to calculate the indices of average real wages and average real earnings reported in Table 2.10. Notice that Feinstein's index of retail prices has not grown as fast as

Table 2.10   Wages, earnings and prices, 1913–20

	Average weekly wage rates	Average weekly earnings	Retail prices	Real wages	Real earnings
1913	100	100	100	100	100
1914	101	101	101	100	100
1915	108	117	121	89	97
1916	118	133	143	83	93
1917	139	170	173	80	98
1918	179	211	199	90	106
1919	215	241	211	102	114
1920	257	278	244	105	114

Source: C. H. Feinstein, *National Income, Output and Expenditure of the United Kingdom*, Table 65, T140 and calculated by author.

wages or earnings by 1920, indicating some real wage and earnings gains relative to 1913. During the middle years of the First World War, however, average real wages and, to a lesser extent, average real earnings, decline relative to 1913. Earnings recover quite quickly, but there is no evidence of any advance in average real wages until after the Armistice. Real earnings were about 15 per cent greater in 1919 than they were in 1913, and remain reasonably constant until 1924, when Bowley carries out his second survey of poverty in northern towns. Feinstein's data offer only limited support for Bowley's contention that there was significant average real wage or earnings growth during the First World War.[290] An average increase of about 2 per cent per annum seems to be a plausible estimate for real earnings growth in the period 1913–20, but most of this occurs after the Armistice. There are some difficulties with the reliability of some of these data, however, and data refinement may influence judgements about the precise extent of these changes.[291]

The distinction between wage rates and earnings is an important one. Depending on the question being addressed, each has its merits and it is not the case that earnings data are always to be preferred to wage-rate data. For the investigation of changes in living standards, earnings data are clearly superior to wage-rate data as they capture the total nominal income prior to taxes and benefits. Both earnings and wage rates need further refinement, however. The most obvious is whether to adjust for hours worked. In the first half of the century, the working week was progressively shortened. The exact length of the working week varied by industry, but a working week of about 54 hours was fairly typical in 1914 (though if the work were outdoors, hours would be somewhat shorter in the winter months). In 1919–20 normal hours were cut to about 47 or 48 per week as the 'eight hour day' became widespread. Across all industries for which the Ministry of Labour collected wage-rate data, Dowie reckons that the reduction in hours in 1919–20 was about 13 per cent.[292] This reduction in the normal working week was not usually accompanied by corresponding reductions in wage rates. As a consequence wage rates per hour rose by roughly the same amount, but this is not reflected in Bowley's wage-rate index, which refers to a normal working week.[293] As Dowie has shown, judgements about changes in living standards during and immediately after the First World War are influenced by the choice of weekly or hourly rates. Bowley's weekly wage-rate series recalculated as an hourly rates index, peaks at 318 in January 1921 (with respect to 100 in July 1914) before falling back to 199 at the end of 1923. This compares with values of the weekly index of 277 and 173 for the same dates.[294]

Despite the lack of evidence for significant weekly real earnings growth during the war (as opposed to the immediate post-war boom), it seems likely that the full employment conditions of the war, coupled with increased female participation, did lead to some improvement in working-class living standards. Average real wages may not have increased by much, but the impact on the household economy of regular wages, plus overtime, taken together with the contribution made by women war workers to the household budget, should not be underestimated. Moreover, the wages of unskilled males were improving relative to their more skilled peers. Whether we can be certain that these changes led to improved working-class nutrition is not clear, however. Dewey argues that contemporary estimates of the average pre-war energy value of diets were about 3000 kcal per capita. Beveridge reckoned that this represented about 3442 kcal per equivalent male.[295] Estimates for the average energy value of diets during the war are given in Table 2.11.

The conclusion that is to be drawn from the evidence presented in Table 2.11 is of nearly constant food supply during the war, very much in line with the conclusions reached by the Sumner Committee on the basis of the analysis of working-class diets from expenditure surveys. Of course, these data only relate to the energy value of diets, are average figures and say nothing about changes in the distribution of resources. Nor is it possible to say with any certainty what impact rationing had from 1917, though it is clear that by the end of the war sugar, butter and cheese consumption had declined markedly compared with 1914 levels.[296] Protein quality was reduced, however, as there was a 'shift in the composition away from livestock products towards cereals and potatoes'.[297]

Table 2.11   Average energy value of UK food supply, 1909–18 (per equivalent man-day)

	1909–13	1914	1915	1916	1917	1918
kcal	3442	3454	3551	3418	3320	3358
1909–13 = 100	100	100	103	99	96	97

Source: P. E. Dewey, 'Nutrition and Living Standards in Wartime Britain', in R. Wall and J. M. Winter (eds), *The Upheaval of War* (1988), Table 6.4, p. 203.

Summary

Prior to the First World War, social investigation highlighted a number of causes of poverty, of which low wages and large family size were generally the most important. Lack of work was often a contributory factor, but was not seen as the principal cause. The nature of poverty varied over the life cycle and was influenced by the pattern of breadwinning, which varied between towns depending upon the opportunity for female and child employment. Old people without younger relatives that were prepared to care for them were especially vulnerable to poverty, with many ending their lives in the workhouse. Irrespective of the incidence of poverty, social investigators emphasised the fragility of the economic position of most working-class households. Unemployment, illness and most importantly, death of family members would invariably mean crossing the line between independent economic survival and destitution and reliance on the parish. Generally, the urban poor experienced poorer health than their rural counterparts, but this depended upon the ability of rural labourers to provide some of their own food. Although urban workers' diets were monotonous and uninteresting, they probably generally provided sufficient energy, although qualitative evidence suggests that women and young girls would receive less of the household's resources. While the First World War was unlikely to have had quite the positive impact Bowley described, there is evidence of a fairly substantial improvement in average earnings in the immediate post-war boom. This, coupled with steadier and more regular employment, along with the continuation in the trend towards smaller families, exerted a powerful influence on many working-class households' economic position. This was reflected in a continuation of the gradual improvement in health that had started well before the beginning of the war.

3

POVERTY AND PROGRESS, 1920–38

Introduction

In the follow-up study of poverty in northern towns in 1924, Bowley points out that in the decade separating the original investigation from the sequel there were 'dominating events'. These include the 'fall in birth rate, loss of life by the war, the rise in prices and the more rapid rise of weekly money wages for unskilled labour, and unemployment'.[298] Together, these were responsible for reducing the incidence of primary poverty to about one-third of its pre-war level. According to Bowley, the increase in real wages was twice as important as the reduction in average family size in reducing the proportion of families below the poverty standard.[299]

We will consider Bowley's post-war findings in detail a little later, but his conclusions are important, since we have seen already that large family size and insufficient income (even when in regular employment) were two of the principal causes of poverty, cited by nearly all investigators prior to the First World War. In the first part of this chapter, the changes in real income are considered before moving on to examine the results of the interwar poverty surveys. The principal cause of poverty in the years between the wars was unemployment and this is considered in Chapter 4.

3.1 Occupation and Class

Table 3.1 shows the distribution of the economically active population by occupational category in 1931. Since 1911, the active population had

Table 3.1   Distribution of economically active population by occupational category, 1931 (percentage by category)

	Males	Females
Self-employed and higher-grade professionals	1.7	1.0
Employers and proprietors	7.6	4.4
Administrators and managers	4.5	1.6
Lower-grade salaried professionals and technicians	1.8	6.0
Inspectors, supervisors and foremen	2.0	0.4
Clerical workers	5.1	10.3
Sales personnel and shop assistants	5.9	8.2
Skilled manual workers	30.1	19.2
Semi-skilled manual workers	23.4	41.4
Unskilled manual workers	17.9	7.5
Total	14,760,000	6,263,000

Source: A. H. Halsey, *Change in British Society* (4th edn, 1995), Table 2.1, pp. 40–1.

increased by nearly 1.8 million males and 0.8 million females, but because of the increase in population, to 46 million by 1931, participation rates had not changed by much.[300] Roughly a third of all women were economically active in the interwar period, the same proportion as before the First World War.[301] Among the economically active population, the relative size of manual working-class male occupational groups had declined a little, and within this group, there were relatively more unskilled workers than there had been before the First World War. A more significant change was the decline of the relative size of female manual occupations. In 1931, just over two-thirds of females were in manual occupations, compared with over three-quarters in 1911. The female occupational groups that had grown, relative to 1911, were clerical workers and sales personnel and shop assistants. In 1931, these two groups accounted for just fewer than one in five economically active women, compared with just fewer than one in ten before the war.

3.2   Wages, Earnings and Prices, 1920–38

Feinstein's indices, showing the behaviour of average money wages and earnings, the cost of living and real wages and earnings, are set out in

Table 3.2. The official cost of living index for the interwar period tabulated here is often criticised for failing to capture accurately the change in retail prices of items important in working-class expenditure patterns in the interwar period.[302] However, altering the expenditure weights of the index to make it more representative of interwar consumption patterns turns out to be empirically unimportant and, despite its shortcomings, the official index is probably a reasonable guide to the change in retail prices during the interwar years.[303] Feinstein uses Chapman's index of average earnings, and the average wage index was originally calculated by Ramsbottom and is by far the most comprehensive estimate of the behaviour of wages for this period.[304] It is based on the average behaviour of wages in 69 manufacturing industries, relating to the end of June and the end of December each year for the period 1920–38.[305]

Table 3.2 shows that while both money wages and earnings fell between 1920 and 1938, retail prices were falling more quickly, producing modest gains in real wages and real earnings. Most of the fall in average money wages and earnings was between 1920 and 1923, and although

Table 3.2   Average wages, earnings and prices, 1920–38, 1938 = 100

	Wages	Earnings	Retail prices	Real wages	Real earnings
1920	139	134	159	87	84
1921	138	126	145	95	87
1922	107	101	117	91	86
1923	95	93	112	85	83
1924	96	95	112	86	84
1925	98	96	113	87	85
1926	98	93	110	89	84
1927	97	95	107	90	89
1928	96	94	107	90	88
1929	95	94	105	90	90
1930	95	93	101	93	92
1931	94	91	95	99	96
1932	92	89	92	100	97
1933	91	89	90	101	99
1934	91	90	90	101	100
1935	92	91	92	100	100
1936	94	94	94	99	100
1937	97	96	99	98	97
1938	100	100	100	100	100

Source: C. H. Feinstein, *National Income, Output and Expenditure of the United Kingdom*, Table 65, T140, recalculated 1938 = 100. Columns (4) and (5) calculated from columns (1)–(3).

wages fell again a little during the slump between 1930 and 1932, they were pretty constant until rates started to improve as recovery got under way in the middle of the 1930s. Average money earnings fell less than average wages, but generally show the same trend. On the other hand, prices fall steadily from 1920 until 1933, before commencing a modest upward trend in 1935. Together, these series indicate an overall increase of about 15 per cent in real wages and just under 20 per cent in real earnings between 1920 and 1938. Of course, this describes average wages for workers who remain in employment, and for many workers in the interwar period, earnings would be interrupted by spells of unemployment or short-time working.

The earnings' censuses provide information that allows a consideration of the extent to which earnings for particular occupations diverged from the average experience. The Board of Trade conducted the first wage census in Britain in 1886. This was followed by a similar inquiry by the Labour Department in 1906.[306] After the First World War, the Ministry of Labour undertook a number of surveys of earnings and hours. There are four inquiries conducted in the interwar period (October 1924, October 1928, October 1931 and October 1935), the results of which are published in the *Gazette*, under the title *Average Earnings and Hours Enquiries*.[307]

All the inquiries were voluntary and are generally restricted to data relating to one week during the month of the survey.[308] Few details are provided in the *Gazette* about the collection of data, though it is clear that the Ministry attempted to ensure consistency of coverage. The interwar surveys were sent to all firms participating in the census of production (all firms employing more than ten people), and a number (about 20 per cent) of smaller firms employing less than ten people, randomly selected. Not all firms were willing participants in these surveys, as a small percentage did not make returns, though the proportion of firms who supplied information to the Ministry increased.[309] Ideally, it would be desirable to have occupation-specific earnings data (both in terms of earnings per week and earnings per 'normal' week net of overtime and short time), disaggregated by age and gender for each industry.[310]

In many respects the early post-First World War surveys are less sophisticated than the 1906 census. Three of the interwar surveys were conducted to complement the census of production in 1924, 1931 and 1935.[311] These do not distinguish earnings by age and only provide average earnings for males, females and 'all workers' (plus the numbers of workers in these categories covered by the survey). The 1928 and

Table 3.3   Average earnings by industry, 1906–35 (shillings per week)

	Male				Female			
	1906	*1924*	*1931*	*1935*	*1906*	*1924*	*1931*	*1935*
Textiles	22.9	51.0	48.0	49.2	13.4	28.6	26.9	27.5
Clothing	24.2	54.8	53.6	54.3	11.2	26.9	26.9	27.8
Coal mining	31.5	53.0	45.2	44.8				
Engineering	–	51.1	50.4	55.0	–	26.3	26.8	28.0
Vehicles	–	57.2	57.3	65.9	–	26.9	28.6	31.8
Shipbuilding	–	54.3	51.8	54.2	–	–	–	–
Chemicals	–	59.0	58.8	60.6	–	25.8	27.7	26.5
Building	–	59.9	58.2	56.2	–	–	–	–
Local government	–	51.6	52.7	52.7	–	27.8	26.2	28.0
Agriculture	18.3	31.5	35	35.7	–	–	–	–

Source: Extracted from A. L. Bowley, *Wages and Income in the United Kingdom since 1860* (1937), Table XI, p. 51. Male refers to earnings of men and boys, female to women and girls.

1931 reports show the proportion of workers on short time and the average number of hours lost (but do not indicate earnings for a normal working week).[312] The 1935 survey distinguishes between adults and juveniles (males over 21 years, youths and boys 16–20, women over 18 years, girls less than 18 years). Average earnings at these benchmark dates for some of the important industries are summarised in Table 3.3.

There was a substantial increase in nominal earnings across the First World War period, for both men and women. With the exception of coal mining, male earnings per week were at least twice as great in 1924 as they had been in 1906, although, of course, prices had also increased, but not quite to such a great extent. Bowley's figures for average male earnings do not suggest that average earnings collapsed in hard-hit industries during the Depression, despite some short-time working. From Table 3.3, it can be seen that for all industries, mean average earnings were only marginally less in 1931 than in 1924 or 1935, although a pro-cyclical 'U' shaped pattern is evident in the data. According to the October 1931 earnings inquiry, in large firms in shipbuilding, for example, 10.6 per cent of workpeople were on short time (of an average duration of 10.8 hours per week). In general engineering the proportion was 26.7 per cent (for 10.7 hours' duration) and in vehicles and cycles, 18.6 per cent of workpeople were on short time (for an average duration of 11.1 hours).[313] Compared with 1924 (and assuming no net short-time working at this date), this would imply, *ceteris paribus*, falls of 2.5 per cent in average earnings in shipbuilding, 6 per cent in general engineering and 4 per cent in vehicles.[314] In the case of women workers, mean earnings were little different in any of the interwar census years and were not markedly lower in 1931 than 1924.[315] In comparison with 1906, however, it is clear that women workers also experienced a significant increase in nominal earnings of roughly the same order of magnitude as men.

More information about the shape of the wage distribution, and how it changes over the course of the interwar period, is provided by Rottier's estimates. His results qualify the conclusion reached on the basis of an examination of Bowley's data. He suggests that the dispersion of earnings did increase markedly between the 1920s and 1930s. For men, the interquartile range more than doubled, and only a small part of this is due to the growth in median earnings as there is a similar increase in magnitude of the coefficient of dispersion (interquartile range/median). Rottier also analysed the difference in earnings behaviour between sectors. The time profile of median earnings in Rottier's group of staple industries (coal mining, wool and cotton spinning and weaving, general engineering and shipbuilding) is different from that of the new industries (chemicals, vehicles, non-ferrous metals, electrical engineering and building). According to Rottier, 'In the staple industries average earnings were markedly lower than in other industries in the worst years of the depression and their fluctuations through time were sharper.'[316] The dispersion of male earnings around the median also increased markedly in staples. It is worth reiterating that these data are pretty crude. The published reports of the interwar earnings inquiries make it impossible to control for differences in age structure, hours worked and methods of payment.

Workers were either paid by time (weekly or hourly) or by some form of payment by results. Before the First World War, time rates of wages were customarily negotiated locally. The 'district rate' as it became known, was jealously guarded by the old craft unions. Over the first half of the century, however, the result of statutory wage fixing and national wage bargaining was to diminish the extent of regional wage variation. During 1917 there was a de facto move to national wage agreements in many manufacturing industries as '... wages of a large proportion of British workers were prescribed by government decree'.[317] In most industries, this move signalled a more formal shift to national bargaining and settlement, as wages were indexed to prices. At that time, plain time rates comprised a basic rate (that varied by district) and a national bonus. For those workers paid by the piece-rates, the situation was similar, although payments by results took a wide variety of forms, with specific formulas that were often bespoke to the industry concerned.[318] For example, in 1914, an individual piece-rate worker of 'average ability' in engineering could expect to earn at least $33\frac{1}{3}$ per cent above occupational time rates. Even the least able were guaranteed the time rate as a minimum. This percentage was incorporated into the 1917 National Agreement, but reduced to 25 per cent in June 1931.[319] Pieceworkers also received national bonuses of similar (though not usually the same) amounts as time workers. These too were uniform across regions.

This process of wage equalisation was augmented by the action of statutory authorities that specified minimum wages under the Whitely Councils and Trades Boards in the immediate post-First World War period.[320] Gradually, during the interwar years, statutory authorities would regulate increasing numbers of workers' wages. As Robertson points out, '... being empowered to set up statutory minimum rates of payment they naturally tended to work towards raising wage payments in specially low-wage districts'.[321] The Ministry was, however, opposed to a national minimum wage.[322] According to Sells, by the end of the 1930s, some form of statutory wage-fixing machinery covered about 2.7 million workers.[323]

One impact of these changes was to reduce the pay differential between occupations and between regions for the same occupation. In terms of relative pay, it is clear that the First World War years witnessed a narrowing of the wage premium between skilled and unskilled workers. Knowles and Robertson provide estimates of wage-rate differentials between adult male skilled and unskilled workers for the period 1914–50.[324] In later work they explored earnings inequality, but this was restricted to a study of engineering and shipbuilding.[325] They calculate wage-rate pay ratios in four industries (building, shipbuilding, engineering, railways) and the police force, plus miscellaneous pay ratios for other industries for a small number of benchmark years. Their original contribution was an examination of the time-series evidence for skill differentials based on representative grades of skilled and unskilled male workers. Robertson, in 1960, summed up the results of all these inquiries with respect to *adult male* differentials:

> The main observed tendency in relative occupational wage rates was for the skill differential to grow smaller during the First and Second World War. After the end of the First World War and in the ensuing depression, relative wages opened out again somewhat, but not to the

pre-1914 extent. They then remained generally stable in the inter-war years.... In the years before 1914 the usual level of unskilled wage rates as a percentage of skilled wage rates was somewhere about 60 per cent. In the inter-war years this figure has become 70 to 75 per cent and since the last war 80 to 85 per cent has been usual. Data on differentials in average earnings between unskilled and skilled may also be derived for a number of industries. They suggest that differentials in average earnings tend to be slightly wider than differentials in negotiated wage rates, but to have been subject to very similar trends.[326]

In a later work, Robertson amplified these conclusions by suggesting that semi-skilled rates fit in 'the gap between skilled and unskilled rates in a way which has meant that the pre-eminent position of the skilled is much less apparent in comparison with semi-skilled than with unskilled wage rates'.[327] Research on changes in relative earnings by Routh provided confirmation that the changes in relative wages could be generalised to changes in relative earnings.[328]

In sum, therefore, during the period 1914–39, most workers saw modest increases in real wages and earnings. This was coupled with a tendency for the wages of unskilled workers to improve relative to their more skilled counterparts. This was the direct result of the establishment of national pay bargaining during the First World War, where increases in wages were made by way of flat rate additions. Moreover, the process of greater wage equalisation was reinforced by statutory mechanisms designed to ensure higher minimum rates of pay for poorly paid workers. Set against this, there is some evidence that the dispersion of earnings in staple industries increased during the Depression, although the earning census data that this conclusion rests upon are subject to quite serious shortcomings.

3.3   Nutritional Adequacy of Diets

We saw in Chapter 2 that despite concern over the health of recruits in Britain during the First World War and the impact that a restricted diet may have had on civilian health, there was little direct evidence of widespread malnutrition. There were a number of social investigations in the interwar period that attempted to address the link between malnutrition and poor health. One of the earliest was commissioned by the Scottish

Committee of Child Life Investigation, which examined working-class diets in rural, urban and mining areas between 1919 and 1924.[329] Paton had been involved in the pre-war investigation of Scottish diets and his studies were carefully executed, but they did not take full account of developments in nutritional thinking with respect to vitamins and minerals. Paton's survey is based upon a number of individual dietary surveys carried out by other researchers between 1921 and 1924, using the method he developed and described in Lindsay's 1913 study. These include the analysis of diets from 11 Glasgow labourers' households (1921), 12 Glasgow unemployed families (1922), 9 Glasgow employed labourers (1924), 17 Glasgow artisans (1923), 12 Dundee labourers (1923), 18 rural workers from Ayrshire, Forfarshire, Perthshire and Stirlingshire and 17 Stirlingshire rural miners' families in 1924.[330]

A considerable amount of anthropometric data was also collected, and Paton found that the rural children at every age were taller and heavier than were children from urban areas. Generally, the diets of rural households provided a male equivalent energy intake of about 3220 kcal per day, compared with 2564 kcal for the Glasgow labourers and 2917 kcal for the Stirlingshire miners. In terms of protein the daily intakes were about 75 g per day for the labourers and miners and 90 g for the agricultural workers.[331] An energy intake of about 3000 kcal per male equivalent is similar to the findings from the pre-war period reported in Table 2.3, although 1921 Glasgow labourers' diets provide less energy than Lindsay's 1912 Glasgow diets. This may be because all of the early 1920s Glasgow diets are for labourers, whereas in 1913 Lindsay had included diets from other classes.

The general objective of the post-war study was to analyse the influence of environmental conditions on the 'growth and nutrition of the slum child'. Despite finding a pronounced difference in the heights and weights of children from rural and urban areas at any given age, Paton could find no evidence for differences in the rate of growth of children between town and country.[332] It is also difficult to make inferences about changes in living standards over time from these aggregate data. As income increases, proportionately more is spent on non-food items. Once basic needs have been met, expenditure on necessities, of which energy-providing foods might well be considered the classic example, is unlikely to increase significantly as income rises.

Hill, who collected 98 weekly rural Essex diets between February and November 1923, carried out a similar comparison to Paton. The equivalent male energy intakes of Hill's diets were 2872 kcal and 74 g of protein.

The Essex diets lacked variation, with most meat reserved for the men, but provided slightly more energy than Rowntree and Kendall's pre-war diet. In comparison with the Scottish urban diets, however, Hill pointed to the higher proportion of carbohydrate in the rural workers' diets. Overall, however, his findings were similar to Paton's. There was little evidence of malnutrition among these Essex agricultural workers' families and the physique of the rural children was better age for age, compared with urban children.[333]

In 1927 and 1928, Dr G. C. M'Gongile, the Medical Officer of Health for Stockton on Tees, investigated the diets of 55 working-class families (roughly half were from the Riverside area in 1927 and half from the new Mount Pleasant estate in 1928), some of whom had been rehoused in a modern housing estate as a result of slum clearance. The death rates of this group increased, which M'Gongile attributed to a poorer diet, which resulted from less money available for food due to the higher rents charged for the new housing. There was little difference in the average income of the two groups, but the percentage expenditure on food was less on the Mount Pleasant estate.[334] While the diets were adequate in terms of energy value for those employed, there was a serious deterioration among unemployed households, and the intake of animal protein was less, especially among unemployed families, once the move from Riverside had been completed.[335] The percentage unemployed on the Mount Pleasant estate was 90 per cent and it was among this group that the increase in death rate was noted.[336]

There are a number of other small-scale investigations of the diets of unemployed families during the 1930s. Ruth Bowley collected five family budgets, where the family head was unemployed, from the south of England in the summer of 1933. In comparison with the 1932 Ministry of Health recommendations, she found that the protein deficiency of the diets varied between 56 and 8 per cent, while energy requirements were typically about 20–25 per cent below the recommended standard.[337] In 1936, Widdowson and McCance made a detailed study of the diets of six Lincolnshire unemployed families and found that the average energy intake for men was 2850 kcal per day, which was about 90 per cent of employed workers' diets.[338] In comparison, their wives' energy intakes were only 2010, or about 70 per cent of their husbands.[339]

The results of the investigation carried out by M'Gongile helped convince the British Medical Association to appoint a Committee on Nutrition, which was 'to determine the minimum weekly expenditure on foodstuffs which must be incurred by families of varying size if health and working capacity [were] to be maintained'. Their 1933 recommendations were important in leading to a revision in the food component of Rowntree's poverty line. The BMA Committee estimated, at 1933 prices, that between 5s and 6s per man per week were needed to provide an adequate diet.[340]

But the most extensive dietary survey of the interwar years produced quite shocking results. In 1936 John Boyd Orr found that about half the population, some 22 million people, had an inadequate diet. This survey utilised estimates of the total food supply of the United Kingdom, in conjunction with household expenditure data collected from 1152 family budget studies, to estimate the consumption of foodstuff by six income groups.[341] These ranged from an income per head of 10s per week in Group I to an income per head of over 45s in Group VI.[342] Dietary requirements reflected the distribution of individuals of different ages within the population. Table 3.4 reveals that, except for those with incomes of less than 10s per head per week, the energy value of the diet met the contemporary recommendation. This was also true of overall protein and fat intake. However, contemporary dietary mineral and vitamin recommendations were only satisfied by Group IV and above, and it is not clear that this group met the prevailing recommendation for calcium intake (the higher figure included a 50 per cent safety margin).

Table 3.4 Nutritional composition of Boyd Orr diets by income group (grams or international units per day)

	Group I	Group II	Group III	Group IV	Group V	Group VI	Recommended allowance
Protein	63.4	76.0	83.6	89.4	94.4	98.3	68
Fat	71.6	98.8	109.6	120.6	130.5	141.5	98
Carbohydrate	348	381	395	403	406	396	–
kcal	2317	2768	2962	3119	3249	3326	2810
Calcium	0.37	0.52	0.61	0.71	0.83	0.95	0.6–0.9
Phosphorus	0.81	1.04	1.17	1.28	1.42	1.54	1.23
Iron	0.008	0.0099	0.011	0.012	0.0127	0.0137	0.0115
Vitamin A (IUs)	774	1250	1624	2015	2210	2875	1900
Vitamin C (IUs)	838	1134	1314	1577	1832	2323	1400

Source: Derived from John Boyd Orr, *Food, Health and Income* (revised 1937), Table VII, p. 40.

The conclusion of Boyd Orr's investigation was that some 4.5 million people had a diet deficient in all constituents. A further 18 million people had a diet deficient in one or more of the nutrients essential for a healthy life, making a total of 22.5 million people whose diet was inadequate in some way.[343] Boyd Orr was clear about the consequences of this for people's health: 'A review of the state of health of people of the different groups suggests that, as income increases, disease and death-rate decrease, children grow more quickly, adult stature is greater and general health and physique improve.'[344] The Ministry of Health's Advisory Committee on Nutrition accepted that Boyd Orr's estimates of food consumption were 'likely to be in accordance with the facts' in broad terms, but were concerned about the inadequate nature of the sample of household budgets and the distribution of working-class incomes.[345] With respect to the last point, however, Bowley endorsed Boyd Orr's results.[346]

The nutritional standard Boyd Orr adopted was not the 'bare subsistence' standard of interwar poverty surveys, however. Instead Boyd Orr's standard was

the optimum . . . not just to provide a diet which will keep people alive, but a diet which will keep people in health; and the standard of health adopted is a state of well-being such that no improvement could be effected by a change in diet. The standard may be regarded, therefore, as the minimum for maximum health.[347]

What this meant in practice was the application of a set of recommendations compiled for the United States Government Bureau of Home Economics.[348] The mineral requirements adopted in this standard were those found necessary for 'positive balance' in experiments, plus 50 per cent. Boyd Orr himself conceded that this margin of safety is 'unnecessarily generous'.[349] Moreover, since all but the poorest group satisfy energy, protein and fat recommendations, judgements on the extent of the nutritional adequacy of the diets of 18 million working-class families were made entirely on the basis of the adequacy of mineral and vitamin content of their diets. The extent of perceived malnutrition is extremely sensitive to the level of dietary recommendation used as a comparator and in Boyd Orr's survey, the use of the United States recommendations had a substantial impact on the conclusion.

3.4   Bowley and the Town Surveys

Bowley's methodological approach to the measurement of poverty in his 1924 survey, *Has Poverty Diminished*, was the same as his pre-war survey *Livelihood and Poverty*, which was itself a refinement of the method devised by Rowntree for estimating numbers in primary poverty in York at the turn of the century. Bowley recognised that there was little scientific basis for estimating appropriate poverty-line expenditures, preferring to think of the analysis as 'conventional rather than absolute', which made the determination of the poverty line 'arbitrary but intelligible' and 'descriptive rather than logical'.[350] What this meant for the standard of living for those living with an income 'at the minimum' he spelt out:

> An income at the minimum will, if the household is well administered with a good tradition of carefulness and a good standard of regularity, appear to provide the necessities and some of the amenities of life; other households with the same income will be squalid and in debt. To hold that the income is sufficient presupposes thrift and care.[351]

Nevertheless, the minimum allows nothing for trade union subscriptions, travel expenditure, amusements, alcohol or tobacco. Bowley was interested in comparisons over time and, to this end, was less concerned with whether the poverty line was the 'best that could be devised', than with the question of whether, on an unchanged standard, poverty was more or less extensive after the First World War than it had been before it began. With respect to his poverty line, Bowley classified households into one of five categories: certainly below, probably below, marginal, probably above and certainly above.

Like his pre-war survey, Bowley's 1924 investigation was based on a random sample of working-class households, varying between 1 in 8 in Stanley to 1 in 36 in Bolton.[352] As Table 3.5 shows, his poverty-line equivalence scale was essentially unaltered from his 1913 survey. Taking the figures for working-class households who were 'certainly' and 'probably' below his poverty line, in the five towns, Bowley found an average level of poverty of 11 per cent in 1912–14. In comparison, the average level in 1923–4 was 3.6 per cent, about a third of the pre-war level. Both these calculations refer to 'assumed full-time wages', however. For 1923–4, Bowley reports estimates of poverty based on household actual income in the week of investigation. On this basis, average poverty levels

Table 3.5   Bowley's 'New Standard' equivalence scale, 1924

	'New Standard'	Adult male equivalence
Man over 18	9s 0d	1.00
Woman over 16	7s 6d	0.83
Youth 16–18	7s 10d	0.87
Boy 14–16	7s 8d	0.85
Girl 14–16	7s 4d	0.81
Child 5–14	5s 0d	0.56
Child 0–5	3s 9d	0.42
Man or woman over 70	5s 10d	0.65

Source: A. L. Bowley and M. Hogg, *Has Poverty Diminished?* (1925), p. 37, column (3) calculated from column (2).

Table 3.6   Working-class families classified in poverty, 1912–24

	Northampton	Warrington	Bolton	Reading	Stanley
Full-time wages, 1912–14	8.0	12	8.0	20	6
Full-time wages, 1923–4	2.0	3.3	2.2	8.1	6.4
Actual income, 1923–4	4.0	7.9	4.9	11.3	7.5

Source: A. L. Bowley and Margaret Hogg, *Has Poverty Diminished?* (1925), Table D, p. 17.

were 6.5 per cent in the five towns, almost double the figure based on assumed full-time earnings. There are no corresponding figures provided for 1912–14, unfortunately. The results for individual towns are reported in Table 3.6.

Bowley identified that the causes of poverty had changed as well. Before the First World War, poverty was largely the result of low wages *relative to the size of the family* or to the death or absence of the principal wage earner. As Bowley remarked in 1913, 'It can hardly be too emphatically stated that of all of the causes of primary poverty ... low wages are by far the most important.'[353] By 1924, in four out of five towns low wages ceased to be the main cause of poverty. Death or absence of the principal wage earner, old age or illness affecting the principal wage earner was now the main cause. Unemployment was not important in these five towns in a normal 'full week', but was, not surprisingly,

important in the week of survey in four out of five cases.[354] Bowley
reflected on the change that had occurred in the intervening 11 years,
suggesting:

> In *Livelihood and Poverty* the opinion was expressed that 'to raise the
> wages of the worst-paid workers is the most pressing social task with
> which the country is confronted to-day.' It has needed a war to do it,
> but that task has been accomplished....[355]

Of course, there were still differences between the towns. In some, one
factor would be more important than in others, especially in Stanley,
which Bowley described as being 'conspicuously different'.[356] But overall,
it was the increase in wages during the war, coupled with a reduction in
family size, that Bowley thought responsible for raising a large number
of families from poverty. Bowley drew particular attention to what this
meant for children. Whereas in 1913–14 more than one in five children
under 14 years old were in poverty, a decade later the proportion had
declined to one in 16. This was offset, to some extent, by the increase in
poverty due to unemployment.

Bowley's survey was important for other reasons as well. He was
a member of the Consultative Committee for the *New Survey of London
Life and Labour* undertaken in 1928 under the directorship of Hubert
Llewelyn-Smith. This inquiry was an ambitious attempt to replicate
Booth's earlier nineteenth-century survey of the metropolis. Bowley's
involvement in the interwar London inquiry led to the adoption of
a poverty line that was identical in conception to the 'northern towns'
surveys. Indeed, the description of the methodological difficulties
associated with the definition and measurement of poverty in the *New
Survey* corresponds closely with the description provided in *Has Poverty
Diminished?*[357] According to Llewelyn-Smith, however, the intention in
the *New Survey* was to 'ensure that so far as is possible the standard of
minimum needs which marks the poverty line shall be directly comparable
with that employed by Charles Booth'.[358] As Lindsey and Lindsey point
out, the *New Survey* failed in this objective.

However, it is difficult to concur with Lindsey and Lindsey's claim that
the *New Survey* also failed to adopt a poverty line suitable for the interwar
period, viewed in an interwar context. They reach this judgement on
the basis of a comparison of the *New Survey* poverty line with Rowntree's
'Human Needs' standard, which was higher than the *New Survey* standard.
But as we shall see, it was Rowntree's 'Human Needs' standard that was

the exception during the interwar period, not the *New Survey* poverty line. The *New Survey* standard was essentially Bowley's northern town poverty line, and it was this approach that was replicated in the vast majority of surveys carried out in Britain between the wars.[359]

Bowley repeats his contention that the poverty is related to 'some minimum standard of economic welfare, which is based on provision of the primary needs of food, clothing, shelter, warmth, etc.'[360] The poverty-line diet was based on 3900 kcal per equivalent man-day, which was a fair bit more than in previous surveys. Although the food component was devised to be 'sufficient for physiological needs', Bowley recognised that 'even here the method of satisfying these needs is largely conventional' and the other components of the poverty line were 'quite definitely conventional'.[361] By the use of the term 'conventional', Bowley was accepting that it was not possible to 'reach any absolute definition of poverty'. He saw his 'minimum standard' as corresponding with 'ordinary conception of the term *at one time and place*' (emphasis added). For Bowley, keeping the definition of poverty 'uniform' allowed comparative investigation of how the incidence of poverty changed over time or varied between different areas.[362]

Bowley adopts the standard used in the 'northern towns' survey, reworked at London prices, which set the poverty line for a London family of two adults and three children at about 41s per week. This was 'virtually the same sum' as the figure Bowley arrived at by recalculating the 1929 income level that would be equivalent to Booth's 'poor', with income between 18s and 21s per week in 1890. Bowley's recalculation of Booth gave an income of between 38s and 40s per week at 1929 prices.[363]

Of course, as we have already seen, Bowley's poverty line was derived from his pre-war 'new standard', which was heavily dependent upon the poverty line devised by Rowntree in his first York survey in 1900. Since Rowntree's objective was to ascertain 'how far the general conclusions arrived at by Mr Booth in respect of the Metropolis would be found applicable to smaller urban populations', the general correspondence between Booth's 1890 definition of 'poor' and Bowley's 1929 recalculation of Booth and his repricing of the 1924 'northern town' poverty line is not surprising.[364] Nevertheless, there are important differences in the way in which poverty is calculated. The equivalence scale used to calculate the poverty line varies between Rowntree and Bowley and, as we saw in Chapter 1, Bowley's is very similar to the one implied in Booth's original inquiry. These standards also vary with respect to the energy and

Table 3.7   Persons in poverty in London, 1929 (persons in poverty as percentage of all working-class persons)

Survey area, 1929	Full-time earnings	Investigation week
East	5.2	10.7
West	4.0	7.8
Total	4.6	9.1

Source: H. Llewelyn-Smith *et al.*, *The New Survey of London Life and Labour*: Vol. VI, *Survey of Social Conditions (2) Western Area* (1935), p. 87.

protein value of the poverty-line diet. In the *New Survey*, Bowley's standard is based upon a daily requirement of 3230–3640 calories per equivalent adult male day and was a more varied diet than Bowley's five towns' survey.[365] In comparison, Booth's used a standard of 3000 kcal and Rowntree's 3500.

The results of the poverty inquiry of the *New Survey* are set out in Tables 3.7 and 3.8. The percentage of families below the poverty line is greater than the number of persons because of the large number of old people living alone who were in poverty, compared with the relatively small number of large families. On both measures, within working-class families, poverty was lower in the western areas than in the east. With respect to the eastern districts, Bowley concluded that:

The reduction of the proportions of persons in poverty in the forty years is enormous, whichever figures we take, and there is no doubt that the measurements are approximately comparable. But when we look at the details we find that in some districts and some age groups the proportion is still very high, especially with the additional burden

Table 3.8   Families in poverty in London, 1929 (families in poverty as percentage of all working-class families)

Survey area, 1929	Full-time earnings	Investigation week
East	6.3	11.0
West	5.2	8.7
Total	5.7	9.8

Source: H. Llewelyn-Smith *et al.*, *The New Survey of London Life and Labour*: Vol. VI, *Survey of Social Conditions (2) Western Area* (1935), p. 88.

of unemployment in 1929.... Over 19 per cent of families in Stepney and Poplar, and over 16 per cent of persons in Stepney and over 19 per cent in Poplar were in poverty in 1929.[366]

Moreover, at both ends of the age distribution, the proportion of persons living in poverty was greater. In the week of investigation, 16 per cent of children in the eastern areas were found to be in poverty (8 per cent if full-time earnings were assumed) and nearly one-quarter of all non-earning men and women over the age of 65 were in poverty.[367] The survey found that over a third of all old people lived alone and about half of those aged over 80 years old. In comparison with earlier periods, Thane sees this as representing a 'decisive shift in the propensity of the generations to share a household following the First World War'.[368]

The numbers living in poverty in London in 1930 amounted to just under half a million or 9.1 per cent of the population. The major causes of poverty identified in the *New Survey* are set out in Table 3.9. As can be seen, there were differences between the eastern and western survey areas. In normal weeks (assuming full earnings), insufficient wages were the major cause of poverty, followed by lack of male wage earner (for whatever reason) and then old age. In the week of investigation, however, unemployment was the principal cause of poverty, while the 'permanent' causes were also proportionately reduced.[369] In June 1929, William Beveridge estimated that 4.8 per cent of the insured workforce in the London survey area were unemployed.[370] For the year the figure was 7.3 per cent compared with 12 per cent for Great Britain as a whole. Unemployment in the docks, public works and building ranged from between 9.4 and 24 per cent, for the rest of the insured population

Table 3.9   Causes of poverty with full-time earnings, 1929 (week of investigation in parentheses)

Causes	West	East	Whole
Old age	19.5 (10)	14 (7)	16.5 (8.5)
Illness or death of male wage earner	33.5 (24)	39.5 (25)	37 (24.5)
Unemployment, short-time work	9.5 (47)	7 (49)	8 (48)
Wages insufficient for number of children	37.5 (19)	40 (19)	38.5 (19)
Total	100 (100)	100.5 (100)	100 (100)

Source: Adapted from H. Llewelyn-Smith *et al.*, *The New Survey of London Life and Labour*: Vol. VI, *Survey of Social Conditions (2) Western Area* (1935), Table XXX, p. 108.

unemployment averaged less than 4.5 per cent. Beveridge observed that 'severe unemployment in London [was] the unemployment of particular industries which have always been notorious for unemployment'. This pattern was quite different from that evident in other regions of Great Britain, where unemployment was high among industries that had been prosperous prior to the Great War.[371]

Bowley's influence on the measurement of interwar poverty extended further, for it was his standard, with little modification, that was adopted by at least four other poverty inquiries during the interwar period: in Merseyside, Sheffield, Southampton and Bristol (where two standards were used). In Caradog Jones's *Social Survey of Merseyside*, the most significant change was Jones's refinement of Bowley's equivalence scale, as set out in Table 3.10.[372] Jones made a 10 per cent allowance for adult males on heavy muscular work and reduced the needs of old people at age 65, rather than at age 70 as Bowley had done.

Following Bowley, Jones treated rent paid, compulsory National Insurance contributions and the cost of travel to and from work as essential items. These were deducted from gross income, allowing net family income to be compared with a poverty line based on 'other primary needs'. Jones repriced Bowley's *New Survey* standard for Liverpool prices, which gave a poverty line of 46s 2d per week for a reference family of two adults and three children. Jones notes that this figure was over 10s more than the income the family would receive in unemployment benefit.[373]

The survey sampled 6780 working-class families in the Merseyside area between the autumn of 1929 and summer of 1930. Jones found that for the entire Merseyside area, 16 per cent of working-class families

Table 3.10 Jones's Merseyside survey equivalence scale, 1929–30

Age	Males	Females
Over 16	1.0	0.8
14–16	0.85	0.8
5–14	0.5	0.5
0–5	0.33	0.33
Over 65	0.6	0.6
Heavy muscular work	1.1	–

Source: D. Caradog Jones (ed.), *Social Survey of Merseyside* (1934), Vol. 1, p. 158.

were living below the poverty line. There were some variations between districts: in Liverpool the proportion was 17 per cent, in Bootle and Birkenhead 15 per cent and in Wallasey 10 per cent, but these were partly a function of the timing of the survey between areas.[374] What this meant, as far as Jones was concerned, was 'A family is deemed to be in poverty if the joint income of its members, supposing it were wisely spent, would not suffice to purchase for them the necessaries of life, taking into account the age and sex constitution of the family.'[375]

On the Registrar-General's overcrowding standard (more than two people per room), 10.9 per cent of the population of Merseyside were living in overcrowded conditions.[376] In districts of inner Liverpool, only 7.6 per cent of families had access to a garden and only 9.8 per cent had access to a fixed bath (about a third of which was shared access).[377] The *Merseyside Survey* found that 'fewer than 3 families out of 4 received over 45s a week', compared with a poverty line of 46s 2d for a reference family of two adults and three children.[378] Hence, low income was of central importance in explaining the causes of poverty. Jones's analysis also revealed a close association between poverty and overcrowding, though these were not invariably related, and between poverty and unemployment and casual employment.[379] Moreover, as with other surveys of the period, large family size and lack of male breadwinner were important additional explanations of poverty. The results of this survey are important because they show that Bowley's comment concerning the virtual elimination of low-wage poverty was premature. Low wages were still an important cause of poverty, though often masked by the growing importance of unemployment.

The *Merseyside Survey* results also differ with respect to the importance attached to old age as a 'cause' of poverty. The proportion of people over 65 years old below the poverty line (as a percentage of all people over 65 in the sample) was slightly less than the average for all ages (14.3 per cent compared with 16 per cent), only marginally greater than for adults aged 21–64 years (13 per cent) and significantly less than infants aged 0–4 years (23.4 per cent).[380] It is likely that Jones would find fewer old people in poverty than Bowley because his poverty-line needs of old people was reduced to 0.6 of an adult at age 65, rather than age 70.

Jones was also provided assistance in the initial stages of the Sheffield Social Survey, although A. D. K Owen, on behalf of the Sheffield Social Survey Committee, directed this inquiry.[381] The Sheffield survey was based on a random sample of 1 in 30 working-class households (3329), using Bowley's standard modified for changes in prices between October

Table 3.11 Overall expenditure equivalence scales, Sheffield survey 1931–2 (excluding fuel)

	Poverty-line expenditure	Equivalence scale
Man or woman over 65	4s 5½ d	0.64
Adult man	6s 11½ d	1.00
Adult woman	6s 1½ d	0.88
Youth 14–15 years	5s 10½ d	0.84
Girl 14–15 years	5s 7d	0.80
Schoolchild	3s 10½ d	0.55
Child 0–4	2s 11d	0.42

Source: A. D. K. Owen, *A Survey of the Standard of Living in Sheffield* (1933), p. 19 and column (3) calculated from column (2).

1931 and January 1932. Nearly half of these households were dependent upon the income of an adult male wage earner (45.2 per cent) and just over one-quarter depended on the income of an adult male wage earner and a subsidiary earner (27.1 per cent). In total, in 5.7 per cent of households there was no wage earner and 7.6 per cent had no adult male wage earner. It is a fair assumption that nearly all of the former and a fair proportion of the latter would have been in poverty. The rest had two or more adult male wage earners, with or without subsidiary earners (14.4 per cent), and it is unlikely that any of these families would have been in poverty.[382]

The Sheffield poverty line was worked out on the basis of the overall expenditure equivalence scale, given in Table 3.11, which was roughly comparable to that of Jones. This produced a poverty-line income for a reference family of two adults and two schoolchildren and an infant of 24s 11½d per week, excluding rent, travel and National Insurance (22s 10½d plus 2s 1d fuel).

Owen interpreted this poverty line as a 'minimum subsistence standard', based on 'objective and measurable criteria', and should not be interpreted as a 'satisfactory human needs standard'.[383] Although Bowley would have presumably quarrelled with the scientific pretensions, the rest accords with his views: 15.4 per cent of working-class families were below the poverty line in the week of study with another 3.5 per cent 'on the margins' of poverty. Had all these families been on full-time earnings, Owen estimated that only 5.0 per cent would have been in poverty with another 0.9 per cent on the margins.[384] The importance of

Table 3.12   Relationship of working-class households
to the poverty line, 1931–2

Position relative to poverty line	Percentage
>50% above poverty line	60.8
<50% above poverty line	20.3
Marginal	3.5
<33% below poverty line	9.9
>33% below poverty line	5.5

Source: A. D. K. Owen, *A Survey of the Standard of Living in Sheffield* (1933), p. 28.

unemployment as a cause of poverty is not surprising given that the survey was undertaken in the middle of the Depression. Table 3.12 shows the relationship of all working-class families in Sheffield to the poverty line. Just under two-thirds of families were more than 50 per cent above the poverty line, and about one working-class household in 20 was more than one-third below the poverty line.

Although unemployment was the primary cause of poverty in Sheffield (66.6 per cent), other factors also played a part. In order of importance, these were widowhood (10 per cent), old age (6.8 per cent), illness or temporary incapacity (6.6 per cent), insufficient earnings (5.2 per cent) and permanent incapacity for work (4.8 per cent).[385] Overall, therefore, the principal conclusion of the survey was the overriding importance of the impact of unemployment as a cause of poverty, despite the fact that over two out of every five families below the poverty line were in receipt of public assistance.[386]

The social survey of Southampton was primarily an ambitious attempt to replicate Booth's street classification by income/occupational type, using mass interview techniques in the summer of 1928. But in addition, Ford also carried out a poverty-line analysis of a random sample of working-class families in the winter of 1931. He found 21 per cent of working-class families below the 'poverty datum line', which for two adults and three schoolchildren he fixed at 32s plus 8s rent in November–December 1931.[387] He preferred this term, because he felt, following Clay, that the expression 'poverty line' implied an absolute standard, whereas 'poverty datum line' conveyed the arbitrary nature of the standard.[388] Again, the poverty line was Bowley's 1924 five towns 'bare subsistence standard' with minor modifications.[389] These conclusions

Table 3.13   Causes of poverty in Southampton, November–
December 1931

Cause	Per cent
Natural head of family dead	2.35
Natural head of family ill	4.70
Natural head of family old	9.86
Short time or unemployment	66.20
Wages insufficient for number of children	11.74
Miscellaneous	5.15

Source: Derived from P. Ford, *Work and Wealth in a Modern Port* (1934),
p. 129.

were based on a random sample of 1 in 46 working-class families in
November and December 1931. Quite simply, the reason this inquiry
found higher levels of poverty than earlier surveys was due to higher
levels of unemployment at the time of the Southampton survey. Ford
found that of the 559 families in his sample, 119 were below the poverty
line, but of these, 76 were in poverty because of unemployment alone.[390]
The causes of poverty identified by Ford are set out in Table 3.13.

Fully two-thirds of all cases of poverty were due to unemployment,
a figure almost identical to the result of the Sheffield survey carried out
at the same time. Indeed, Ford estimated that if unemployment had
been at the level prevailing in the autumn of 1929, when the Merseyside
survey was carried out, 14 or 15 per cent of Southampton working-class
families would have been in poverty. Ford also considered poverty in
terms of household composition and labour force participation. Not
surprisingly, he found that fewer families were in poverty in households
where there were subsidiary earners or two adult earners. Poverty was
highest among working-class families reliant on a sole male breadwinner
or where there were no earners. Clearly, in the case of multiple or joint
breadwinning, the potential impact of unemployment was lessened.[391]
In fact, however, these were a substantial minority of households. From
the sample, 246 families (44 per cent) had additional wage earners,
although opportunities for adult female labour force participation were
less than in Bowley's textile towns.[392]

Figures for the composition of family income are given in Table 3.14.
It is clear that sole male breadwinning was a relatively rare household
type, accounting for just fewer than one-third of all working-class families
in Ford's sample, compared with just under half in Sheffield. Over half

Table 3.14   Breadwinning and the composition of family income in Southampton, 1931

Breadwinning type	Percent
Wages of head of family only	32.2
Wages of other earners only	0.2
Income from benefit only	14.5
Wages of head and others' earnings	20.2
Wages of head and income from benefit	13.1
Wages from other earners and income from benefit	10.2
Wages of head, other earners and income from benefit	9.7

Source: Derived from P. Ford, *Work and Wealth in a Modern Port* (1934), p. 141.

of all families had more than one source of income, although social benefits contributed to household income in about a third of all cases, and about half as many again were solely reliant on benefit. The majority of families survived on a patchwork of income from various earners and social benefits.

The relationship between Ford's poverty line and benefit and poor relief scales, changed over time and depended upon household composition. In all cases, relief was below Ford's 'poverty datum line', but the gap between benefit scales and Ford's poverty line tended to narrow during the Depression, although less so for families with children. For a household of two adults, Ford's poverty datum line for 1928 was 26s 6d plus 8s rent, whereas unemployment benefit was 24s and outdoor relief was 18s 6d. By the winter of 1931, however, Ford's poverty datum line was 23s 6d, and although unemployment benefit had been reduced to 23s 3d, it left a smaller deficit of 3d plus 8s rent. However, for families with children, the position was different. A family of two adults and three schoolchildren were entitled to unemployment benefit of 30s in 1928 and outdoor relief of 27s, compared with Ford's poverty line of 36s plus 8s rent – a shortfall of between 14s and 17s or about one-third. In the winter of 1931, unemployment benefit had been reduced to 29s 3d and Ford's poverty line was 32s plus 8s rent.[393]

The final application of the Bowley poverty line was in Bristol in 1937 by Tout. His investigation was based on the application of two different poverty lines. Using the *New Survey* standard, Tout found that 6.9 per cent of working-class families were in poverty in the week of the investigation and 4.1 per cent if full-time earnings were assumed.[394] This conclusion was reached on the basis of information from a random sample of working-class households (some 4526 families) obtained between May and October 1937.[395] However, Tout's main inquiry used a slightly modified version of George's poverty line, the results of which we will consider shortly.

3.5   A New Calculation of the Poverty Line

In 1937 George attempted to revise components of the various interwar 'bare subsistence' measures of poverty to make them compatible.[396] George maintained that, with one exception, all of the interwar poverty measures 'used the standard based on the poverty line calculated by Rowntree . . .'.[397] As we saw in Chapter 1, this is only partly true. Bowley made several important modifications to Rowntree's 1899 poverty line but also adopted a more appropriate equivalence scale. The interwar surveys generally adopt both Bowley's poverty-line standard, which it is reasonable to see as being based on Rowntree, and Bowley's equivalence scale, which was not the same as Rowntree's standard.

In his 'New Calculation', George argues that 'since the technique of the poverty-line was first adumbrated, new calculations have arisen which, if given effect, must alter certain of the standards used by Rowntree and since followed'.[398] These were particularly important with respect to the physiological recommendations of 'minimum' food requirements, especially those relating to children and infants, but also applied to other categories of poverty-line expenditure. George was heavily influenced by the British Medical Association's 1933 nutritional recommendations, which stressed the importance of vitamins and minerals. All of the interwar standards that applied some version of Bowley's bare subsistence standard were inadequate with respect to the BMA's 1933 recommendations. This was especially true of milk consumption, which was a relatively expensive food, and was required in significantly greater quantities than Bowley allowed for and disproportionately so by children and infants.[399]

This had two important consequences. Satisfying the BMA recommendations increased the poverty-line cost of food for all family types. As importantly, because in some instances the vitamin and mineral needs of children and infants were greater than adults, and these were relatively expensive to meet, the existing food equivalence scale, based on energy requirements, was inappropriate. This had the effect of making children relatively more expensive and thus raising the poverty line for families with children more than those without children. George also

Table 3.15 'New calculations' of interwar poverty lines at 1936 prices

Survey	2 Adults	2 Adults, plus child, 10	2 Adults, plus children, 10 and 4
Bowley, 5 northern towns	15s 4d	19s $4\frac{1}{2}$d	22s 3d
New Survey	16s 7d	20s $6\frac{1}{2}$d	22s 2d
Merseyside	14s 6d	18s $2\frac{1}{2}$d	20s 11d
Southampton	15s 2d	18s $11\frac{1}{2}$d	21s 9d
'New Calculation'	17s 8d	23s 10d	28s 5d

Source: R. F. George, 'A New Calculation', Tables (a)–(c), p. 91.

argued that given the wide variety of cheap clothing that was available, Rowntree's poverty-line expenditure was inappropriate in the late 1930s, which partly offset the increased poverty-line cost of food, although for young women George made an extra allowance. For cleaning materials and lighting costs, George argued that Rowntree's standard was reasonable, and reduced the fuel allowance somewhat.[400] The impact of these changes, for the interwar surveys considered here, is set out in Table 3.15.

Notice that George's 'New Calculation' gives a higher poverty line for all family types than does any other study hitherto discussed. Almost all of this increase is due to revisions to the food component. Because the food needs of young children are increased as a proportion of adult requirements, the disparity between George's calculations and those due to other investigators is greater for larger families. It is not possible to say, on the basis of published material, what the precise impact of George's revision would be for the measurement of poverty in these towns, other than it would clearly increase the proportion regarded as being below the poverty line. Some indication of just how many can be gleaned from Rowntree's second survey of York, which also uses the 1933 BMA recommendations.

3.6 Rowntree's Human Needs of Labour

Rowntree still exerted an important influence on poverty research in the interwar period. Most interwar poverty surveys reference his first York survey and, as we have seen, although it was Bowley's poverty line that was adopted in the Merseyside, London, Sheffield and Southampton inquiries, Bowley's methodology owed a great deal to Rowntree's primary poverty measure. Rowntree also carried out his second social survey of York in 1936. Rowntree eschewed the labour-saving advantages afforded by Bowley's sampling method and, instead, repeated his 1899 house-to-house investigations of the entire working-class population of York. By 1935 these numbered 16,362 families. Firms employing about 60 per cent of workers covered by the survey also provided wage information.[401] Although it was Rowntree's intention to repeat his 1899 investigation 'to find out what changes had occurred in the living conditions of the workers during the thirty-six years which had elapsed', Rowntree used a different poverty line in his second York survey, making direct comparison with the results of his first inquiry potentially misleading.[402] This new poverty line was the standard devised in his *Human Needs of Labour*, revised 1937 (first published in 1918), and, for a family of two adults and three children, was equivalent to 43s 6d per week for urban families, after paying rent, or 53s for urban families and 41s for rural families, including rent at 1936 prices.[403]

This poverty line was still welded to a methodology based on the income necessary for the 'maintenance of physical efficiency'. However, this new standard reflected advances in nutritional thinking based on the BMA recommendations of 1933. These were designed to ensure both 'health and working capacity' and were not bare subsistence or minimum figures. For a 'normal man of average stature', they recommended an intake of 3400 kcal, made up of 100 g of fat, 100 g of protein (half of which should be animal protein) and 500 g of carbohydrate.[404] Moreover, for the first time it was recognised that vitamins and minerals were 'necessary constituents of any diet', but no specific intakes were recommended. Instead, Rowntree followed the BMA practice of costing a diet that would satisfy the quantitative constraints outlined above, but which included foods known to be vitamin rich.[405] Unlike the diet adopted for the first York survey, Rowntree's Human Needs diet included meat.

The BMA requirements for women and children expressed in terms of male equivalence are given in Table 3.16. In the same way that Rowntree chose to ignore the equivalence scale of Atwater in his first survey of York, his 'Human Needs' standard ignored the BMA's equivalence scale. Instead, for children of all ages, Rowntree adopts an equivalence of 0.65 of an adult male.[406] In practice, Rowntree's equivalence scale was simple: 1.0 adult male in moderate work, 0.83 for an adult woman and 0.65 for all children under 14. Notice that this is

Table 3.16   1933 BMA equivalence scale

Adult female	0.83
Boy 14 years and over	1.00
Girl 14 years and over	0.83
Child 12–14 years	0.90
Child 10–12 years	0.80
Child 8–10 years	0.70
Child 6–8 years	0.60
Child 3–6 years	0.50
Child 2–3 years	0.40
Child 1–2 years	0.30
Child 0–1 year	0.20

Source: B. S. Rowntree, *The Human Needs of Labour* (revised 1937), p. 64.

a significantly higher allowance for the needs of children than any of the other interwar surveys. The diet that he devised that would satisfy the 1933 BMA standard cost 5s 5d per male equivalent per week, or 20s 6d per week for a family of two adults and three children. This compares with 18s 5d (at 1936 prices) for the diet he devised in his 1918 *Human Needs*. According to Rowntree, this increase represented the cost in advancement in nutritional knowledge.[407]

For non-food items, Rowntree had no extrinsic standard available. The cost of accommodation of 9s 6d was the 'predominant rent, including rates, for a non-parlour house with three bedrooms'.[408] For clothing, Rowntree based his figure of 3s for men, 1s 9d for women and 1s 1d for children, or 8s per week for a family of two adults and three children on information provided by men and women 'with first hand experience at how low a cost it was possible to clothe a family'.[409] From the evidence obtained from 'a number of working people', Rowntree considered that the cost of fuel and light for a reference family averaged 4s 4d per week over the year.[410] For sundry items, Rowntree distinguished between 'household sundries', which by questionnaire he estimated cost 1s 8d for a reference family, and 'personal sundries'. This latter category represents a substantial shift from his position outlined in *Poverty*. By 1937, Rowntree's poverty line included the cost of expenditure on unemployment and health insurance, sick and burial club contributions, trade union subscriptions, the cost of travel to work, stamps, writing paper and stationery, a daily newspaper and a small allowance for beer, tobacco, presents, holidays, travelling and books, etc., to a total of 9s per week for a reference family.[411]

In 1921 Rowntree had conducted a survey of 67,333 women workers' families in 11 cities.[412] He found that the proportion of working women that supported dependants varied greatly by age. In the *Human Needs*, he argues that under 7.5 per cent of working women had dependants at age 18–21, rising to 28 per cent at age 36–40, falling to 6 per cent for women over 60. Therefore, he fixed a poverty line, or 'minimum wage', for women workers assuming that 'it was not normal for women to have to support dependants'.[413] Rowntree estimated the minimum sum for women workers was 30s 9d, based on 18s for lodgings, 5s 3d for clothing and 7s 6d for personal sundries.[414]

In sum, Rowntree's 'Human Needs' poverty line was a combination of the BMA's nutritional recommendations, modified so as to simplify the equivalence scale between adults and children, estimates of prevailing market cost of housing, working-class declared expenditure on household sundries and fuel and light, working-class estimates of perceived minimum expenditure on clothing and Rowntree's own assumptions concerning 'reasonable' expenditure on personal sundries. What was new about Rowntree's 'Human Needs' standard was his attempt to identify his poverty line with a minimum wage. The 'Human Needs' standard also allowed expenditure for social participation. Rowntree made this explicit when he writes:

> A clear distinction must be drawn between the principles that should guide us in fixing minimum wages and those which should determine wages above the minimum. The former should be based on the human needs of the worker, the latter on the market value of the services rendered.[415]

He applied his 'Human Needs' standard in his second social survey of York and found that 31.1 per cent of the working-class population of York were below this standard (some 17,185 persons).[416] Rowntree reached this conclusion by following essentially the same method as he had done in 1900. However, in 1936 Rowntree confined himself to measuring primary poverty, eschewing a second attempt to quantify secondary poverty because he thought the concept 'too rough to give reliable results' and the realisation that conceptions of 'obvious want and squalor' had changed markedly over the 40 years separating the inquiries.[417]

Rowntree also calculated the proportion in poverty in York in 1936 using his 1899 poverty line. Allowing for changes in prices, the 1899 poverty line (excluding rent) for a reference family of two adults and three children, would have been 30s 7d at 1936 prices compared with a figure of 43s 6d (excluding rent) for the 1936 poverty line at 1936 prices. In 1899 Rowntree found 1465 families (7230 persons) in primary poverty. This represented 15.46 per cent of working-class families and 9.91 per cent of the total population of York. In 1936, using the 1899 poverty line, Rowntree found 1067 families (3767 persons) in primary poverty, which represented 6.8 and 3.9 per cent of the working-class and total population respectively.[418]

Rowntree thought that the reduction in primary poverty in York, between 1899 and 1936, from just under 10 to just under 4 per cent, was the result of three factors: reductions in family size, increases in real wages and improvements in social services.[419] This analysis is a reflection of a change in the relative importance of the causes of poverty between the two surveys. In Table 3.17, the percentage of poverty due to various causes is recorded for both surveys (using the 1899 poverty line). The substantive conclusions would not be much altered if the 1936 poverty line were used instead.

What is immediately obvious from this table is the changing relative importance of low wages and unemployment. According to Rowntree, over half of primary poverty was due to low wages in 1899, yet 40 years later low wages were a relatively minor cause – though, of course, this conclusion is reached on the basis of applying the 1899 poverty line that made *no allowance* for social participation. Rowntree estimated that on average real wages had increased by about 30 per cent between the dates

Table 3.17 Causes of primary poverty in York, 1899 and 1936 (%)

Cause of primary poverty	1899	1936
Death of chief wage earner	15.63	8.97
Illness	5.11	5.58
Old age		17.92
Unemployment	2.31	44.53
Irregularity of work	2.83	5.87
Largeness of family (more than 4 children)	22.16	7.97
Low wages for regular work	51.96	9.16

Source: B. S. Rowntree, *Poverty and Progress* (1941), p. 110.

of his first two surveys and, at the same time, working hours had decreased from about 54 to 48 per week.[420] Not surprisingly, however, unemployment had assumed a vastly more important role as a causal factor in poverty by 1936. Unemployment duration in York appears to have been uncommonly high, however. Rowntree provides information on the duration of unemployment for a sample of 569 unemployed families, 21.9 per cent of which had been unemployed for between 2 and 4 years, 23.6 per cent for between 4 and 6 years and 17.9 per cent for over 6 years.[421]

Despite the introduction of non-contributory old-age pensions in 1908 for those over 70 years and contributory pensions in 1925 for the over 65s, old age was still a major cause of poverty during the interwar period. This was partly a reflection of increases in life expectancy, as more people were living to a greater age, but also because pensions were quite meagre.[422] Many old people were dependent on help from relatives, yet it is clear from the testimony of old people that if children would not help, they would 'rather starve than force them to do so by applying for out-relief'.[423] It is not surprising that relatively fewer families were in poverty in 1936 for reasons of large family size, as the birth rate and average completed family size had fallen since the turn of the century, though not as dramatically as might be imagined. In 1901 average household size was 4.6, and in 1931 it was 4.1, before falling to 3.5 by 1939.[424]

But what of Rowntree's progress? Rowntree claimed that in 1936, workers in York were better housed, better fed, better clothed and showed a marked improvement in health when compared to 40 years earlier.[425] The improvement in health was reflected in reduced infant mortality rates (from 160.6 per 1000 in 1898–1901 to 54.6 per 1000 in 1936) and reduced death rates (from 17.2 per 1000 to 11.6 per 1000 over the same period).[426] But Rowntree meant more than this when he talked of progress. He also placed great emphasis on recreation activities and new forms of leisure available to workers in the 1930s, many of which were unheard of at the turn of the century (including cinema, wireless, bicycles, libraries, cheap books, swimming baths, parks and public gardens, theatre, music halls, cheap travel facilities and opportunity for adult education).[427] He concluded by arguing, 'These things have had a profound effect on the lives of the workers and on all those with limited means, far more pronounced than on the wealthier classes who have never lacked means of recreation.'[428] While historians would not dispute this contention, most would want to stress the way in which access to leisure in the late 1930s was still influenced by class, age and gender.[429]

Tout in his survey of Bristol provided the most optimistic picture of the extent of poverty in Britain during the 1930s. His inquiry was carried out in the summer of 1937 at the trade cycle peak and official estimates of unemployment in Bristol had declined from a peak of 27,806 in January 1931 to 11,651 in September 1937. Applying a modified version of George's poverty line, Tout found that 10.7 per cent of the working-class families in his sample were below the poverty line (7.2 per cent if full-time earnings were assumed). However, Tout did not apply the BMA's nutritional recommendation with respect to milk consumption of children and infants, so it cannot be directly compared with the figures given in Table 3.18.[430] However, the rank ordering of causes of poverty was similar to other surveys, irrespective of the standard applied. Tout used family income net of rent, travel to work and compulsory insurance and was based on a food requirements equivalent scale similar to other contemporary surveys.[431] As Table 3.18 shows, despite the timing of the survey, Tout found that unemployment was still the single most important cause of poverty. Roughly one-third of all families were in poverty because of unemployment.

The sensitivity of the findings of interwar poverty surveys to the poverty line employed has been investigated. Hatton and Bailey recalculated the *New Survey* for 22,016 households, for which income records survive, using a variety of different poverty lines. This sample from the original inquiry gives 10.5 per cent in poverty using the *New Survey* poverty line, a little higher than the 9.8 per cent originally found. They demonstrate that the poverty headcount is very sensitive to the

Table 3.18   Causes of poverty in Bristol, summer 1937

Cause	Per cent of families
Unemployment	32.1
Insufficient wages	21.3
Old age	15.2
Absence of adult male earner	13.3
Sickness or incapacity	9.0
Self-employment or hawking	6.5
Other	2.7

Source: H. Tout, *The Standard of Living in Bristol* (1937), p. 46.

choice of standard. In particular, using empirical estimates of equivalence, rather than those embodied in the original *New Survey* poverty line, nearly doubles the numbers of old people in poverty, although the use of empirically estimated scales of equivalence only increases the overall proportion in poverty to 12.1 per cent. This is because a large number of old people have incomes close to the *New Survey* poverty line.[432] The assumption of interwar poverty investigators, that old people's needs were equivalent to 0.6 of an adult male, has a large bearing on the numbers defined in poverty and is not supported by empirical estimates of equivalence.

Hatton and Bailey also re-estimate the extent of poverty in interwar London using Rowntree's 'Human Needs' scale. This roughly doubles the headcount measure to 22.2 per cent.[433] They calculate the impact of interwar welfare provision by adding back to household income all state insurance contributions and deducting all state benefits. On this basis 17.2 per cent of households in London were in poverty, 'implying that 7.5 per cent of all households were raised out of poverty' by state provision.[434] These effects are particularly important for elderly households, but quite modest for other types.

Summary

In interwar Britain average real incomes and earnings grew modestly and differentials between skilled and unskilled workers were substantially less than they had been before the war. The nutritional adequacy of diets also improved, though those for unemployed workers were still below the standard devised to judge adequacy at the time. The causes of poverty, as identified by social investigators, also changed in importance. Unemployment was a principal cause of poverty after 1929, though it would be wrong to assume that poverty due to low wages had completely disappeared, despite the growth in statutory wage regulation. Moreover, old age was still an important cause of poverty, though many of the interwar social surveys fail to identify the extent of old-age poverty because they treat the needs of the elderly as being only 60 per cent of those of adult males. This assumption is not supported by empirical estimates of the needs of old people.

Judgements about the extent of poverty in the interwar period and how it varied between regions depends on the poverty standard applied. The summary results of interwar poverty standards are given in Table 3.19.

Table 3.19   Summary of interwar poverty results, percentage of working-class families in poverty

Investigator	Town	Date	Poverty line	Percentage
Rowntree	York	1899	Primary Poverty	15.46
Bowley	Warrington	1923–4	Bowley	7.9
	Northampton	1923–4	Bowley	4.0
	Stanley	1923–4	Bowley	7.5
	Reading	1923–4	Bowley	11.3
	Bolton	1923–4	Bowley	4.9
Llewelyn-Smith/ Bowley	London	1929–30	Bowley (modified)	9.1
Jones	Merseyside	1929–30	Bowley (modified)	16.0
Owen	Sheffield	1931	Bowley (modified)	15.4
Ford	Southampton	1931	Bowley (modified)	21.3
Rowntree	York	1936	'Human Needs'	31.1
Tout	Bristol	1937	Bowley (modified)	6.9
Tout	Bristol	1937	George	10.7

Note that these social investigators used three different poverty standards and some express their results relative to the working-class population, while others refer to the entire population of the town or city. The first standard, used by Bowley in his immediate post-war investigation, was directly derived from *Livelihood and Poverty*. Bowley used this 'bare physical efficiency standard' in his five northern towns' survey and the *New Survey*, as well as by Jones in Merseyside, Owen in Sheffield and Ford in Southampton. The second, Rowntree's, has no direct precedent. His 'Human Needs' standard was significantly more generous than his original 1899 'merely physical efficiency' measure and was designed to allow a degree of social participation. The third standard, George's, was similar to Rowntree's 'Human Needs' scale except he made no allowance for personal sundries.

Bowley's 'bare physical efficiency' standard has more in common with Rowntree's 1899 standard than Rowntree's 'Human Needs' measure. A comparison between these two poverty lines is given in Table 3.20, though it should be noted that although both have been repriced for October 1936 prices (using the official cost of living index), Rowntree's 'Human Needs' measure is based on his 1918 calculations, rather than his revised 1937 estimates.[435] The figures relate to expenditure required for a reference family of two adults and three schoolchildren and the large difference between them is immediately apparent.

Table 3.20   Bowley's and Rowntree's poverty line compared

	Bowley: 'Bare physical efficiency'	Rowntree: 1918 'Human Needs'
Food	18s 8½d	19s 11d
Rent	8s 5d	9s 6½d
Clothing	4s 3½d	9s 6d
Fuel	3s 3d	4s 4½d
Insurance	1s 6d	1s 6d
Sundries: household	1s 5d	2s 10d
Sundries: personal	–	10s
Total	37s 7d	57s 8d

Source: A. M. Carr-Saunders and D. Caradog Jones, *A Survey of the Social Structure of England and Wales* (2nd edn, 1937), Table LXVIII, p. 179.

The differences between Rowntree's 1918 and 1937 'Human Needs' standards are not that important in this context. The former was based on a diet that provided 3500 kcal and 115 g of protein per adult male equivalent, whereas the revised standards used the BMA recommendation of 3400 kcal and 100 g of protein.[436] The amounts for rent and clothing also differed, but only in terms of price, not conception. Nevertheless, while the food and rent component of Rowntree's and Bowley's standards is essentially similar, the substantial gap between them is accounted for largely by the inclusion of expenditure for personal sundry items and a more generous clothing allowance in Rowntree's 'Human Needs' poverty line.

Not only is this difference in the conception of poverty, and how it should be measured, important with respect to assessing progress in the interwar period, the differences between Rowntree's 'Human Needs' standard and Bowley or Rowntree's 'bare subsistence' standard are also important for evaluating the generosity of the level of state benefit recommended in the 1942 Beveridge Report, as we shall see in Chapter 5.

4

UNEMPLOYMENT AND POVERTY IN BRITAIN BETWEEN THE WARS

Introduction

Following the closure of Palmer's shipyard, 200 men from Jarrow marched to London in order to petition Parliament so that the government would '... realise the urgent need that work should be provided for the town without delay'.[437] Photographs of the 1936 Jarrow march are one of the most enduring icons of the interwar years. Keith Joseph probably had this kind of image in mind when he favourably contrasted the 'gaunt, tight-lipped men in caps and mufflers of the 1930s', with the unemployed of the early 1970s.[438] The interwar period has become synonymous with mass unemployment, although paradoxically, it was also a time of relative economic prosperity for some Britons. In these years, despite unprecedented high unemployment, the economy grew at a modest rate, living standards improved for those with work and new consumer goods became available that enhanced leisure activity and lessened some of the drudgery of domestic chores. In interwar Britain, many homes and factories were electrified; the ownership of wireless sets became commonplace and the growth in ownership of motor cars transformed social life for those wealthy enough to own them. For the middle classes, and for some sections of the working classes, the modernity of the interwar period was as important as persistent joblessness was for those excluded from the benefits of economic progress. This dichotomy of experience is perhaps best summed up by the phrase 'poverty and progress', which, as we have seen, was the title chosen by Rowntree for his second social survey of York in 1936. This chapter will investigate the extent to which

100

unemployment was a cause of poverty and the efficacy of the state response to increased numbers of people who were workless.

4.1   Interwar Unemployment

Before we consider the relationship between unemployment and poverty, it is necessary to be clear about some of the 'facts' about unemployment in interwar Britain.[439] Estimates of the rate of unemployment require data on numbers unemployed and the size of the labour force. As Booth and Glynn point out, during the interwar period, 'unemployment was effectively defined by the method of measurement, which was on the basis of voluntary registration at labour exchanges'.[440] Unemployment statistics rely upon data resulting from the operation of the National Insurance scheme. From 1911, the Ministry of Labour published figures for the total number of insured workers unemployed. They distinguished between the 'temporally stopped' that were expected to return to work within six weeks and the 'wholly unemployed'.[441] During the interwar period, about two-thirds of the labour force were covered by this scheme, after it had been considerably expanded in 1920. Important groups were still excluded, however. Agricultural workers, domestic servants, teachers, nurses and many local authority workers were not covered by National Insurance, although it was extended to agricultural workers in 1936. The 1931 population census enumerated 19.5 million people as gainfully employed, whereas only 12.5 million were covered by National Insurance at this date.[442] In Table 4.1 the unemployment insurance data are shown along with unemployment rates derived from trade union records. The close correspondence in these data is likely the result of the dominance of highly unionised industries covered by the insurance. The trade union records themselves refer to unemployment rates in a relatively small sample of the labour force (about 0.7 million in 1910).[443]

Various attempts have been made to try to correct the interwar data to make them more representative of the experience of the entire economy. The most reliable estimates are due to Feinstein, reported in Garside, using unemployment data from the 1931 census in conjunction with National Insurance records.[444] These figures are reported in Table 4.2. Paradoxically, the unemployment rate among the insured section of the labour force, henceforth the 'insured workers' unemployment rate', is greater than the unemployment rate for the entire economy, the 'total

Table 4.1 Unemployment rates, 1913–26

	Trade union (per cent unemployment)	National Insurance (per cent unemployed)
1913	2.1	3.6
1914	3.3	4.2
1915	1.1	1.2
1916	0.4	0.6
1917	0.7	0.7
1918	0.8	0.8
1919	2.4	n.a.
1920	2.4	3.9
1921	14.8	16.9
1922	15.2	14.3
1923	11.3	11.7
1924	8.1	10.3
1925	10.5	11.3
1926	12.2	12.5

Source: W. R. Garside, *British Unemployment, 1919–1939* (Cambridge, 1990), Table 1, p. 4.

Table 4.2 Employment and unemployment, 1921–38 (000s)

	Employees at work	Unemployment		Percentage unemployed	
		Insured persons aged 16–64	Total workers	Insured workers as a proportion of insured employees	Total unemployed as a proportion of total employees
1921	15,879	1840	2212	17.0	12.2
1922	15,847	1588	1909	14.3	10.8
1923	16,068	1304	1567	11.7	8.9
1924	16,332	1168	1404	10.3	7.9
1925	16,531	1297	1559	11.3	8.6
1926	16,529	1463	1759	12.5	9.6
1927	17,060	1142	1373	9.7	7.4
1928	17,123	1278	1536	10.8	8.2
1929	17,392	1250	1503	10.4	8.0
1930	17,016	1979	2379	16.1	12.3
1931	16,554	2705	3252	21.3	16.4
1932	16,644	2828	3400	22.1	17.0
1933	17,018	2567	3087	19.9	15.4
1934	17,550	2170	2609	16.7	12.9
1935	17,890	2027	2437	15.5	12.0
1936	18,513	1749	2100	13.1	10.2
1937	19,196	1482	1776	10.8	8.5
1938	19,243	1800	2164	12.9	10.1

Source: W. R. Garside, *British Unemployment, 1919–1939* (1990), Table 2, p. 5.

unemployment rate'. This is because people in those industries outside the scheme also experienced unemployment, but not generally to the same extent as those covered by the scheme. So although the insured workers' unemployment data underestimate the *extent* of unemployment (because some people working in industries not covered by the scheme would be unemployed), it underestimates the *rate* of unemployment.

Overall, the magnitude of Feinstein's adjustment to the unemployment scheme data was considerable. Between 1921 and 1938, average unemployment is 14.2 per cent as recorded by the insured workers' data. Feinstein's revisions suggest that average unemployment for all workers was 10.8 per cent during this period.[445] Nevertheless, despite these revisions to the data, it is still reasonable to view the interwar years as witnessing a long period of fluctuating but constantly high level of unemployment, which began at the end of 1920 and continued until the beginning of the Second World War. Unlike most industrialised economies, Britain experienced two depressions in the interwar period: one in 1921 and another in 1930–3. The output of the economy fell more severely in the former than the latter period but unemployment increased sharply in both, from an official annual rate of just less than 4 per cent in 1920 to just under 17 per cent in 1921. Throughout the rest of the interwar period, according to official statistics of insured workers, there were never less than a million unemployed. The worst year for recorded unemployment was 1932 when nearly 3 million were 'on the dole', though the *increase* in unemployment from the trade cycle peak of 1929 was not quite as great as in the period 1920–1. In 1932 the unemployment rate for 'insured workers' peaked at just over 22 per cent and the rate for 'all workers' was 17 per cent.

4.2   The Characteristics of Interwar Unemployment

Of course, there was no one type of person unemployed, but unemployment tended to be more pronounced in the north of Britain, Wales and Scotland. Older men who had worked in heavy industry had higher rates of unemployment than other groups of people. Both these general statements need careful qualification, however. Unemployment was worse in some areas than in others, primarily because the Depression hit some *industries* harder than others. The regional and industrial patterns of unemployment, for three benchmark years, are summarised in Table 4.3.

Table 4.3   Regional and industrial variations in interwar unemployment

	Regional unemployment rates for insured workers (per cent)		
	June 1929	June 1932	June 1937
South East	4.4	12.3	4.9
East Anglia	5.8	15.4	6.9
South West	7.7	16.1	6.5
West Midlands	9.0	22.0	6.2
East Midlands	8.4	19.7	7.5
North West	12.7	25.3	12.7
Yorkshire and Humberside	11.5	27.0	12.3
North	15.2	36.4	16.8
Wales	18.2	37.4	20.7
Scotland	11.0	26.8	14.0
Great Britain	10.4	22.1	10.8

	Unemployment rates for insured workers in selected industries (per cent)		
	1929	1932	1937
Coal mining	19.0	34.5	16.1
Cotton textiles	12.9	30.6	10.9
Shipbuilding	25.3	62.0	24.4
Motors, cycles and aircraft	7.1	22.4	5.9
Electrical engineering	4.6	16.8	3.1
Chemicals	6.5	17.3	6.8
Building	14.3	30.2	14.6
Distributive trades	6.2	12.6	8.9
Road transport	12.0	22.2	12.3

Source: N.F.R. Crafts, *British Economic Growh during the Industrial Revolution* (1985), Table 8.4, p. 170.

As Table 4.3 shows, the old staple industries, that had dominated the British economy prior to the First World War, were particularly badly affected. In 1932, roughly two-thirds of shipbuilders were unemployed, along with a third of textile workers and nearly two-fifths of all miners. Because these industries were based in the North, Wales and Scotland, the Depression was much more severe in an area described as 'outer Britain' (north of a line drawn between the Bristol Channel and the Wash). In some towns within these depressed areas, the position was even worse. In Jarrow, for example, which was dominated by Palmer's shipbuilding until the yard closed in 1933, three-quarters of the insured workforce were unemployed.[446] Hilda Jennings's study of Brynmawr, a town in the South Wales coalfield, revealed how long-term unemployment could be devastating for a small community dependent on coal mining and the manufacture of iron, steel and tinplate.[447] A sample of 1202 unemployed men revealed that just fewer than 19 per cent had been unemployed for less than 2 years and about 20 per cent had been unemployed for 5 years or more. With the exception of the 7 per cent who had never worked, the rest had been unemployed between 2 and 5 years. The vast majority of these chronically unemployed men were aged between 40 and 65 years old.[448]

It is necessary to remember, however, that unemployment is a 'stock-flow' concept. In any week, new people enter unemployment and some people without jobs find work. An average figure of 17 per cent unemployed in 1932, the worst year of the Depression, could be consistent with 17 per cent of all workers being unemployed for a whole year, or all workers being unemployed for 17 per cent of the year, or anything between these two extremes.[449] As Thomas points out, 'Neither the risks of becoming unemployed nor the chances of finding a new job are shared equally by everyone in society.'[450] Moreover, because it is likely that the negative impact of unemployment on an individual's health is liable to be greater the longer he or she is unemployed, information on the length of average spells of unemployment, and how this changes over time, is important if the social and personal consequences of joblessness are to be fully considered.

Thomas maintains that the increase in unemployment in the Depression was not the result of a dramatic increase in the inflow rate to unemployment and 'must, therefore, be accounted for by a rise in the average duration of joblessness'.[451] Data on the duration of unemployment during the 1920s and 1930s are available from a number of sources. In 1944, Beveridge argued that

In September, 1929, nearly 90 per cent of applicants had been unemployed for less than six months and less than five per cent had been unemployed for twelve months or more. In August, 1936, the number of persons with short unemployment (less than six months) was much the same as in September, 1929, about 850,000, but constituted only 64.4 per cent of the unemployed: those unemployed twelve months or more were one quarter of the whole.[452]

For Beveridge, the increase in long-term unemployment in the 1930s was the 'Legacy of the Great Depression'.[453] The Pilgrim Trust expressed similar views, 'Apart from this small stagnant pool [the less than 5 per cent long-term jobless], we must think of pre-depression unemployment as a fairly rapidly moving stream.'[454] In contrast, 'In the middle of 1933, when the last of the men thrown out by the depression and not reabsorbed had passed on into the long-term class, 25 of every 100 unemployed had no work during the last year.'[455] This created what the Pilgrim Trust described as a 'social problem of the first order'.[456]

However, while the unemployment insurance data are a reasonably accurate guide to the number of long-term unemployed after 1931, Crafts has shown that they understate the long-term unemployed prior to this date. This is because prior to 1931, many of the long-term unemployed, who had exhausted their entitlement to benefit, received poor relief instead. Although these people would still be counted as unemployed, they would not feature in the data for long-term unemployment. In consequence, Beveridge's figures for 1929 underestimate significantly the numbers in this category. Crafts suggests that Beveridge's estimate of 45,000 long-term unemployed in September 1929 should be raised to 89,000, but this still means that long-term unemployment increased during the 1930s, as the corresponding figure for August 1937 was 288,000.[457] Over the same period the average duration of unemployment increased from about 22 weeks in September 1929 to about 43 weeks in December 1935, before falling slowly to about 38 weeks in June 1938.[458]

We saw in Chapter 2 that Beveridge and Lavers's study of unemployment in York before the war had identified that roughly one in four workers had been unemployed for over a year in June 1910. It may be that York was atypical and that nationally long-term unemployment was considerably less than this figure before the Great War, but if York is in any way representative, it would imply that the 1920s labour market was somewhat exceptional, notwithstanding Crafts's important revision to Beveridge's work.

As Table 4.4 shows, there were two further aspects to the pattern of long-term unemployment in interwar Britain that need to be considered. First, long-term unemployment was much more acute in 'outer Britain'. Second, it was highest among workers aged over 45 years. For example, while the average duration of unemployment was 17 weeks in the South East in February 1938, in the northern region it was 71.2 weeks, over four times as high. Among older workers, duration figures were proportionately even worse. In the South East average duration was 20.4 weeks for workers over 45 years, while in the northern region it was 112.8 weeks – over five times higher.

Table 4.4 Disaggregated statistics on duration of male unemployment, February 1938

Region	Age	Claimants unemployed over 1 year (%)	Claimants unemployed over 5 years (%)	Average duration of unemployment (weeks)
Great Britain	All	20.5	4.4	38.6
	18–24	12.6	0.5	14.8
	25–34	14.3	2.0	27.7
	35–44	21.0	3.9	38.8
	45–54	25.5	5.9	48.1
	55–64	37.0	10.2	48.4
London	All	5.8	0.2	15.5
	18–24	1.9	0.0	11.0
	25–44	4.4	0.0	13.9
	45–64	10.0	0.5	20.7
South East	All	6.6	0.3	17.0
	18–24	2.9	0.1	13.0
	25–44	6.0	0.3	16.2
	45–64	9.2	0.4	20.4
South West	All	8.6	1.3	20.0
	18–24	2.2	0.1	11.6
	25–44	5.5	0.6	15.4
	45–64	14.5	2.4	29.3
Midlands	All	15.9	3.3	30.3
	18–24	3.1	0.2	11.9
	25–44	10.2	1.4	21.2
	45–64	26.7	6.4	48.8
North East	All	18.2	3.6	34.2
	18–24	4.1	0.1	13.4
	25–44	12.8	1.5	25.1
	45–64	28.6	7.0	53.3
North West	All	23.1	4.2	40.8
	18–24	9.4	0.4	20.1
	25–44	20.4	2.7	35.9
	45–64	32.4	7.6	41.8
Northern	All	35.5	9.9	71.2
	18–24	11.9	1.0	24.4

Region	Age	Claimants unemployed over 1 year (%)	Claimants unemployed over 5 years (%)	Average duration of unemployment (weeks)
	25–44	30.8	6.9	59.0
	45–64	49.6	16.5	112.8
Scotland	All	29.7	6.1	56.1
	18–24	14.2	0.8	27.2
	25–44	29.3	4.6	52.6
	45–64	41.3	11.5	84.8
Wales	All	30.7	8.9	61.8
	18–24	9.3	0.7	20.5
	25–44	23.9	5.7	45.5
	45–64	45.8	15.2	104.8

Source: N. F. R. Crafts, 'Long-Term Unemployment in Britain in the 1930s', *Economic History Review*, 40 (1987), Table 2, p. 421.

Overall, the percentage of long-term unemployed (over one year), and chronic long-term unemployed (over five years), was significantly higher in 'outer Britain'. In Wales and Scotland nearly one in three of the unemployed had been unemployed for at least a year, in the northern region the position was marginally worse, whereas in the North East and North West, about one in four or five of all unemployed claimants were long-term unemployed. In the northern region, nearly one in every ten of the unemployed had been unemployed for over five years. This compares with one in every 500 who were chronic long-term unemployed in London (unemployed for longer than five years). In these relatively prosperous regions, long-term unemployment was 5 or 6 per cent of the total unemployed and chronic long-term unemployment was rare.

The incidence of unemployment also varied by age and gender. For most of the interwar period, unemployment rates among females were significantly less than those of men, but this is partly a function of the way in which unemployment data were collected, as we shall see in a moment. At any given date, those with consistently the lowest rates of unemployment were juvenile workers aged less than 20 years old. This group also had the shortest average duration of unemployment. It is worth noting Eichengreen's caution with respect to lower unemployment rates among juvenile workers in interwar Britain. It may be that there were disincentives for juveniles to register as unemployed since, unlike adults, juveniles were required to attend junior instruction centres.[459] Hence, in part, lower levels of recorded juvenile unemployment could be a consequence of the regulations governing the administration of unemployment benefit.[460] Among adults of both sexes, unemployment rates among prime-aged workers (30–39) were lower than those among older workers aged 45–64. Not surprisingly, the highest age-specific rates were among men aged 60 and over. Nevertheless, as Beveridge was to note, the risks of becoming unemployed were the same across all age cohorts over 35, but older workers had a lower probability of finding new work and leaving the unemployment register.[461] Younger adult male workers aged 21–29 also had relatively high unemployment rates, possibly because of dissatisfaction with what contemporaries referred to as 'blind alley' or 'dead end' jobs.[462] The age distribution of adult male unemployment followed a 'U' pattern, where it started off fairly high for young men in their twenties and then fell to low levels among prime-aged males, before rising sharply among older men.

Women accounted for less than 14 per cent of the total volume of unemployment in 1933. This, in turn, reflected women's lower levels of labour force participation, as only one-third of women over 14 years were in the labour force during the interwar period. Despite this, recorded rates of female unemployment were lower and the average duration of unemployment was shorter. Thomas argues that when women lost their jobs they were more likely than men to leave the labour force. One consequence of this was that it lowered the age structure of women's employment.[463] The effect of unemployment benefit legislation can also be seen in Table 4.5 as female unemployment dropped by half between February 1931 and November 1932, while recorded male unemployment remained about the same, partly because of the effective disqualification of many married women under the provisions of the October 1931 Anomalies Act.[464] Prior to 1930, married women who had exhausted their entitlement to unemployment insurance, were disqualified from receiving 'extended benefit' if their husbands were working. In addition, Deacon reckons that there were about 3 million claimants who had their benefit disqualified between 1921 and 1930, due to the operation of the 'genuinely seeking work' clause.[465] It was mainly women that were debarred under this

Table 4.5   Unemployment rates by age and sex

	April 1927	February 1931	November 1932	February 1938
Males				
16–17	2.1	–	4.6	4.1
18–20		15.8	16.3	8.2
21–24	8.8	23.3	23.5	12.5
25–29	11.0	21.3	22.7	11.1
30–34	9.3	22.0	21.9	11.4
35–39	9.2	22.3	21.4	13.0
40–44	9.5	22.3	22.4	13.5
45–49	10.8	24.4	23.1	15.1
50–54	11.3	27.1	26.5	17.6
55–59	13.0	28.5	26.9	19.9
60–64	15.1	34.5	32.0	23.6
18–64	10.2	23.1	22.9	13.6
Females				
16–17	2.2	–	3.1	5.5
18–20		13.3	7.9	8.3
21–24	5.1	18.4	9.1	10.6
25–29	4.3	20.5	9.3	10.7
30–34	4.1	24.1	11.8	11.7
35–39	4.5	27.2	10.9	12.8
40–44	4.3	26.5	9.4	13.8
45–49	4.6	27.8	17.3	15.1
50–54	5.2	30.4	18.3	17.3
55–59	4.8	32.9	20.6	19.8
60–64	5.5	30.6	16.4	24.5
18–64	4.8	20.3	10.4	11.6

Source: Mark Thomas, 'Unemployment in Interwar Britain', in B. Eichengreen and
T. J. Hatton (eds), *Interwar Unemployment in International Perspective* (1988), Table 3.6,
p. 117.

clause and, of course, disqualification prevented these women register-
ing as unemployed.

In terms of skill level, working with data from the 1931 population
census of England and Wales, Thomas finds that unskilled males were
the most vulnerable to unemployment and female higher professionals
the least vulnerable. In general terms, the risk of unemployment
decreased with higher social class, as is evident from Table 4.6. It is noteworthy, however, that unemployment rates among semi-professional
groups were high compared with other social classes and this is true of
both men and women.

Table 4.6   Unemployment by occupational class, 1931

Social class	Percentage male unemployed	Percentage female unemployed
Ia Higher professional	1.77	0.17
Ib Lower professional	4.87	2.74
Ic Semi-professional	14.53	17.16
II Employers, managers	1.38	0.88
III Clerical	5.61	4.33
IV Foremen, supervisors	5.09	4.40
V Skilled manual	12.06	12.93
VI Semi-skilled manual	11.94	9.71
VII Unskilled manual	21.53	11.13

Source: Adapted from Mark Thomas, 'Unemployment in Interwar Britain', in B. Eichengreen and T. J. Hatton (eds), *Interwar Unemployment in International Perspective* (1988), Table 3.9, p. 123.

4.3   The Health Consequences of Unemployment

Evaluating the health consequences of unemployment is a difficult task. Many contemporaries were convinced that the Depression had resulted in a deterioration in people's health, especially among those who had experienced prolonged periods of unemployment. The debate about the impact of the Depression on the health of Britons has continued ever since. Attempting to establish a causal link between unemployment and ill health is demanding precisely because ill health is also associated with poverty – and unemployment and poverty are highly correlated.

One of the most careful analyses of the impact of unemployment on health undertaken in the late 1930s, remained wisely equivocal on this issue. In *Men without Work*, the Pilgrim Trust concluded that, 'with regard to the effects of unemployment on the health of the men concerned – as opposed to their families – it is difficult, here too, to distinguish the actual results of unemployment from conditions associated with it'.[466] Moreover, since the physical health consequences of unemployment might be very long term, observations on the health of individuals are required over periods in which they move from employment to unemployment, and ideally, back into employment. Longitudinal data of this type are rare and most studies have to rely upon (unsatisfactory) aggregate time-series or cross-section data.[467]

It is also difficult to distinguish the impact of unemployment on psychological and physical health since clearly they are related, but the initial consequence of unemployment was likely to be an impairment of psychological health. Prolonged unemployment might take years to manifest symptoms of physical ill health, which may be reflected in higher mortality rates decades later. In contrast, the psychological impact is likely to be apparent much sooner, possibly immediately, and consequently it is easier to observe. There is a clear dichotomy between those writers who have argued that the ill-health effects of unemployment are the consequence of the reduction in income and financial security brought about by unemployment and those who have argued that work confers many other benefits on individuals. For these writers, it is the absence of these benefits during spells of unemployment that leads to deterioration in an individual's health.[468]

E. Wright Bakke's 1933 inquiry of the unemployed in Greenwich revealed a heterogeneous response to unemployment, depending upon age, skill, marital status and personality. Bakke appreciated the stock-flow nature of unemployment and the fact that most people's experience was of a relatively short duration.[469] Among the long-term unemployed, Bakke thought that the unemployment insurance scheme, while preventing the worst ill effects of unemployment (starvation, ill health and poverty), could not 'relieve the ill effects of no work'. Although unemployment benefit increased the feeling of security among the unemployed, the lack of work 'continue[d] to take the heart out of men, and replace[d] ambition and industry with discouragement'.[470] This study also demonstrated the significant variation in individual response to unemployment, although Bakke claimed that it was 'the most ambitious [that] lost heart most quickly'.[471]

The Pilgrim Trust's detailed 1936 investigation of long-term unemployment, *Men without Work*, was based on a random sample of 1086 unemployed workers in England and Wales (938 men and 148 women). These were drawn from those men who had been unemployed between November 1935 and November 1936 in Deptford (London), Leicester, Liverpool, Blackburn, Crook (County Durham) and Rhondda.[472] The Pilgrim Trust considered the impact of unemployment on health, including its psychological effect, and they show the way that the impact of long-term unemployment varied between skilled and unskilled, between the single and married and between the young and the old. Generally, they found that older, skilled men were less ready to accept long-term unemployment.[473] It may be that the time path of response to unemployment is important here. Dr James Halliday reported in 1935 that unemployed men in Britain were subject to a higher incidence of psychoneurotic disease than employed men, although the incidence was lower among the long- and very long-term unemployed than those men who had been unemployed for between 6 and 12 months.[474]

Jahoda's study of the impact of unemployment in Monmouthshire, which was carried out in 1938, but not published until 1987, is illuminating in this context.[475] It centred on an analysis of the workings of the Subsistence Production Society (SPS), in which unemployed men produced goods for their own subsistence. A similar society operated in Wigan.[476] The central objective was to 'overcome the disastrous economic and human consequences of unemployment'.[477] When the scheme started, in June 1935, about 45 per cent of the male population were unemployed, most of whom had previously worked in coal mining. Despite initial resistance to the scheme, by March 1938, 8.9 per cent of the unemployed in the eastern valley of Monmouthshire were members of the SPS. Of these, nearly 83 per cent were aged 35 and over, many of them chronic long-term unemployed (the average duration of unemployment for SPS members was six years).[478] The industrial workshops of the SPS scheme consisted of furniture making, handicrafts, boot repairing, and tailoring (supplied by SPS weaving and knitting workshops). Cakes and bread were provided by an SPS bakery, made from flour produced in an SPS flour mill; meat and milk from livestock raised and slaughtered on SPS farms and abattoir, and butchery and vegetables, fruit and honey cultivated on SPS farms. As Fryer observes, this was a 'social experiment on such a grand scale that it almost beggars the imagination'.[479]

Membership of the SPS had a generally positive impact on psychological well-being, especially for older workers.[480] Fryer suggests that membership conferred a significant improvement in 'consumption power', which was important for the psychological health of the unemployed.[481] Jahoda found that most of the unemployed were 'resigned', though relatively few of the Monmouthshire unemployed were in states of 'despair' or 'apathy', due to the moderating impact of unemployment benefit.

In 1934, Beales and Lambert had identified a similar response. Their study was based on the experiences of 25 individuals, of different age, sex, occupation and location. They argued that 'in prolonged unemployment the victim's reaction ... passes through a series of phases. There is a rough progression from optimism to pessimism, from pessimism to fatalism.'[482] In a review of the evidence on unemployment and

psychological health in 1938, Eisenberg and Lazarsfeld provided the
definitive statement of the staged response to unemployment:

> First there is shock, which is followed by an active hunt for a job,
> during which the individual is still optimistic and unresigned; he
> still maintains an unbroken attitude. Second, when all efforts fail, the
> individual becomes pessimistic, anxious and suffers active distress:
> this is the most crucial state of all. And third, the individual becomes
> fatalistic and adapts himself to his new state but with a narrower scope.
> He now has a broken attitude.[483]

This type of analysis has found few disciples among modern researchers,
however. Marsh argues that the evidence is 'based on unsystematic
research, colourful autobiographies, memoirs or intensive unstructured
interviews with the unemployed' and there is little agreement on the
number of stages or what explains transition from one stage to another.[484]
Historians, too, have been generally quite sceptical. While the evidence
for 'demoralisation' among the unemployed is widespread, it did not
necessarily lead to passivity. McKibbin argues that, while the loss of work
could cause 'dismay or even despair', it is difficult to accept that 'the
unemployed disintegrated, that their mental faculties withered, that
they lost interest in work, that they became apolitical or that there
was some sort of progressive decline'.[485] One of the features of the interwar labour market that stands out is its high level of rapid turnover.
According to Thomas, this was due to the operation of the insurance
system, prevalence of casual employment and low job attachment.[486]
It is hard to reconcile this with impaired search activity. Indeed,
neo-classical explanations of the causes of unemployment point to
increased search activity in the interwar period, arising from relatively
generous benefits.[487]

Whiteside has shown how rising unemployment was accompanied by
rising claims for sickness and disablement benefit, which in 1938 struck
one Ministry of Health official as 'inconsistent with the claim that is often
made ... that the general health of the nation is generally improving'.[488]
There were, of course, good reasons why people would prefer to be
classified sick in the 1930s rather than unemployed: being sick avoided
the work search and availability tests of the 'dole'. However, the Pilgrim
Trust noted that sickness benefit was liable to be significantly less than
unemployment assistance because the former did not cover dependants.[489] Moreover, Whiteside notes that there was reciprocal causality

between unemployment and health: sickness could cause unemployment as well as unemployment causing sickness.[490]

There are a number of empirical studies that have tried to establish a causal relationship between unemployment and mortality. For the Pilgrim Trust, Singer reported that maternal and infant mortality rates increased with unemployment in England and Wales for the period 1928–33.[491] Using county borough unemployment and maternal mortality data, Singer claimed that there were approximately 850 extra deaths due to the slump. If the county boroughs were representative of the country, then the increase in mortality due to puerperal disease was estimated at 3200. Singer argues that this was due to nervous strain, malnutrition and economies in social services.[492] However, although Singer's analysis was undoubtedly pioneering, as Stern points out, 'it is virtually impossible to establish a causal effect of unemployment on mortality or morbidity from data aggregated for different individuals'. This is because both the incidences of ill health and unemployment are also strongly related to income.[493] Over a longer time period, using time-series data for 1936–76, Brenner concluded that if unemployment increased by more than 1 million in five years, it would result in 50,000 more deaths from general illness and 167,000 deaths from cardiovascular disease.[494] His results have been resoundingly criticised by health economists, however.[495] Nevertheless, it is widely agreed that a fall in income and/or increased stress is the most likely link between unemployment and ill health. Exactly how such things as length of time unemployed; socio-economic class; family status; age; gender and a host of lifestyle factors might affect this relationship still remains uncertain.[496]

During the interwar years official surveys on the health of the unemployed gave little cause for concern, as their findings failed to identify any serious health consequences of unemployment poverty. This view rested on two sorts of empirical evidence collected at the peak of the Depression in 1932: an investigation of mortality rates in 8 counties and 16 county boroughs with high unemployment rates and a comparison between the mortality rates in county boroughs with 'high' and 'low' incidence of unemployment.[497] The Ministry of Health was of the opinion that 'depressed areas' always displayed worse rates of morbidity and mortality and, if anything, the gap was closing compared with the position in 1921.

Most regional medical officers of health expressed similarly optimistic views in their annual reports and these were endorsed by further empirical investigations conducted by the Ministry of Health in 1933. Little

evidence of malnutrition or unemployment-related health problems
were evident even in the most depressed areas.[498] The Ministry claimed
that 'though specifically sought for, evidence of widespread malnutrition there is none' and there was 'no available evidence of any general
increase in physical impairment, in sickness or in mortality, as the result
of the economic depression or unemployment'.[499] Although the Chief
Medical Officer, Sir George Newman, 'attached particular importance
to the effects of unemployment on health', the conclusions he drew from
his analysis of the reports by the regional medical officers were often
somewhat misleading. Harris points out that 41 of the 66 medical officers who responded to Newman's inquiries said 'they were personally
aware of a deterioration in the health of the population as a result of
unemployment'.[500]

Charles Webster has convincingly demonstrated how the political
motivation of the medical officers of health, coupled with the subjective
definition of 'malnutrition', make official health (morbidity) statistics
for the interwar period almost worthless. So, for example, in many
depressed areas, the reported incidence of subnormal nutrition was less
than half of the average of all areas. School medical officers in Bootle
reported malnutrition rates 12 times greater than those reported in
Liverpool, while agricultural areas of Wales 'suffered from appalling
malnutrition, while the mining areas seemed to be virtually free of the
problem'.[501] Moreover, Webster argues that many contemporary commentators pointed to the dire health consequences of unemployment
poverty in the depressed areas, much of which might be concealed by
the behaviour of *average* health statistics.[502]

Mortality data, especially infant and maternal mortality statistics,
provide direct evidence of changes in the health of the people, which is
not subject to the same subjective treatment in recording as the interwar
morbidity data. These mortality statistics have been used to attempt to
establish a causal relationship between unemployment and ill health,
but this is a complex problem, as we have already seen. Consider the
behaviour of infant mortality rates by social class first of all. In Chapter 1,
Richard Titmuss's evidence of wide disparities in the incidence of
infant mortality by socio-economic class was discussed for the pre-First
World War period. Despite falling infant mortality rates for all classes
between 1911 and 1930–2, the gap between rich and poor widened.
The mortality rates of infants born to parents where the father was enumerated as social class I, fell faster than the mortality rates of infants
born to parents where the father was in social class V.

This inequality in the *relative* improvement of infant mortality by socio-economic class reflected the poorer health of children born into working-class families, especially with respect to their nutritional attainment, which in turn affects resistance to infectious disease. However, Titmuss's conclusions were based on an evaluation of the Registrar-General's statistics for the 1920s and early 1930s. Winter analysed the Registrar-General's statistics for 1939 and found that by the eve of the Second World War, the implied health inequalities by socio-economic class were less than they had been prior to the First World War. Table 4.7 summarises the findings of Titmuss for 1911 to 1930–2 and of Winter for 1939.

Infant health, at all ages, improved markedly between 1911 and 1939, from an average of 130 to 51 deaths per 1000. The decline in infant mortality was true for children born into both manual and professional workers' families and remains the most important conclusion to be drawn from the analysis of these data. This improvement was concentrated in

Table 4.7 Infant mortality rates by socio-economic class, 1911–39 (per 1000 legitimate births)

	1911	1920–2	1930–2	1939
Neonatal mortality				
Class V	42.5	36.9	32.5	30.1
Class I	30.2	23.4	21.7	18.9
Excess class V	12.3	13.5	10.8	11.2
Percentage excess	40.7	57.7	49.7	59.3
Post-neonatal mortality				
Class V	110.0	60.1	44.5	30.0
Class I	46.2	15.0	11.0	8.0
Excess class V	63.8	45.1	33.5	22.0
Percentage excess	138.1	300.1	304.5	275.0
Mortality 6–12 months				
Class V	50.0	24.6	19.4	10.4
Class I	18.3	5.8	3.6	2.3
Excess class V	31.7	18.8	15.8	8.1
Percentage excess	173.2	324.1	438.9	352.2
Infant mortality				
Class V	152.5	97.0	77.0	60.1
Class I	76.4	38.4	32.7	26.9
Excess class V	76.1	58.6	44.3	33.2
Percentage excess	99.6	152.6	135.5	123.4

Source: J. Winter, *The Decline of Mortality, 1870–1950*, Table 2, p. 107.

the later months of infancy as there were 'only very modest changes in neonatal mortality'.[503] Furthermore, the national average data by socio-economic class do not show a consistent pattern of changes in infant mortality during the Depression. It is true that the improvement was faster for professional workers, but the extent of the disparity in improvement by socio-economic class during the interwar years is dependent upon the choice of mortality statistic. In the case of mortality between 6 and 12 months, the health gradient by class worsens during the Depression (comparing 1920–2 with 1930–2). Notice this is not true for infant mortality rates. In all cases, however, the percentage excess of infant mortality among manual workers' families, compared with professional workers, worsened after the First World War. This is true for all measures of mortality of infants under 12 months old and at all dates during the interwar period, although by 1939 the extent of the disparity between social classes had considerably lessened.

Table 4.8 Index of infant mortality rates in England and Wales and selected urban districts, 1926–39 (England and Wales, 1926–9 = 100)

	1926–9	1930	1931	1932	1933	1934	1935	1936	1937	1938
England and Wales	100	86	94	93	91	84	81	84	83	76
Greater London	87	77	93	96	86	96	83	94	86	81
Chelsea	93	57	60	74	111	93	86	76	84	114
Hackney	89	71	86	77	73	80	69	90	61	80
Hampstead	79	83	87	77	54	76	70	94	77	81
Kensington	107	99	109	140	104	133	113	104	119	111
Stepney	106	109	111	86	91	121	87	141	86	90
Wandsworth	81	77	89	90	73	83	79	83	91	66
Birmingham	104	87	100	97	94	96	93	90	86	87
Bradford	120	107	101	107	114	89	91	119	100	84
Coventry	97	79	84	101	91	76	66	74	71	80
Leeds	126	97	110	126	116	101	110	109	99	89
Liverpool	140	117	134	130	140	114	120	109	117	106
Manchester	129	110	121	123	107	99	101	110	109	99
Merthyr Tydfil	139	131	150	104	129	109	107	113	113	111
Stockport	117	81	113	103	119	77	81	109	81	80
Wigan	153	153	147	130	157	96	140	117	131	141

Source: J. M. Winter, 'Infant Mortality, Maternal Mortality, and Public Health in Britain in the 1930s', *Journal of European Economic History*, 8 (1979), Table V, p. 449.

Table 4.8 provides evidence of the behaviour of infant mortality rates by urban area for the period 1926–38, expressed relative to the average for England and Wales between 1926 and 1929. On the basis of this evidence, Winter argues that it is not possible to make a case for unemployment causing deterioration in health during the Depression, as infant mortality does not increase markedly in the depressed areas compared with prosperous ones.[504] For England and Wales as a whole, the average infant mortality rate was significantly lower in 1938 than it had been in 1926–9. During the worst years of the Depression in 1931–3, Winter's data do actually reveal a slight increase on 1930 levels in many areas, though not in all. It is difficult to argue that this increase is any greater in depressed areas, rather than prosperous areas, however. A note of caution is necessary here since there is a large variance in these data on a year-on-year basis in some areas, which makes the identification of change difficult at this level of aggregation.

Harris's analysis of the impact of the Depression on the height of schoolchildren lends some support to Winter's view. In a study of changes in the height of school-age children and changes in unemployment in three groups of towns in Britain between 1923 and 1938, Harris found little evidence of a negative association between changes in average height and changes in unemployment.[505] Harris concluded that although the incidence of unemployment was significantly greater in the depressed areas, wages were not that much greater than unemployment benefit. Under these circumstances, at an aggregate level, it is unlikely that unemployment per se affected family living standards to such an extent that it would be evident in deterioration in the height of schoolchildren, when compared with the children of relatively low-waged counterparts.

Of course, the impact of long-term chronic unemployment among a sizeable minority of the unemployed might not be evident in aggregate data. As Webster writes, the behaviour of infant mortality at a lower level of aggregation does provide stronger support for believing that some high-unemployment areas experienced deteriorating health during the Depression:

The infant mortality rate average for England and Wales for 1931–5 was 62, and for 1936–40 it was 56. By contrast, the comparative rates for Scotland, almost never alluded to by ministry officials in London, were 81 and 74. Scotland was thus some 10 years behind England and Wales in its control of infant mortality.... Even within small areas there were sharp differences from district to district. Hence in Oldham in

Table 4.9 Age-standardised mortality ratios for England and Wales, 1921–32 (all occupied and retired = 100 in each period)

Social class (age)	I	II	III	IV	V
Men 1921–3 (20–64)	82	94	95	101	125
Men 1930–2 (20–64)	90	94	97	102	111
Women 1930–2 (20–64)	81	89	99	103	113

Source: Richard Wilkinson, 'Class Mortality Differentials, Income Distribution and Trends in Poverty 1921–81', *Journal of Social Policy*, 18, 3 (1988), Tables 1 and 2, pp. 308–9.

1931, seven of the 12 wards recorded an infant mortality rate of more than 140, while four of these wards experienced a rate above 170.[506]

In contrast to the behaviour of relative class-specific infant mortality rates, differentials in the relative mortality experience of adult men by social class suggest that mortality experience was becoming more equal. Table 4.9 reports standardised mortality ratios (SMRs) by economic class for adult men in 1921–3 and 1930–2. At the later date, the SMR for men in social class I relative to V was significantly lower than it had been in 1921–3. This aggregate observation is confirmed by Pamuk's detailed analysis of changes in mortality by socio-economic class between 1921 and 1981 based on 143 occupations.[507] As part of a wider thesis, Wilkinson has argued that narrowing health differentials in England and Wales during the interwar period reflect a reduction in the incidence of poverty. He argues that the increase in unemployment was partially off-set by increases in the number of people in employment and generous unemployment benefit.[508]

Support for Wilkinson's argument is provided by the Pilgrim Trust's investigation. With respect to the health of the long-term unemployed, they concluded that 'the economic level at which families were living in many homes visited was such as to cause nervous anxiety and in some instances physical deterioration'. However, they also suggest that long-term unemployment per se was not necessarily the cause, because 'there is little reason to believe that many wage earners have an income not that very different from that of some of the homes in the sample'.[509] They applied George's poverty line (with minor amendment to the fuel component) to the income of the households. The results of their analysis are reported in Table 4.10.

Table 4.10   Long-term unemployment in relation to the George poverty line

	Number of families	Percentage
Families in 'deep poverty' (incomes more than 10% below poverty line)	159	17
Families in 'moderate poverty' (incomes less than 10% below the poverty line)	120	13
Families on 'subsistence level' (incomes less than 10% above the poverty line)	137	14
Families living 'a little above the poverty line' (incomes between 10 and 25% above)	174	19
Families living 'well above the poverty line' (incomes between 25 and 75% above)	251	27
Families living in 'moderate comfort' (incomes more than 75% above the poverty line)	91	10
Total number of families	932	100

Source: Pilgrim Trust, *Men without Work* (1938), Table XXXI, p. 109.

About one-third of long-term unemployed families were living below the George poverty line in November 1936 and 80 per cent of these cases were wholly dependent on unemployment assistance. There was also significant regional variation in the incidence of poverty among the families of the long-term unemployed, with the proportion below the poverty line in Liverpool being nearly half, whereas in most of the other towns it was nearer one-quarter. In addition, the incidence of poverty was greatest in families with large numbers of children under working age.[510] They argue that poverty of this kind 'is not necessarily associated' with unemployment because an 'unemployed man with a large family is living at something near the level at which the labourer in steady employment is living'.[511] This suggests that the impact of the Depression on health, by the mechanism of increased unemployment, was likely to be less than is sometimes assumed.

There is another way that the Pilgrim Trust's study illuminates the study of unemployment and its impact on health in interwar Britain. They observed that the distribution of resources was unequal within long-term unemployed families. The Pilgrim Trust thought that mothers made sacrifices to ensure that their children had sufficient food as 'in most unemployed families the parents, and in particular the wives, bore the burden of want, and in many instances were literally starving themselves in order to feed and clothe the children reasonably well'.[512] We saw in Chapter 3 that the limited evidence on the energy consumption of unemployed families suggests that women received about 70 per cent of the male intake. This conclusion was endorsed by the findings of the Women's Health Enquiry Committee, based on a questionnaire survey of the health of 1250 working-class women, in which over one-third self-reported illness suggesting very poor health. Again, part of the reason was because women were according priority to the needs of their children and husbands. As Margery Spring Rice wrote,

> Naturally they suffer, as the father does too, from the poverty of the home, the lack of sufficient food and clothes and warmth and comfort, but it is undoubtedly true that even in these respects the mother will be the first to go without. Her husband *must* be fed, as upon him depends the first of all necessities, money. The children must or will be fed, and the school will if necessary supplement. Equally husband and children must be clothed, not only fairly warmly but also for school or work fairly decently. She need not be.[513]

Neither Wilkinson nor Pamut present data on aggregate female mortality by socio-economic class in the early 1920s, so comparison for the period 1930–2 is not possible. However, information on maternal mortality is available and the interpretation of these data has divided historians.[514] Maternal mortality statistics record those deaths that are directly *attributable* to pregnancy and childbirth, but in addition there are also deaths *associated* with pregnancy and childbirth, though these are not included in the maternal mortality statistics.[515] National average maternal mortality rate increased from 4.11 per 1000 live births between 1919 and 1922 to 4.31 per 1000 in 1930–3.[516] At the peak of the Depression, however, in 1933 and 1934, maternal mortality rates were similar to what they had been in the closing years of the nineteenth century.[517] The 1932 Final Report of the Departmental Committee on Maternal Mortality and Morbidity claimed that 'at least one half of maternal deaths occurring in this country were preventable'.[518] The report attributed impaired health during and after pregnancy to 'neglected health during early womanhood', and the findings of the Pilgrim Trust and Women's Health Committee with respect to diet and the distribution of family resources are consistent with this conclusion.[519]

From 1934, however, maternal mortality fell quickly, and was 2.61 per 1000 by 1940. This fall is usually seen as the result of both the introduction of sulphonamide drugs, which reduced the risk of infection during childbirth, and better nutrition, which increased the resistance to infection.[520] By 1937 official opinion was stressing the dramatic improvement in maternal mortality. A Report on an Investigation into Maternal Mortality concluded that 'motherhood in this country has reached a comparatively high level of safety'.[521] The extension of social services also played a part in this decline. Following the 1936 Public Health and Midwives Act the number of maternal and child welfare centres increased, providing antenatal examinations as well as limited post-natal support.

4.4   Unemployment and the State

Social policy in the interwar period was dominated by governments' attempts to provide some measure of support for the unemployed while keeping costs within politically acceptable bounds. As Table 4.11 shows, the rate of benefit in 1920 was 15s per week for men and 12s for women. Nothing was paid for the dependent wives of unemployed men or their children until November 1921. The nominal value of unemployment benefit levels increased modestly during the interwar years, although benefits were cut in 1928 and in 1931. Despite these reductions, however,

Table 4.11   Scales of unemployment insurance benefits, 1919–40 (shillings per week)

	Single men	Single women	Wife	Child	Family of two adults and three children[a]
Dec. 1919	11	11	0	0	11
Dec. 1920	15	12	0	0	15
Nov. 1921	15	12	5	1	23
Aug. 1924	18	15	5	2	29
Apr. 1928	17	15	7	2	30
Mar. 1930	17	15	9	2	32
Oct. 1931	15	13	8	2	29
May 1934	17	17	9	3	35
Feb. 1935	17	17	10	3	36
Aug. 1940	20	18	10	4	42

[a] Assuming male unemployment.
Source: Beveridge, *Social Insurance and Allied Services*, Cmd 6404, p. 216 and calculated by author. Rates for means-tested unemployment assistance were generally lower from 1934.

the real value of benefits rose considerably as retail prices were generally falling between 1920 and 1933. Moreover, when dependants' allowances are taken into consideration, unemployment benefit for a family of two adults and three children of 36s per week was just below Bowley's poverty-line standard of 37s 7d at 1936 prices (see Table 3.20).[522] Set against this background of more generous treatment, the government attempted to limit the cost of unemployment relief through the imposition of a 'genuinely seeking work' clause and means-tested benefit. As Deacon demonstrates, between March 1921 and March 1930 nearly 3 million claimants were disallowed benefit under the provision of the 'genuinely seeking work' test, the majority women.[523] Between 1931 and 1938 about one-third of claimants had their benefit reduced by the means test and a substantial minority had their claim completely disallowed.

The unemployment insurance system had never been designed to cope with widespread unemployment of the kind experienced in the interwar period, and it could not do so. Those that had exhausted their entitlement to unemployment insurance, were either treated 'as if' they still had entitlement or were forced to seek assistance from the parish. On 1 January 1936, 26 per 1000 of the population were in receipt of poor relief. This figure is slightly in excess of the proportion in receipt of poor relief prior to the First World War (between 1911 and 1914 the rate varied between 21.8 and 24.8 per 1000), though the immediate pre-war years were ones of relatively good employment.[524] However, as Gilbert points out, the Mond scale, which was adopted in London in 1922 as a direct consequence of the Poplar Guardians' struggle with local government, was gradually taken as a national reference point, and led to a more liberal treatment of families in receipt of poor relief.[525]

In addition, for much of the interwar period, many people who had exhausted their entitlement to unemployment benefit were provided with benefit 'as if' they had entitlement to insurance benefit as long as they could show they were looking for work. Benefit in this category was referred to by a variety of terms during the interwar period, including: out of work donation, uncovenanted benefit, extended benefit, transitional payments and public assistance. These benefits mark the introduction of a clearly defined two-tier system, with unemployment insurance available as of right, as long as the person had entitlement, and was looking for work, and public assistance for those insured workers who were looking for work, but had no current entitlement to unemployment benefit.

Since the introduction of unemployment insurance in 1911, it had been a condition of unemployment benefit that claimants be 'capable and available for work but unable to obtain suitable employment'.[526] With the abandonment of actuarial principles of insurance, and in response to the rapid increase in unemployment from the middle of 1920, governments did their best to limit the numbers of people eligible for unemployment insurance benefits through the operation of a 'genuinely seeking work' clause. From March 1921 claimants had to prove they were 'seeking work' and from February 1922, applicants for uncovenanted benefit had to be prepared to accept any work 'which they are reasonably capable of performing' and their benefit was subject to a means test.[527] The interpretation of the provision of this Act was left to the discretion of individual local employment committees. In 1924 the minority Labour government withdrew the means test, increased the value of unemployment benefit and made 'extended' benefit of unlimited duration. At the same time, however, it extended the genuinely seeking work test to all applicants for benefits and made the rules tougher and appointed a committee to review unemployment insurance.

According to Gilbert, the Blanesburgh Committee's report had an 'almost entirely bad' effect on the workings of unemployment insurance, as it maintained that 'no useful distinction could be made among various kinds of unemployment'.[528] Ultimately, this view would be embodied within the 1927 Unemployment Insurance Act. In the mean time, Baldwin's Conservative government continued with a 'tightening-up campaign', and, as a consequence, the proportion of disallowed claims increased, from 9.9 per cent at the end of 1924 to 14.7 per cent in 1926 and 17 per cent in 1927.[529] The means test was reintroduced in 1925, which particularly affected women as it led to the proportion of women disallowed being 2.5 times greater than the proportion of men disallowed. Moreover, there were significant regional variations in disallowance rates, with the Merthyr Tydfil Committee refusing only 2.6 per cent of claimants between July 1924 and April 1925, compared with Hackney, which disallowed 36 per cent of claims between September 1925 and June 1926.[530]

The 1927 Unemployment Insurance Act (effective April 1928) removed the distinction between insurance benefit and extended benefit and abolished the means test. All claimants now had to prove that they were 'genuinely seeking whole-time employment but unable to obtain such employment'. As Deacon notes,

The seeking work test was a futile and sometimes brutal ritual. No one pretended that the work which claimants were supposed to be seeking actually existed, least of all the Minister involved. By aimlessly 'tramping round', the unemployed were to earn the benefit and reassure Whitehall that the incentive to seek work, any work was being maintained.[531]

The 'genuinely seeking work' clause was finally abolished in March 1930 by the second minority Labour government, who also appointed a Royal Commission on Unemployment Insurance, which reported in June 1931. The increase in unemployment following the onset of the slump and reduction in disallowed claims led to the increasing indebtedness of the Unemployment Fund. The report recommended limiting the duration of unemployment benefit to 26 weeks, increasing the rates of weekly contribution, reducing the rate of benefit and tightening the rules for qualification for transitional benefit. Furthermore, it identified a number of 'anomalies', including the provision that a married woman should only be entitled to benefit if 'she had not abandoned insurable employment' and 'that having regard to her industrial experience and to the industrial circumstances of the district, she can expect to obtain insurable employment in the district in which she is residing'.[532] Although the recommendations for changes to benefit levels and contribution conditions were *initially* rejected, the Anomalies Regulations were accepted, and came into force in October 1931, making it much harder for women to qualify for transitional benefit.[533]

The growing economic crisis in 1931 forced the Labour government to reconsider the economy measures recommended by the first Royal Commission. The manner in which events unfolded in the late summer of 1931, culminating in the abandonment of the gold standard, the government being forced out of office and the formation of a 'National' government in its place, are beyond the scope of this book.[534] The incoming government, however, quickly implemented most of the Royal Commission's other recommendations. Benefits were cut by 10 per cent, the two-tier system was explicitly reintroduced with the duration of standard unemployment benefit limited to 26 weeks, and an extra provision was made that qualification required the claimant to have paid 30 contributions in the previous two years. Those who did not qualify for standard benefit were subject to a household means test, administered by local public assistance committees (PACs) with transitional benefit determined 'according to need'.[535]

There was local variation in the severity of the administration of the means test, but in the first two months of its operation 800,000 claims for transitional benefit were considered, of which a fifth were disallowed completely.[536] Between November 1931 and January 1935 only about half the applicants for transitional benefit were granted benefit at the full rate of unemployment benefit, while about one-third were given benefit at about three-quarters of the full rate.[537] Although some PACs were more generous than others, there is no real evidence that the means test was administered more leniently after the first few months of operation. As Deacon and Bradshaw point out, although 'the proportion of claims which were disallowed completely had fallen from 18 per cent to 14 per cent by 1934 ... this was matched by a similar rise in the proportion given benefit at a reduced rate'.[538]

The 1934 Unemployment Act transferred responsibility for the unemployed who had exhausted entitlement to unemployment insurance to unemployment assistance boards (UABs). Boards were empowered to determine national regulations for the payment of relief scales. The creation of UABs went some way to meeting the recommendations of the minority report of the second Royal Commission on Unemployment Insurance in 1932.[539] However, the benefits paid by UABs were governed by nineteenth-century principles of 'less eligibility', so complex rules were devised to ensure that benefits were lower than the wages of unskilled labourers. In general, UAB rates were a little below unemployment benefit rates for adults (whether single or couples), but significantly less for dependants.[540] Moreover, the UABs continued to apply a household means test. In October 1938 one-third of claimants had their assistance benefit reduced on the grounds of household income.[541] Unemployed individuals might fail to qualify for public assistance if the household contained other working members earning a wage. Furthermore, the value of 'non-essential' household items was also taken into account and unemployed people were expected to sell such goods before relief was granted.

For those who were subject to unemployment insurance, rather than assistance, the numbers of disallowance claims for unemployment benefit were distinctly pro-cyclical during the 1930s. Taking disallowance due to dismissal for misconduct, voluntary quitting and failure to accept 'suitable' employment together, there were just over 129,000 cases in 1933, rising to just under 243,000 in 1937, before falling back to about 139,000 in the summer of 1939.[542] In a variety of ways, as a direct consequence of the administration of unemployment assistance programmes, unemployed workers and their families could be forced to rely on poor relief. That there was not a greater disparity between the health of the employed and the unemployed was due to the generosity of unemployment benefit increasing, at the same time as the administration of relief was tightened up.

Summary

This chapter has shown that while unemployment was persistently high during the interwar period, and concentrated in particular trades and regions, the duration of unemployment was surprisingly short for many people, especially in the 1920s. Nevertheless, there was a hard core of chronically long-term unemployed in some parts of the depressed areas. Attempting to identify the impact unemployment had on health is far from easy. Most studies of the impact of unemployment on health stress how the effect of joblessness depends upon a number of factors, including income. In 1930s Britain, the negative effect of unemployment on health was mitigated by fairly generous unemployment benefit. However, it is also clear that stringent attempts were made to limit the qualification for benefit and to reduce benefit subject to 'means' in a way that caused significant hardship and resentment. The overall impact of unemployment on health is difficult to ascertain because unemployment is highly correlated with poverty and both are associated with ill health. It seems more sensible, therefore, to consider the impact of unemployment–poverty, rather than concentrate on the separate health effects of unemployment. Here, the evidence is mixed, but within the family there are good reasons to believe that women's health was likely to suffer most as a consequence of unemployment–poverty during the Depression.

5

1940s BRITAIN

Introduction

The Second World War led to a labour famine of immense proportions, despite the mass mobilisation of womanpower.[543] With the onset of war, however, unemployment actually continued to increase from 1.23 million in September 1939 to 1.5 million in February 1940, before beginning to fall in March 1940.[544] In that month, there were still about 34,500 insured workers unemployed in engineering.[545] The Ministry of Labour resisted Treasury pressure to introduce wage fixing and maintained a restricted system of collective bargaining. From May 1940, strikes and lockouts were made illegal, with disputes resolved by compulsory and binding arbitration of the Industrial Court.[546] Despite excess demand for labour, average wages and earnings increased fairly modestly. This was partly due to the successful implementation of a 'social contract' between the government and trade union leaders. This was brokered by Ernest Bevin, the Minister of Labour in Churchill's coalition government and former leader of the Transport and General Workers' Union. The wartime social contract coupled trade unionist sense of responsibility in moderating wage claims to government control of price and profits and is generally seen as a milestone in the creation of a social democratic state.[547]

Overall, during the war wages increased less fast than earnings, but both kept ahead of the increase in retail prices. Exactly how far ahead is a matter of some dispute, however. While the information on the change in wartime wages and earnings is of a high quality, it is fairly widely appreciated that the official Ministry of Labour cost of living index does

129

not accurately capture the changes in retail prices experienced by consumers during the war.[548] This is important both for the accurate assessment of changes in real incomes, but also for considering changes in the number of people thought to be in poverty before and after the war. Most, though not all, writers would agree with Townsend's assessment that 'there was a levelling of standards during the war years of 1939–45, maintained by the Labour government for at least the first few years after the war'.[549]

5.1   Wages, Earnings and Prices

Following the outbreak of war, prices increased sharply – by 12 per cent in the second half of 1939. The view of the Chancellor of the Exchequer, and of economists advising the government in the early months of the war, was to instigate cuts in the real wages. This involved government fixing wages, implicitly at levels below those warranted by increases in consumer prices, so as to be able to 'find resources for the war effort'.[550] In 1940, Keynes was advocating a system whereby wages would be indexed to movements in a 'bare necessities' cost of living index, but upon investigation, the Ministry of Labour discovered that the official index was, itself, little more than this already. Bevin and officials at the Ministry of Labour resisted pressure to fix wages and henceforth, Treasury policy was directed at stabilising prices by subsidising the cost of items in the Ministry of Labour cost of living index.[551]

But in one key respect, opponents of Bevin got their way – surreptitiously, at least. Because of its limited coverage, and large weight accorded to food items, the official cost of living index provided a poor guide to changes in prices facing consumers, even before government subsidies were targeted at its constituent items. The extent of these subsidies on food was considerable and many items were also subject to maximum price orders. By February 1944, Nicholson estimates that the unsubsidised price of bread would have been 5d per 4 lb loaf more expensive than the prevailing 'market price' of 9d, the difference for flour would have been 7d per 6 lb, home-killed meat 3¼d per lb, eggs 1¼d per dozen and potatoes 3½d per 7 lb, sugar 1½d per lb, cheese 2¼d per lb, bacon ½d per lb and tea would have been 2d per lb more expensive.[552] Moreover, important foodstuffs, clothing, fuel and other necessities were rationed during the war and while rationing was generally regarded as 'fair' and commanded popular support, the price of non-rationed items in short supply were subject to severe inflationary pressure.[553] Calder writes that 'The stability of the cost of living index was only maintained by disingenuous and tortuous manoeuvres' and that as the war progressed, 'Shortages and queues, the physical symptoms of inflation, grew worse.'[554] As can be seen from Table 5.1, column 1, subsidies and maximum price orders had the effect of controlling the increase in the official Ministry of Labour retail price index, bringing measured price inflation nearly to a halt after 1941.

In the immediate post-war years, several economists examined the extent of the bias in the official index during the war, as the Ministry of Labour revised the official cost of living index in July 1947. The official index prior to 1947 was based on expenditure weights identified from pre-First World War patterns of working-class expenditure.[555] The index was designed to show the 'average percentage increase in the cost of maintaining unchanged the standard of living prevailing in working-class families prior to August 1914'. But by the late 1930s the Ministry recognised that the coverage of the index and expenditure weights used in its construction were inadequate.[556] In October 1937 the Ministry announced that it was undertaking an inquiry to 'obtain a representative

Table 5.1   The cost of living and the war (1938 = 100)

| | Official Ministry of Labour | Allen: working class | Seers: | | Feinstein: retail price |
			working class	middle class	
1938	100	100	100	100	100
1939	102	103	102	103	103
1940	119	120	119	120	117
1941	128	132	130.5	136	129
1942	129	142	140	146	137
1943	128	146	144.5	153	142
1944	130	149	147.5	157	145
1945	131	150	149	164	148
1946	131	152	151.5	171	154
1947	131	160	161.5	183	163

Sources: D. Seers, 'The Increase in Working Class Cost of Living since before the War', *Bulletin of the Oxford Institute of Statistics*, 10,4 (1948), pp. 140–61 and 'The Cost of Living, 1938–48', *Bulletin of the Oxford Institute of Statistics*, 11, 4 (1949), pp. 127–47. R. G. D. Allen, *Bulletin of the London and Cambridge Economic Service*, 11 August 1947, p. 75 and 18 February 1948, pp. 18–19 and C. H. Feinstein, *National Income Output and Expenditure in the United Kingdom* (1972), T140, rebased 1938 = 100.

collection of "budgets" giving particulars of the weekly expenditure of working-class households'.[557] Before the official cost of living index could be revised, however, war intervened. The summary results of the 1937/8 working-class family budget inquiries were published in the *Gazette* in December 1940, but the official index was not revised until 1947, when a new 'interim index' was published.[558]

In 1947, the White Paper on National Income and Expenditure included details of price changes in the main categories of consumption between 1938 and 1946.[559] This information, used in conjunction with expenditure weights derived from the 1937–8 Ministry of Labour household budget inquiry, enabled investigation of the extent of bias in the wartime official cost of living index. Table 5.1 reports estimates due to Allen and to Seers, based on slightly different data and assumptions, although as can be seen, they largely agree.[560] Overall, the official Ministry of Labour cost of living index underestimates increases in the cost of living between 1938 and 1947, by about half.[561] According to Seers, this shows the 'combined effect of the distorted weighting system of that index together with the official policy of concentrating subsidies on items with a high weight in the index'.[562] It is also clear that the 60 per cent increase in the cost of items commonly purchased by working-class consumers was significantly less than the increase in the cost of items purchased by middle-class families. For the middle class, the extent of consumer price increases was about 83 per cent in June 1947, compared with average prices in 1938. Feinstein's retail price index is very similar to Seers's series, as Table 5.1, column 5 shows.

We are now able to consider the evidence on average earnings and wages growth in conjunction with changes in the cost of living. Table 5.2 reports Feinstein's estimates of wages, earnings and prices along with estimates of real earnings and prices derived from these series, between 1938 and 1950. Although average wages increase by about 50 per cent during the war and average earnings by about 75 per cent, taking full allowance of the change in retail prices shows that average real wages were more or less stationary over the course of the war.

The increase in wartime earnings is considerably greater than wartime wages. Increased hours of work provide an important explanation for this trend during the early years of the war, but there is also another important factor. In addition to a basic rate of wages or piecework price, and flat rate national bonus, some workers also received additional special bonuses. Many firms rewarded reliable labour with 'time-keeping bonuses' and there were various forms of collective output premiums.

Table 5.2 Average earnings, wages and prices, 1938–50 (1938 = 100)

Year	Wages	Earnings	Retail prices	Real wages	Real earnings
1938	100	100	100	100	100
1939	101	n.a.	103	98	n.a.
1940	112	130	117	96	111
1941	122	142	129	95	110
1942	131	160	137	95	117
1943	137	176	142	97	124
1944	144	179	145	99	123
1945	151	178	148	102	120
1946	163	185	154	106	120
1947	169	199	163	104	122
1948	178	217	175	102	124
1949	182	226	180	101	126
1950	186	237	185	101	128

Source: Calculated from C. H. Feinstein, *National Income Output and Expenditure in the United Kingdom* (1972), T140, but with 1938 = 100.

The existence of special bonuses, or supplementary payments, is an important factor in explaining the growing divergence between wage rates and earnings – so-called 'earnings drift'.[563]

Average real earnings grew only modestly, by about 20 per cent between 1938 and 1945, but continued to grow in the immediate post-war years. In 1950, average real earnings were about 28 per cent higher than they had been in 1938. Real earnings per hour increased by more than this amount because of the widespread reductions in hours worked in the late 1940s, from a typical working week of 47 or 48 hours to one of 44 hours. Of course, the changes indicated in Table 5.2 are significantly less than estimates of the growth in real earnings based on the official retail price index.

At a political level, the waging of total war strengthened the desire for more egalitarianism in many aspects of life. As Routh put it, 'In periods of rapid change, with social relationships under strain, flat-rate claims are made because they express and generate a sense of solidarity between occupations at different levels in the same union or federation of unions.'[564] Although the extent of wartime levelling remains a matter of some dispute, these desires help explain the propensity for flat-rate advances in wages. As we saw in Chapter 3, most of what we previously knew about wage-rate pay ratios during this period is due to the research of Knowles and Robertson, who provide estimates of wage-rate differentials between adult male skilled and unskilled workers, 1914–50.[565]

In all the industries they studied, the unskilled/skilled pay ratio narrowed considerably during the first half of the twentieth century. Most of this levelling occurred during periods of war when wages were either indexed to changes in the cost of living, or where movements in the official consumer price index acted as a wage guide. These war bonuses were mainly flat-rate lump sums. Because price inflation was significantly greater in the First than the Second World War, the flat-rate indexation of wages to changes in the cost of living during the Great War had a more pronounced effect on adult male pay ratios than it did during the Second World War. Knowles and Robertson demonstrate that there was considerable convergence in the unskilled/skilled pay ratio by 1950 across the industries they studied. In all five industries, the unskilled earned about four-fifths of skilled workers in 1950.

Moreover, data on the distribution of income suggest that there was some levelling in favour of the working class. Dudley Seers claims that between 1938 and 1949, after tax, there was a transfer of about £450 million (at 1938 prices) from property owners and £150 million from the salaried and self-employed, which combined with a £100 million increase in the public's total income, increased farmers' income by £50 million and working-class wage earners' income by £650 million. This represented an increase in the share of working-class incomes of nearly one-quarter.[566] The general data on the distribution of personal pre-tax incomes suggest that there was some overall levelling up during the war, which was reinforced by progressive fiscal policy.[567]

The extent to which the redistribution of personal incomes favoured poorer groups within the bottom 30 per cent of the income distribution remains uncertain, however. According to the Royal Commission on the Distribution of Income and Wealth, the share of pre-tax incomes going to the bottom 30 per cent was identical in 1938/9 and 1949/50. After tax, the share of the bottom 30 per cent increased from 15.4 to 15.9 per cent. Post-tax levelling did occur, but in the form of a redistribution from very rich to rich coupled with a modest improvement in the share of the middle income range.[568]

5.2   Nutrition in Wartime

The object of government policy, as laid down in the last full year of peace, was to 'ensure that supplies of essential foodstuffs at controlled prices are available to meet the requirements of all types of consumers and in all parts of the country, if, and when, an emergency arise'.[569] During the period 1934–8, two-thirds of the energy value of Britons' diets and half their protein came from imported food. With the loss of shipping during the battle of the Atlantic, to German aircraft and submarines, shipping space for essential war materials was at a premium. Bulky food imports were halved from about 22 million tons per annum pre-war to between 10.6 and 11.5 million tons in 1942–4.[570]

As the war progressed the aims of the Ministry of Food also changed. In particular, controls were more wide-ranging than 'essential foodstuffs' and the Ministry became a protector of vulnerable groups such as children, pregnant women and invalids. Most importantly, however, it interested itself in the nutritional impact of wartime food policy.[571] Between 1940 and 1949 the Ministry of Food carried out inquiries into working-class food consumption.[572] These were large-scale, annual, random, surveys of between 5000 and 9000 working-class households from selected towns.[573] From the beginning of the war, the government was being urged to adopt rationing as part of a policy that assumed responsibility for the nutritional adequacy of Britons' diets.[574] Following the sharp rise in the official cost of living index in the first four months of the war, various systems of rationing were introduced, starting in January 1940, based on detailed plans drawn up in the last years of peace.[575]

Food rationing was introduced in January 1940 for bacon, ham, sugar and butter (by weight), though at quite generous quantities.[576] This was followed by meat (by price) in March 1940, tea in July 1940, jam and marmalade in March 1941, cheese in May 1941 and eggs in June 1941, which were subject to 'controlled distribution'. Clothing was rationed (by a points system) from June 1941 and in July 1941 a ceiling was placed on domestic coal consumption.[577] The points system was widened to include tinned foods (meat, fish and vegetables) in November 1941. In January 1942, the list of items rationed by points was extended to include dried fruit, rice, sago, tapioca and pulses, and in February 1941 tinned fruit, tomatoes, pears and soap were added to the list. The extent of rationing continued to grow through the remainder of 1942.[578] In April condensed milk and breakfast cereals were rationed, followed by syrup, treacle, chocolate and sweets in July, biscuits in August and oats (flaked and rolled) in December.[579] In 1940 only about 25 per cent of food expenditure was on rationed or controlled foods, but by 1943, this figure had grown to about 60 per cent.[580]

Food eaten away from home, in restaurants or lodging facilities was 'off rations', but the food-providing establishments were themselves rationed on the same basis as individuals, given certain assumptions about the number of person meals served. However, it was up to the establishment concerned to decide how to allocate the quantities of rationed foods. For example, if a meat ration was provided for a certain number of person meals, this could be used in as many or few meals as the caterer saw fit, as long as the balance was made up of meals excluding this item (that is, the total number of person meals remained the same). Moreover, there were no supply constraints. The more person meals served, the larger the establishment's ration.[581]

The Ministry utilised the 'off-ration' meal to supplement the diet of key war workers. In industrial canteens, which were required at any factory employing more than 250 people, an enhanced ration scale was implemented, which ensured that they were able to provide more rationed items than restaurants. In December 1944 there were 18,486 industrial canteens and an additional 4718 restaurants, which received rations on the industrial scale because they largely catered for war workers.[582]

In addition the government promoted (and subsidised the capital expenditure of) British Restaurants, originally designed to cater for victims of civilian bombing, and the Rural Pie Scheme (RPS), commencing in the spring of 1942, which was designed to provide food for agricultural workers for whom industrial canteens or a British Restaurant was not available. By December 1943 there were over 2 million British Restaurants serving a total of over 0.6 million meals daily. In addition, the RPS served over 5000 villages distributing over 1.25 million meals each week. In 1947 there were still 850 British Restaurants, but their numbers steadily declined after government withdrew financial support.[583]

Since 1906 local education authorities had been given powers to provide free or subsidised school meals. Only 151,535 children received free school meals and 560,879 children were receiving free milk in 1937–8, from a total of about 5 million school-age children.[584] The 'milk-in-schools' scheme, which was started in 1934, was clearly more successful, especially if figures for elementary schoolchildren are considered. By 1939, the scheme provided one-third of a pint of milk for nearly half of all elementary schoolchildren, for free or at low cost by 1939.[585] In 1941 this scheme was extended because of a desire to ensure adequate nutritional intakes among schoolchildren, a concern that was partly fuelled by the mobilisation of large numbers of women for war work. The numbers of school meals provided in Great Britain grew from about a quarter of a million prior to the war to 1 million in October 1942 and 1.85 million in February 1945.[586] By the end of the war about

40 per cent of schoolchildren were receiving a 'heavily subsidised' meal, which provided about 1000 kcal.[587]

Nutritional planning was not a feature of pre-war food planning, but was forced upon government as a consequence of the shipping losses due to U-boat attack in the Atlantic. The restrictions imposed upon shipping space in conjunction with the general reduction in the volume of imports, compelled consideration of relative priorities in food supply.[588] It was clear that it was relatively easy, given the climate and soil type, to produce milk, vegetables and potatoes.[589] During the summer of 1940, the scientific advisor to the Ministry of Food advocated the nutritional enhancement of margarine with vitamins A and D, which made it nutritionally similar to the butter that it was increasingly replacing in most family diets. This was followed in June 1941 with the addition of synthetic vitamin B1 to flour, though the augmentation of flour ceased to be necessary once the 85 per cent milling of flour became compulsory in March 1942, as higher-extraction flour already contained sufficient natural vitamin B1. High-extraction flour was also fortified with calcium.

In addition to these schemes designed to enhance the vitamin content of basic foods, the nutritional intakes of pregnant women and infants were directly targeted by the Vitamin Welfare Scheme, introduced in December 1941. This scheme was designed to ensure adequate intakes of vitamins A, C and D in these vulnerable groups, reflecting concern over reduced consumption of fruit, butter and eggs. Initially cod liver oil and blackcurrant purée were provided free of charge to children under two years (replaced with Lend/Lease orange juice in April 1942 and subject to a charge), but later the scheme was amalgamated with the operation of the National Milk Scheme, so that pregnant women and children under five who qualified for cheap or free milk also qualified for orange juice and cod liver oil on the same basis. By 1944 nearly half of all potential beneficiaries were receiving orange juice and about one-fifth were receiving cod liver oil.[590] Zweiniger-Bargielowska points out that following the controlled distribution of milk and eggs, the priority classes, accounting for just under a third of consumers, received nearly half of the available supply of milk.[591]

Rationing continued in the post-war period, with some foods that had not been rationed in wartime, such as bread, added to the list of rationed items. Since the provision of food under Lend–Lease arrangements considerably augmented wartime supply, the ending of Lend Lease led to reduced consumption, though early post-war food shortages in Britain were not on the same scale as in other European countries, such as

France and Belgium. However, excluding cheese and meat, the 1945 level was at least equalled by 1949. With the ending of food rationing in 1954, consumption grew steadily in the late 1950s and early 1960s.[592]

The wartime diet was 'nutritionally adequate and healthy but also dull and monotonous'. The consumption of bread, potatoes and milk increased in comparison with pre-war, while that of butter and other fats, sugar, meat, bacon, fish, fruit and fresh eggs decreased.[593] As Zweiniger-Bargielowska writes, the Ministry's own judgement was that people were 'compelled to satisfy their physical needs by filling up with larger quantities of the bulky and less attractive vegetable and cereal foodstuffs still obtainable'.[594] The overall impact of the Ministry's schemes on dietary intakes, as opposed to changes brought about by increases in income and changes in the relative price of particular foods, is difficult to assess. From data on average per capita consumption of nutrients, it is likely that the Ministry's efforts were reasonably successful, however. Although the available daily energy of average wartime diets in 1940 and 1941 was 2800 kcal per capita, somewhat less than the 3000 available pre-war, the consumption of calcium and iron 'increased substantially during the war', as did vitamin B1 and riboflavin. Moderate increases also occurred in vitamin C and niacin intakes. Moreover, the reduction in energy intakes was made good by 1944. The average wartime diet also contained significantly less animal protein. Only in the case of vitamin A was average wartime intake less than pre-war.[595]

Moreover, the results of the wartime national food surveys, where detailed evidence of food purchases from 600–700 families were recorded, suggested that there was little difference between the diets of working- and middle-class families, 'reflecting the general levelling out of food distribution during the war'.[596] According to Zweiniger-Bargielowska, class-based differentials in nutritional intake, which had characterised the British diet during the first half of the century, 'disappeared with the introduction of rationing and food controls during the Second World War', as Table 5.3 shows. Moreover, the war represents a watershed, as the diets of rich and poor remained reasonably similar 'in terms of both quantity and nutrient intake'.[597] Whether the full extent of the reduction in dietary class differentials can be attributed to rationing and food policy, seems more contentious, however. The general increase in incomes, which started in the late 1930s, accelerated during the war and was maintained during the 1950s and 1960s, is also likely to have been important in narrowing the variations in dietary intake by economic class.

Table 5.3 Energy and protein intakes per capita in the United Kingdom by social class, 1932–5 to 1950

	Middle-class kcal	Working-class kcal	Relative energy(%)	Middle-class protein (g)	Working-class protein (g)	Relative protein(%)
1932–5	3275	2859	114	96	80	120
1936–7	3159	2557	123	89	70	127
1944	2403	2387	101	74	73	101
1945	2402	2375	101	77	76	101
1946	2336	2307	101	78	78	100
1947	2307	2308	100	77	77	100
1950	2506	2468	101	79	77	102

Source: Extracted from Ina Zweiniger-Bargielowska, *Austerity in Britain* (2000), Table 1.5, p. 45.

5.3   The 'Human Needs' Index

The Oxford Institute of Statistics instigated regular inquiries into working-class food consumption and food prices. This information was used to investigate the change in the cost of a working-class 'Human Needs' diet during the Second World War and immediate post-war period, which was published biannually in its *Bulletin* in the spring and autumn.

The Institute of Statistics biannual food consumption surveys were small-scale inquiries carried out between 1940 and 1949, by one or two university teachers or social workers, assisted by students. For most of the 1940s, about 200 families also recorded food consumption over a two-week period, for payment of a small sum. In all the households selected the head was a manual worker with at least one dependent child with no lodgers. Details of family income, household composition and main expenditure were collected by questionnaire.[598] Not all households provided details of family income, however.[599] The households were from 'larger industrial towns', with Liverpool and Southampton being 'two of the largest contributors' to the sample.[600] In the late 1940s, the geographical coverage of the survey included Birmingham, Bolton, Liverpool, Sheffield, Southampton and Swindon.[601] By the late 1940s, the Institute's food consumption surveys suggested that about one-third of working-class household income was spent on food (and about one-twelfth on accommodation).[602]

Food price information was collected from market stalls and food outlets in working-class districts. It would appear that the geographical coverage of the food price survey was not the same as the food consumption surveys. It was these food price data that were used to reprice the nutrition constant 'Human Needs' index, which was reported in the *Bulletin* from March 1941 and was originally based on data relating only to Oxford. It was extended to include London and Reading in 1948 and during the 1950s the geographical coverage of the investigation was further expanded to cover a number of Midland towns, but by that stage the food consumption surveys had ceased. The purpose of the investigation was to document the change in cost of foods that would ensure adequate nutrition. Unlike the food component of the official retail price index that reprices a constant bundle of foods, the Institute 'Human Needs' index repriced a 'nutritionally constant' index, although from time to time, small refinements were made to the nutritional standard applied.

The Institute of Statistics 'Human Needs' index was clearly inspired by Rowntree's 1937 (revised) *Human Needs of Labour*. However, for the most part, the Institute only concerned itself with a 'Human Needs' diet and not with other categories of 'Human Needs' expenditure identified by Rowntree.[603] The 'Human Needs' diet was a 'diet that would supply adequate nutrition for a small outlay', for Rowntree's reference family of two adults and three children under 14 years old.[604] Originally, this was based on Rowntree's diet from his second social survey of York, which met the BMA 1933 nutritional recommendations. The Institute used this standard until the autumn of 1942. After April 1943, the Institute's 'Human Needs' diet met revised Ministry of Health nutritional requirements until 1945, when they were superseded by those published in the British Medical Council's *Memorandum on Nutritive Values of Wartime Foods*.[605] The diet was devised from foods that could be purchased 'without undue difficulty' and reflected rationing and shortages of accustomed foods. Indeed this was the reason for most of the differences between the Oxford diet and Rowntree's.[606] Moreover, the equivalence scale used by the Institute was more sophisticated than Rowntree's and varied by nutrient, as Table 5.4 makes clear.[607] While the equivalence scale for energy requirements is very similar to those used in interwar poverty surveys, for other nutrients the 'Human Needs' equivalence scale is very different, reflecting advances in nutritional knowledge – especially for calcium and iron where children's needs are significantly greater than those of adults.

The cost of the 'Human Needs' diet for five people in the autumn of 1936 was 21s 10½d. By the spring of 1941, the cost had risen by 1.51 times and by the end of the war the cost was 1.65 times higher. In the

Table 5.4   Nutritional requirements for 'Human Needs' index, 1941–9

	kcal	Protein	Calcium	Iron	Vitamin A	Vitamin B1	Vitamin C
Adult male	1.0	1.0	1.0	1.0	1.0	1.0	1.0
Adult female	0.83	0.86	1.0	1.0	1.0	0.83	1.0
Child 7–12 yrs	0.7	0.93	1.75	1.3	1.0	1.05	1.0
Child 5 yrs	0.5	0.71	1.63	0.8	1.0	0.75	1.0

Source: T. Schulz, 'Human Needs Diets from 1936 to 1949', *Bulletin of the Oxford Institute of Statistics*, 11 (1949), Table V, p. 316.

spring of 1949, the cost of the 'Human Needs' diet was 2.22 times greater than at the time of Rowntree's second social survey of York. This compares with an increase in the Ministry of Labour's cost of living index food component of 1.29, 1.30 and 1.34 at the same dates.[608] There was, therefore, a considerable divergence between the change in the official series (or the Seers adjusted index), based on repricing a constant bundle of goods, and a 'nutritional constant' series. The reason for this divergence is the substitution of more expensive foods for those that are rationed or in short supply in the 'Human Needs' index. The fact that many of the rationed items were subject to price control and subsidy had the effect of minimising the rise in the official cost of living index, but in the 'Human Needs' index, the reduced nutritional intake provided by the subsidised, or rationed, foods was made good with foodstuffs that increased in price to a considerably greater extent.[609]

The Institute also calculated the cost of 'Human Needs' maintenance for a person living alone in May 1943, which included food, clothing, fuel and light. The cost of the 'Human Needs' diet for a single woman was 8s 4d, although if six meals were eaten in British Restaurants, this cost would have risen to 12s 3¾ d. The figures for a single man were calculated as 10s 5½ d and 14s 5d respectively.[610] Clothing was rationed during the war and assuming that all clothing coupons were spent on utility clothing, the cost was estimated at about 2s per week, the same as the cost for fuel and light. In addition Schulz made an allowance of 1s 6d for cleaning materials and 2s 6d for sundries (newspapers, wireless licence and personal expenses).

Table 5.5 sets out the comparative cost of these items in 1950. Comparable items in 1950 would have increased the poverty line to 24s1d, or 28s 1¼ d if an allowance was still included for six meals eaten away from home. However, subjective as these judgements are, it seems less reasonable

Table 5.5 'Human Needs' scale for single women, 1943 and 1950

	1943	1950	1943 (6 meals out)	1950 (6 meals out)
Food	8s4d	11s11$\frac{1}{2}$d	12s 3$\frac{3}{4}$d	17s0$\frac{1}{2}$d
Clothing	2s0d	3s6$\frac{1}{2}$d	2s0d	3s6$\frac{3}{4}$d
Fuel and light	2s0d	2s7d	1s6d	1s11$\frac{1}{4}$d
Household	1s6d	2s6d	1s3d	2s1d
Sundries	2s6d	3s6d	2s6d	3s6d
Total 1943 poverty line	16s4d	24s1d	19s6$\frac{3}{4}$d	28s1$\frac{1}{4}$d
Extra clothing		2s8$\frac{1}{4}$d		2s8$\frac{1}{4}$d
Extra household replacements		10d		8$\frac{1}{4}$d
Total 1950 poverty line		27s7$\frac{1}{4}$d		31s5$\frac{3}{4}$d

Source: T. Schulz, 'Human Needs of a Single Person', *Bulletin of Oxford Institute of Statistics*, 12, 6 (June 1950), Table VIII, p. 166.

to include this allowance in 1950 than 1943. Schulz maintains that the 1943 wartime clothing and sundries allowance was excessively stringent by 1950 standards and indicates additional expenditure of 2s 8$\frac{1}{4}$d and 10d per week 'if we grant a somewhat higher standard of "human needs" in peace-time than in war-time'.[611]

5.4   Poverty and the Second World War

Social investigations of poverty, following the methodology developed by Rowntree and Bowley, were a rarity after the 1930s. This was possibly because there was a feeling that 'want' had been abolished. In 1941 the University of Liverpool undertook an investigation of wartime poverty. This concentrated on three types of households: a household consisting of a couple and young children, a widow supporting children of school age and a couple in old age.[612] Two poverty standards were used: Rowntree's 1937 'Human Needs' standard, with modified food and rent components, and the Merseyside poverty-line standard, which, as we saw in Chapter 3, was based upon the *New Survey* poverty line. The former standard was applied to households in work, while the less generous Merseyside poverty line was seen as being more appropriate when the household was reliant upon state assistance.

The Liverpool survey devised specimen diets for each household type that took account of rationing and wartime shortages. The diets provided 3400 kcal per equivalent male adult per day, derived from 100 g of protein and fats and 500 g of carbohydrate. The cost of the diet was ascertained from prices quoted in the Ministry of Labour *Gazette* in conjunction with those gleaned from 'private sources'.[613] With respect to rent, 'minimum reasonable' accommodation appropriate for each household type was assumed. The assumptions made for the 'Human Needs' standard were more generous than those using the Merseyside poverty line.[614] The cost of different types of accommodation was taken from the Merseyside survey and repriced using the Ministry of Labour's rent index.

Not surprisingly as Table 5.6 shows, comparing the two standards for the representative household types, the 'Human Needs' standard exceeds the poverty-line standard by between 62 and 85 per cent. In October 1936, Rowntree's 'Human Needs' standard exceeded the 'poverty line' standard by 50 per cent. The main reason why the gap between these two standards had increased was because of the modifications made to the food component of the 'Human Needs' standard that reflected wartime shortages and rationing.[615] Notice that the 'poverty line' standard is quite similar to state benefits for all three of these reference households, although it is possible that the old age couple could receive benefit somewhat in excess of this poverty line. This analysis

Table 5.6 'Human Needs' and poverty-line standards compared with household expenditure, October 1940

Household type	'Human Needs'	Poverty line	State benefit [a]	Actual expenditure
Couple with 3 children	66s	40s 9d	38s 6d–41s	45s
Widow with 2 children	48s 6d	29s 0d	28s–37s 3d	26s 4½d
Old age couple	38s 4d	20s 9d	20s–32s	37s 6d

[a] The figures for state benefit depend upon the circumstances of the claimant and the type of benefit. In the case of an adult male worker who is unemployed with dependants, the figures refer to public assistance or unemployment insurance. For the widow with two dependants, the range refers to public assistance and soldiers' widows' pension. The old age couple is the state pension and state pension plus supplement from the Assistance Board. There are also other cases that bisect the range of benefit given here. See Liverpool University, *The Cost of Living of Representative Working-Class Families*, pp. 17–19 for a full discussion.

Source: Extracted from Liverpool University, *Cost of Living of Representative Working-Class Families* (1941), Table 4, p. 13, Table 5, p. 17 and text.

excludes sickness benefit, which made no allowance for dependants. The figures for actual expenditure relate to the budgets of a single household of the same composition in the circumstances described for November 1940 (male unemployed with dependant, widow with two dependent children and old age couple). Only in the case of the last household does actual expenditure compare favourably with the 'poverty line' standard. Most likely this is because of the payment of a supplementary pension, which was introduced in 1940.

Thane has shown how changes in the administration of state support for the old during the war revealed the 'discovery of secret need', following the introduction of supplementary assistance in 1940. The Old Age and Widows' Pension Act transferred responsibility for the old to the Unemployment Assistance Board. Formerly, responsibility for old people had rested with local authorities, where a direct lineage to the Poor Law Board was discernible. The number of old people applying for assistance dramatically exceeded the government's expectation and by 1941, the Assistance Board was helping to support about a third of all old age pensioners.[616] Nevertheless, the 1942 Nuffield College Reconstruction Survey did not believe that supplementary pensions had eradicated poverty, since as Thane points out, the 'basic sum could not cover clothing replacement or medical treatment and was usually not adequate to buy a nourishing diet suitable for frail old people or adequate fuel'.[617] It is clear, however, from the Liverpool survey, that relative to interwar poverty standards, supplementary pension had a significant impact on pensioner income. The Liverpool survey suggests that an old age couple would be only just below Rowntree's 'Human Needs' standard.

It is not clear what further can be drawn from such a small-scale study conducted near the beginning of the war and we are forced to turn to more indirect sources of information. The wartime evacuation of 1.5 million mothers and children from metropolitan and urban areas, thought by the government to be at risk from enemy bombing, provides evidence on some aspects of material provision and health of the poor, though the latter needs to be treated with great caution. Once the initial wartime evacuation was completed, health departments started to receive complaints and appeals from a variety of concerned parties and individuals concerning the clothing of evacuee children in rural reception areas. Much of this centred on the inadequacy of children's footwear, but as Titmuss writes: 'A large number of Welsh local authorities that received evacuees from Liverpool spoke of "children in rags", in a condition which "baffles description", and of clothing which was so dirty and verminous that it had to be destroyed.'[618]

The clothing of working-class children from Liverpool was unlikely to have been exceptional. Indeed, there is much more general evidence of complaints about the adequacy of children's footwear.[619] For Titmuss, the failure of parents to send their children away properly equipped is testament to the financial hardship that many Britons still endured at the end of the 1930s. In 1939 the average number of people registered unemployed was just under 1.5 million and there were over 1 million people in England and Wales in receipt of poor relief. For these families, the purchase of adequate clothing for their children was clearly 'beyond their immediate resources'.[620] 'Many wartime evacuee children experienced enuresis and a disturbing number were infected with head lice, scabies, impetigo and other skin complaints.'

Titmuss thought the problem of bed-wetting exaggerated, but where evidence existed of children's lack of control over urination, it was likely caused by an 'acute sense of insecurity', which, in most cases, passed within a few weeks.[621] Equally graphic descriptions of 'verminous' children soon reached health departments following the evacuation. As James McCullum, a 38-year-old science teacher who was appointed billeting officer in the Highland town of Kingussie, was to write: 'The evacuees in this area were from a slum-clearance scheme in Edinburgh, and so some (at least 10%) were in a shocking condition of neglect, families with mothers as well as unaccompanied children – lousy, afflicted with impetigo and ringworm etc.'[622]

Not all reception areas made inspections of children, but in those that did, the conclusions varied from one area to another; with infection levels of head lice varying from between 22 and 50 per cent in areas receiving children from Merseyside and between 8 and 35 per cent in children from London.[623] These findings seem to be broadly consistent with infection rates revealed in the Mellanby inquiry for the Ministry of Health in January 1940.[624] Reports such as these clearly shocked both public and government alike, largely because of under-recording in pre-war school medical officers' reports.[625] Indeed, Titmuss thought the lack of 'social facts' concerning the conditions of life of a large proportion of urban workers and their families in the late 1930s extended to other indicators of poverty, such as the number of insanitary houses and the proportion lacking baths and lavatories.

Some benchmark estimates for these indicators of living conditions are available for the war years, however. In 1939, 40 per cent of houses were without fixed baths in Bootle, the same number as Hull in 1943. In Salford, 52 per cent of houses were without fixed baths in 1943, roughly the same number as was found in Glasgow in 1944. In 1946 about 25 per cent of the houses of Birmingham were without bathrooms and 12 per cent had no separate lavatories. In 1947 an investigation by the Social Survey for the Ministry of Works found that 13 per cent of all urban households in Britain had no fixed bath. With respect to the poorest economic groups in urban areas, the number without fixed baths was 29 per cent.[626]

Whether the revelations of the living conditions of British town dwellers that were exposed by evacuation were directly responsible for a reformist impetus among the middle class now seems much more debatable. Titmuss argued that during the summer of 1940, the 'mood of the people changed', as Britons of all classes perceived an imminent threat to national survival, but much of this thesis is now disputed.[627] As Macnicol points out, Whitehall considered that the symptoms of inner-city poverty revealed by evacuation were largely the result of working-class mores. Much middle-class opinion was also deeply conservative.[628]

Nevertheless, during the early phases of the war, there were progressive elements of social policy. The quality of hospital care provided by the Emergency Medical Service for air-raid casualties is possibly the best example.[629] The 1941 Determination of Needs Act is another. This Act abolished the household means test and seemed to 'hold out the possibility of a more humane system of means testing'.[630] Under the provision of this Act, where claimants were living with non-dependent relatives who were wage earners, only earnings over 20s per week would be relevant. Moreover, in cases where claimants were dependent on others, the Act made an allowance for their personal income sufficient for their basic expenditures in the assessment of claimants' income.

These provisions allowed 200,000 additional pensioners to receive supplementary pensions, but despite increased state assistance for the elderly, Thane has shown the ways in which there was a 'complex reciprocity of old people's relationships with others'. It was not uncommon for old people to give their ration coupons to children or grandchildren, for example, and refused medical help for fear that relatives would have to cover the cost.[631]

5.5   Poverty and the State

There is an obvious relationship between the empirical investigation of poverty and the history of the development in social policies designed to alleviate poverty in Britain. During the first half of the twentieth century social investigation almost certainly had a positive impact on the development of social policy, but it was during the war years that the relationship between investigator and social policy maker was the closest. In June 1941 William Beveridge was appointed to chair a committee on reform of workmen's compensation and social insurance. For the wartime generation and those that immediately followed, the report of this committee, *Social Insurance and Allied Services*, published on 1 December 1942, and better known as the Beveridge Report, was viewed as a milestone in British social policy. It was widely believed that by exceeding his brief, Beveridge made wide-ranging recommendations for the reform of social policy that provided 'adequate' provision for Britons from 'the cradle to the grave'. The publication of his report, with its vision of a new Britain free from the giant evils of want, ignorance, disease, squalor and idleness, captured the mood of the people of war-torn Britain at a time when, finally, the pendulum of war had begun to swing their way.[632] Recent writers have tended to be more critical of Beveridge's proposals, however.

The Beveridge plan was predicated on the assumption that post-war governments would commit themselves to maintaining 'full employment', though the precise meaning of this term was somewhat ambiguous.[633] Those workers who were unemployed would qualify for unemployment benefit, from a social insurance fund. The same was true of poverty caused by ill health or disability or that due to the premature death of the principal wage earner. Poverty due to large family size would be mitigated by the payment of a child allowance. However, the extent to which large family size was an important cause of poverty had diminished considerably during the first half of the century as average household size had steadily fallen.[634] Beveridge also regarded child allowances as an important incentive for the employed, since he wished to avoid the situation where benefits during periods of unemployment were greater than earnings in employment. Family allowances provided a way of restoring the gap between the net family income of the employed and unemployed.[635] Beveridge initially viewed poverty due to old age as analogous with other causes of poverty, which was also suitable for social insurance palliative. Because of the financial implications associated with a recommendation of universal qualification for old age benefit (before sufficient funds had been accumulated), Beveridge recommended a 'transitional period' lasting 20 years from the commencement of the scheme. However, the 1946 Act dispensed with this idea of a transitional period. All men over 65 years and women over 60 years would qualify for the full pension, irrespective of entitlement by virtue of contribution.[636]

The extent to which Beveridge's report, and the subsequent enactment of his recommendations by the post-war Labour government, did really provide for this 'New Jerusalem' is now widely contested. First, it was participation in the labour market, rather than citizenship, that determined entitlement in Beveridge's plan. As Lewis points out, despite Beveridge's refusal to call housewives 'dependants' and viewing their work as 'vital', Beveridge's proposals strengthened the notion of a 'male breadwinner' welfare state in which women would be dependent on, and support, male participation in paid employment.[637] Indeed, contemporary feminist groups had been quick to point out the way in which Beveridge's plan disadvantaged married women. The Women's Freedom League were strongly critical of Beveridge's proposals and campaigned against them through their fortnightly journal the *Women's Bulletin* for the remainder of the war.[638] Some groups of women were in an especially vulnerable position precisely because there was no male breadwinner, as Hills *et al.* write:

> His view of the position of married women – seven eighths of whom he thought would 'follow no gainful occupation' in peace-time resulted in a system which catered for widowhood as a contingency to be covered, but not divorce, lone-parenting or caring, and which was ill-adapted for a world where the majority of married women [were] to have [their own] earnings.[639]

Second, he decided to work within established parameters of early twentieth-century social policy. He was wedded to actuarial principles of insurance based on a flat rate of contribution and benefit and eschewed a more progressive system based on earnings-related benefits and contributions or finance through progressive taxation.[640] According to Glennerster and Evans, this 'made irreconcilable his objectives of subsistence adequacy and universal coverage'.[641] It also imparted an inherently regressive bias to his recommendations.[642]

Thirdly, and most importantly from the perspective of this study, Beveridge's proposals did not abolish 'want', despite the fact that the majority of post-war Britons were experiencing the benefits of the 'golden age' of full employment and economic growth in the 1950s. To complete the circle, the implementation of Beveridge's reforms was subsequently hailed by Rowntree as the most important explanation for the tremendous reduction in poverty in the immediate post-war years in his third, and final, social survey of York in 1950. Veit-Wilson argues the converse. He believes that Beveridge's 1942 recommendations retarded the relief of poverty in Britain for a generation following the ending of the Second World War.[643] The argument hinges on the relationship between Beveridge's recommendations and the two poverty lines formulated by Rowntree for his first and second social surveys of York in 1899 and 1936.

The relationship between Beveridge's proposed scale of benefits and contemporaneous definitions of poverty has received a fair amount of attention over the years, and the question whether Beveridge's proposals were generous relative to definitions of interwar poverty has polarised historians of the welfare state. Rowntree's 1941 conclusions on the changing cause of poverty were critical for the development of Beveridge's views. As Glennerster and Evans write, 'The main reasons for economic insecurity and poverty had altered from low wages to unemployment and old age.The importance of this change is difficult to underestimate for Beveridge.'[644] For it was this that largely convinced Beveridge that poverty could be eradicated by social insurance, and it is equally clear that Beveridge's assumptions and recommendations were heavily influenced by the results of interwar poverty surveys. As his biographer, Jose Harris, points out, Beveridge viewed his proposals for welfare reform in the context of measures to tackle various 'interruptions of earnings', which were all amenable to social insurance. Unlike the position at the beginning of the century when low earnings were the principal cause of poverty, against which it was not possible to insure, the single most important cause of interwar poverty was unemployment.[645]

Beveridge was intent that the committee should make a report that reflected his own views and Beveridge presented many of his ideas in the form of memoranda to the committee for consideration during the winter of 1941–2. In his second memorandum, issued in January 1942, Beveridge made it clear that he believed that it was possible to abolish poverty through a social insurance scheme, affecting an income transfer within the working class. He was of the opinion that Rowntree's 1936 survey had shown that the aggregate extent of working-class income above the poverty line was eight times higher than the aggregate deficit below it, thus making it possible to consider such a redistribution possible – though he did not think that transfers should be wholly intra-working-class.[646] Beveridge had sought the advice of A. L. Bowley, Seebohm Rowntree, R. F. George and Dr H. E. Magee, who formed the subsistence subcommittee.[647] Beveridge adopted a proposal for a flat rate of benefit, despite empirical evidence that the cost of living varied on a regional basis, especially with respect to rent.[648]

The 1937–8 Ministry of Labour inquiry into working-class expenditure revealed that average expenditure on accommodation was 10s 9d per week. Beveridge wished to adopt a figure 'below rather than above the average', because these working-class households were generally well above subsistence level. Beveridge settled on 10s per week for households (6s 6d for individuals), partly because Rowntree had found an average expenditure of 9s 6d in 1936.[649] Beveridge recognised that including a fixed payment for rent in his scale would lead to inequity, but rejected the arguments of 'some members of the sub-committee', the Fabian Society and the Association of Municipal Corporations that benefits should be based on rent actually paid. He did so for reasons based on ease of administration and belief in the principle that equality of contribution should be accompanied by equality of benefit.[650]

Veit-Wilson has written that Beveridge distinguished between 'want', which implied insufficient income for both minimum subsistence and social participation and 'subsistence', which meant consumption essential for physiological needs.[651] This perceived distinction in Beveridge's terminology allows a simple mapping onto Rowntree's two poverty lines – his 'physical efficiency' poverty line first developed in his 1899 study and his 'Human Needs' poverty line, first applied in his second social survey of York in 1936. However, there is serious disagreement here about what Beveridge really intended with respect to the level of state benefit. Harris notes that Beveridge was inclined towards Rowntree's more generous revised 'Human Needs' poverty line, because Beveridge felt that a more stringent scale would 'be rejected decisively by public opinion'.[652] Nevertheless, Beveridge still viewed state benefit as a means of augmenting individual provision, rather than acting as a substitute for thrift.

With respect to social insurance, Beveridge maintained that the 'minimum income' needed for people of working age for 'subsistence during interruption of earnings', ought to be sufficient to cover expenditure on food, clothing, fuel, light and household sundries, and rent, plus 'some margin must be allowed for inefficiency in spending'.[653] The minimum food expenditure for an adult man and woman, Beveridge reckoned, was 13s per week at 1938 prices (7s for an adult man, 6s for an adult woman). This would be sufficient to purchase food that would meet either the 1933 BMA nutritional recommendations or the 1936 and 1938 League of Nations Reports of the Technical Commission on Nutrition. For clothing, Beveridge recommended a figure of 1s 6d each for an adult man or woman. This was considerably below the average expenditure in the 1937–8 Ministry of Labour inquiry (2s 4¼d for a man and 2s 6¼d for a woman), but a little above the figure allowed in interwar poverty surveys.[654] For fuel and light, Beveridge recommended 4s for an adult couple, or 2s 6d for an individual adult. In addition, Beveridge allowed for a margin of 2s per week for a couple or 1s 6d for an individual adult.[655] Beveridge's recommendations are summarised in Table 5.7.

Retired persons' needs were generally judged to be less than adults of working age. Food requirements were placed at about 85 per cent of adults of working age (6s per week for men and 5s 6d for women), which was significantly higher than assumed by interwar poverty investigators (normally 60–65 per cent). Beveridge claimed that the clothing requirements of old people were only two-thirds of those of adults of working age, for the temporary disruption of earnings. But for the purpose of ascertaining the appropriate allowance for clothing in old age pensions, long-term clothing needs had to be taken into account. Beveridge adopted a figure of 1s 4d per week for a man or woman, which was two-thirds of Rowntree's 1936 poverty-line recommendation for long-period clothing expenditure. The amount of necessary 'margin' was deemed to be identical, but rent benefit was allowed at a rate that was 85–90 per cent of an adult of working age (8s 6d for a retired couple or 6s for a single person).[656] Only fuel and light benefit was set at a figure higher than for adults of working age, at 5s for two adults or 3s for one person. As can be seen from Table 5.7, the cumulative impact of

Table 5.7 Beveridge's 1942 recommendations for adults, by expenditure group at 1938 prices

	Man and woman of working age	Man of working age	Woman of working age	Retired man and woman	Retired man	Retired woman
Food	13s	7s	6s	11s 6d	6s	5s 6d
Clothing	3s	1s 6d	1s 6d	2s 8d	1s 4d	1s 4d
Fuel and light	4s	2s 6d	2s 6d	5s	3s	3s
Margin	2s	1s 6d	1s 6d	2s	1s 6d	1s 6d
Rent	10s	6s 6d	6s 6d	8s 6d	6s	6s
Total	32s	19s	18s	29s 8d	17s 10d	17s 4d

Source: W. Beveridge, *Social Insurance and Allied Services* (November 1942), Cmd 6404, Table IX, p. 87 and Table X, p. 88.

these assumptions was to make the recommendations for retirement pensions about 92–96 per cent of those for adults of working age experiencing 'temporary loss of earnings'. For the benefits applicable to children, Beveridge also distinguished between those of working age and dependent children. It should be noted that the figures for dependent children of differing ages appear illustrative. Beveridge was concerned to demonstrate that a figure of 7s per week would be a reasonable 'average subsistence allowance at 1938 prices...instead of the 5s which is common to assume in discussing children's allowances in the past'.[657]

All of Beveridge's recommendations for benefits were calculated at 1938 prices. His recommendations for different household types are given in Table 5.8. He noted that in November 1942, the 'cost of living is about 30 per cent above the level for 1938'. He assumed that prices would remain fairly stable between November 1942 and the end of the war, after which time they 'will settle at about 25 per cent above 1938'. Beveridge noted that this would imply a figure of 40s per week for an adult couple of working age and about 24s per week for an individual man or woman (ignoring the difference between the separate benefit levels recommended for men and women). For children, Beveridge thought it reasonable 'to take a provisional post-war rate of 9s per week', an increase of nearly 30 per cent on 1938 prices. But because of extra provision in the social security budget, by way of school meals and free or cheap milk, Beveridge recommended a post-war benefit level of 8s per child.[658] However, retail price increases were about 60 per cent, rather than 30 per cent, between 1938 and the end of the war.

Although Beveridge recognised that social insurance would cover most risks, it would not cover all needs. As a consequence Beveridge recommended a system of 'assistance' based upon an individual means test – later to be termed National Assistance. The level of benefit paid for assistance is vague in *Social Insurance and Allied Services* (*SIAS*). But the report is clear that:

> It must meet those needs adequately up to subsistence level, but it must be felt to be something less desirable than insurance benefit; otherwise the insured persons get nothing for their contributions. Assistance therefore will be given always subject to proof of needs and examination of means.[659]

Assistance was envisaged for pensioners in the transitional period, persons who did not qualify for insurance benefit, by virtue of having made insufficient contributions, people failing to fulfil the conditions of benefit, persons with abnormal needs and those in need through causes not suitable for insurance.[660] Assistance was to be paid in accordance with need, once due allowance had been taken of the individual's economic circumstances, based on 'what is necessary for subsistence'. This in turn was to be governed by the level of recommended social insurance benefit.[661]

So, it is important to be clear about what recommendations are being referred to when discussing the Beveridge Report. There are a number of possible sets of figures: Beveridge's *insurance* recommendations at 1938 prices, Beveridge's recommendations with respect to *assistance*, Beveridge's post-war projections or the amounts actually allowed in the 1946 and 1948 Acts.

How did Beveridge's insurance benefit recommendations compare with contemporary poverty standards? As we have seen, Rowntree formulated two separate measures of poverty. The first, used in his first social survey of York in 1899, was seen by him as a subsistence standard.[662] As we have seen, on the basis of the application of this poverty line, Rowntree found 9.9 per cent of the population of York (15.4 per cent of the working-class families) were without the means for 'bare physical efficiency'. He classified these people as a being in 'primary poverty'. The second was used in his follow-up social survey of York, carried out in 1936. This used a more generous 'Human Needs' poverty line. Applying this standard, Rowntree found that 31.1 per cent of the working-class population of York were in poverty.

Table 5.8   Beveridge's *SIAS* recommendations, 1938 prices

	Including rent	*Excluding rent*
Man (of working age)	19s	12s 6d
Woman (of working age)	18s	11s 6d
Couple	32s	22s
Couple plus 1 child	39s	29s
Couple plus 2 children	46s	36s
Couple plus 3 children	53s	43s
Couple plus 4 children	60s	50s
Retired man	17s 10d	11s 10d
Retired woman	17s 4d	11s 4d
Retired couple	29s 8d	21s 2d

Source: *SIAS*: man, woman and couple paragraph 221, dependent child paragraph 228, retired person paragraph 225.

To compare these recommendations with Rowntree's poverty lines, we need to take account of the change in prices. Some authors have chosen to do this by expressing all the measures at 1948 prices, but this is not the most straightforward way of proceeding as the measurement of price changes during the war is tricky (for reasons that have already been discussed). It is easier to revalue Rowntree's poverty line at 1938 prices because the extent of price increases is much smaller and not disputed, only about 6 per cent as measured by the official Ministry of Labour cost of living index. In addition, no plausible revision to the official series, by extending its coverage or revising the weights attached to each constituent item, would substantially alter this conclusion.

Tables 5.9 and 5.10 set out these calculations for both of Rowntree's poverty lines. Revaluing Rowntree's 1899 standard at 1938 prices produces a poverty line that is dramatically lower than his 'Human Needs' scale – especially for single adults and couples.

We are now in a position to compare Beveridge's 1942 recommendations with both of Rowntree's poverty lines (Table 5.8 column 3 and

Table 5.9   Rowntree's 'Human Needs' poverty scale at 1936 and 1938 prices, excluding rent [a]

	1936 prices		1938 prices	
	Employed	*Unemployed*	*Employed*	*Unemployed*
Man (of working age)	25s 10d	22s 9d	27s 4$\frac{3}{4}$d	24s 1$\frac{1}{2}$d
Woman (of working age)	21s 3d	17s 6d	22s 6$\frac{1}{4}$d	18s 6$\frac{1}{2}$d
Couple	31s 11d	27s 8d	33s 10d	29s 4d
Couple plus 1 child	38s 1d	35s	40s 4$\frac{1}{4}$d	37s 1$\frac{1}{4}$d
Couple plus 2 children	41s 2d	38s 8d	41s 2d	40s 11$\frac{3}{4}$d
Couple plus 3 children	43s 6d	40s 5d	46s 1$\frac{1}{4}$d	42s 10$\frac{1}{4}$d
Couple plus 4 children	48s 10d	45s 9d	51s 9$\frac{1}{4}$d	48s 6d
Retired man	15s 3d		16s 2d	16s 2d
Retired woman	12s 6d		13s 3d	13s 3d
Retired couple	22s 4d		23s 8d	23s 8d

[a] For an unemployed man, Rowntree deducted 1s 7d for unemployment and health insurance, 6d for trade union subscriptions and 1s for travel to and from work. In the case of unemployed women, Rowntree deducted 1s 3d for unemployment and health insurance, 6d for trade union subscriptions, 1s for travel and 1s for personal sundries. (This item was very generous for an employed woman compared with an employed man and Rowntree did not consider it necessary during periods of unemployment.) Conversion to 1938 prices on the basis of 1936 prices × 1.06, rounded to nearest ¼d.

Source: B. S. Rowntree, *Poverty and Progress* (1941), p. 30 and calculated by author.

Table 5.10   Rowntree's physical efficiency (PE) poverty scale at 1936 and 1938 prices (excluding rent)

	1899 PE scale at 1936 prices	1899 PE scale at 1938 prices
Man (of working age)	11s	11s 8d
Woman (of working age)	9s 11d	10s $6\frac{1}{4}$d
Couple	16s 4d	17s $3\frac{3}{4}$d
Couple plus 1 child	20s 9d	22s
Couple plus 2 children	25s 2d	26s 8d
Couple plus 3 children	30s 7d	32s 5d
Couple plus 4 children	35s	37s $1\frac{1}{4}$ d

Source: B. S. Rowntree, *Poverty and Progress* (1941), p. 102 and column (2) calculated by author.

Table 5.10 column 3). In Table 5.11 this comparison is achieved by taking the ratio of Beveridge's recommendations to those of Rowntree (all excluding rent and at 1938 prices). A ratio greater than unity indicates that Beveridge's proposals were more generous than Rowntree's and for ratios less than unity the converse is true.

An examination of Table 5.11 reveals how potentially misleading Viet-Wilson's conclusion could be. By concentrating solely upon the relationship between Beveridge's recommendations and Rowntree's poverty scales as they applied to a *couple*, he ignores the very great variation in Beveridge's recommendations by household type.[663] While for a working couple it is clear that *SIAS* benefits proposals were halfway

Table 5.11   Beveridge and Rowntree compared

	Beveridge/'Human Needs'	Beveridge/physical efficiency
Man (of working age)	0.52	1.07
Woman (of working age)	0.62	1.09
Couple	0.75	1.27
Couple plus 1 child	0.78	1.31
Couple plus 2 children	0.88	1.35
Couple plus 3 children	1.00	1.33
Couple plus 4 children	1.03	1.35
Retired man	0.73	–
Retired woman	0.86	–
Retired couple	0.89	–

between Rowntree's 'Human Needs' and physical efficiency scale, for couples with three or four children Beveridge's recommendations were at least as generous as Rowntree's 'Human Needs' scale. Sufficient, that is, to secure social participation. The real anomaly were his recommendations for single working men and women. Here he suggested benefit levels that were little more than those devised for Rowntree in his 1899 survey, only just sufficient to meet the needs of 'bare physical efficiency' as prescribed in 1899.

A note of caution is needed with respect to the interpretation that should be placed on the comparison between Rowntree's 'Human Needs' and Beveridge's recommendations for retired people. As can be seen from Table 5.9, Rowntree's 'Human Needs' for retired men and women were about 60 per cent of those of single men and women under 65 years old. Beveridge's recommendations were more generous. His proposed benefits for retired individuals were about 92–96 per cent of those for adults. This explains the relatively high value of Beveridge's proposals for retired people compared with Rowntree's standard. But it should be remembered that Beveridge was proposing a reduced level of benefit that was already only set at only 0.6 of a person below retirement age. It is clear that this feature of his recommendations is important for understanding the incidence and extent of post-war poverty.

Beveridge also made recommendations for benefit levels after the war. These were based on the figures reported in Table 5.8, but with some adjustment for an increase in prices of 25 per cent and deductions for improved services and other benefits, especially with respect to free milk and cheap school meals. In 1946, the National Insurance Act integrated all the existing schemes of social insurance into a single system under a new Ministry of National Insurance. National Insurance was compulsory for all people of working age in paid employment, and in return for weekly contributions benefits were available to cover unemployment, sickness, maternity and retirement pensions, etc. as of right. The 1948 National Assistance Act abolished the Poor Laws and provided supplementary benefit on the basis of 'need', assessed by an individual means test. The 1946 National Insurance Act and 1948 National Assistance Act provided a unified scheme of benefits for unemployment, sickness and retirement. These benefits were 26s per week (for the male breadwinner), 16s for a wife and 7s 6d for the first child dependant.[664] This was backed by means-tested benefit, on an individual rather than household basis, for people falling outside of the scheme.

Summary

Britons became significantly better off during the war and immediate post-war period. Average real earnings grew by nearly 25 per cent in the decade 1938–48, much less than suggested by the official series because the cost of living increased significantly more than recorded by the Ministry of Labour retail price index during the war. Male adult pay differentials continued to narrow, but not to such a large extent as during the previous conflict. And most importantly, for the first time in a generation, Britain experienced full employment in peacetime. The impact of wartime controls on food consumption was generally positive and class differences in the nutritional adequacy of diets were significantly less pronounced than they had been prior to the Second World War. Generally, social policy became more progressive during the war to the advantage of some sections of the population that experienced a high incidence of poverty, such as old people.

The investigation of poverty practically ceased with the war, although evacuation revealed much about the conditions of poor urban workers' children in the late 1930s. Both Rowntree and Bowley influenced the Beveridge Report, which provided the plan for post-war social insurance legislation. The scales of benefit proposed in the report varied by household type. In the case of a couple, Beveridge's proposals were about half-way between Rowntree's primary poverty measure and 'Human Needs' scale. For a couple with three children or more, Beveridge's proposals were more generous than Rowntree's 'Human Needs' scale. In other cases, Beveridge's proposals were significantly less generous. In particular, the proposed post-war scale of benefits for old people was very near Rowntree's 1899 primary poverty-line measure adjusted for changes in prices. The differences in Beveridge's proposals by household type are clearly important in helping to explain the incidence and extent of post-war poverty.

6

POST-WAR POVERTY, 1950–65

Introduction

Richard Titmuss argued that the assumption of responsibility for citizens' health during the Second World War marked a complete transformation of the role of the state:

> It would, in any relative sense, be true to say that by the end of the Second World War the Government had, through the agency of newly established or existing services, assumed and developed a measure of direct concern for the health and well-being of the population which, by contrast with the role of Government in the nineteen-thirties, was little short of remarkable. No longer did concern rest on the belief that, in respect to many social needs, it was proper to intervene only to assist the poor and those who were unable to pay for services of one kind and another. Instead, it was increasingly regarded as a proper function or even obligation of government to ward off distress and strain among not only the poor but also almost all classes of society.[665]

Much subsequent writing on the development of the welfare state, while noting the important changes, stressed the extent of continuity with the 1930s and the eclectic mix of social philosophy embodied in the 'Beveridge welfare state'.[666] Nevertheless, the 'make do and mend' 1940s Britain of utility design and rationing was gradually transformed into a society of mass consumption and widespread property ownership. The closing years of the 1950s have been characterised as the 'zenith of One-Nation Toryism' and the welfare state had eliminated poverty, or

158

so it was believed.[667] The results of Rowntree's third survey of York were greeted with 'intense press coverage' with the *Manchester Guardian* proclaiming the 'ending of poverty'. A direct corollary of this euphoria was the genuine shock that surrounded the 'rediscovery of poverty' at the beginning of the 1960s.[668] *The Times* greeted the publication of the *Poor and the Poorest* in 1965 with headlines proclaiming, 'Many British Children Living in Hardship and Poverty', while *The Guardian* claimed that 'Poverty Group Brings a Christmas Story to Mr Wilson'.[669] This chapter considers how poverty could have been 'eradicated' and then 'rediscovered' in just 14 years.

6.1 Occupation and Class

About 16 million men and 7.6 million women were economically active in 1961. This represents an increase in the participation rate of women, from about 30 per cent during the interwar period, to about 37 per cent in 1961. Whereas only 11 per cent of married women were in the labour force in 1931, 30 years later it was nearly 30 per cent.[670] The distribution of women's occupations also changed significantly, as Table 6.1 shows. Fewer than half of all women worked in manual occupations (about 47 per cent), compared with just over two-thirds before the Second World

Table 6.1 Distribution of economically active population by occupational category, 1961 (percentage by category)

	Males	*Females*
Self-employed and higher-grade professionals	4.5	1.1
Employers and proprietors	4.8	3.0
Administrators and managers	7.5	2.6
Lower-grade salaried professionals and technicians	4.0	9.2
Inspectors, supervisors and foremen	3.8	0.9
Clerical workers	6.5	25.5
Sales personnel and shop assistants	3.9	10.0
Skilled manual workers	32.3	10.8
Semi-skilled manual workers	22.8	30.9
Unskilled manual workers	9.9	6.0
Total	15,992,000	7,649,000

Source: A. H. Halsey, *Change in British Society* (4th edn, 1995), Table 2.1, pp. 40–1.

War. Over one-third of all economically active females worked in clerical occupations or as sales personnel or shop assistants. Among males, about 86 per cent participated in the labour force and the proportion of manual occupations had declined from just fewer than three-quarters of the total to just under two-thirds (about 65 per cent). The most significant change here was the contraction of the relative size of male unskilled occupations and the expansion of higher occupational class work. Relatively more men were occupied in self-employed, higher-grade professional or administrative and managerial occupations.

From the perspective of an investigation of poverty, it is important to note the decrease since the interwar years in the relative numbers of the economically active population in low-paid unskilled manual work and the increasing relative numbers in higher-paid occupations, along with the increased participation of married women. Of course, this says nothing about those who were not economically active, and the proportion of people over retirement age had increased substantially since before the First World War. Nearly 12 per cent of the population was over 65 years old in 1965 compared with only 5.2 per cent in 1911.[671] This was mainly due to increases in life expectancy. Also important was the reduction in the birth rate (leading to proportionately more old people) and decrease in family size. Average family size was smaller, as was the variance around the mean size of households.[672] In 1961 average household size was 3.1 compared with 4.1 in 1931 and 4.6 in 1901.[673] This is clearly important given the emphasis placed upon large family size as a cause of poverty at the beginning of the century. The fact that women were having fewer children, marrying earlier and completing childbirth at a relatively younger age also had implications for female labour force participation. In turn, married women's employment increased household income, and dual incomes provided greater financial security against the consequences of unemployment or ill health.

6.2   Wages, Earnings and Prices, 1948–65

The years spanning a generation or so after the end of the Second World War were 'golden years' of full employment and sustained increases in real incomes. Unlike the experience following the First World War, depression did not follow a post-war boom. Between 1945 and 1960 unemployment remained under 2 per cent. The last time unemployment levels were so low in peacetime was briefly glimpsed in

1920.[674] This exceeded even the most optimistic expectations of what was meant by 'full employment' at the time of the 1944 White Paper, which committed government to maintain a 'high and stable' level of employment after the war.[675] Moreover, not only was there work, but also it was increasingly well-paid work, as Table 6.2 shows. Between 1948 and 1965, average money wages more than doubled and average money earnings nearly tripled. But retail prices increased too – though not by as much as money wages. Nevertheless, inflation eroded a significant proportion of the gain in average money wages. Real wages increased by about 15 per cent on average, or just under 1 per cent per annum, but real earnings increased by nearly half (47 per cent), or just over 2.5 per cent per annum.

Despite this relative prosperity, changes in the distribution of personal incomes moved against the bottom 30 per cent of income units. Whereas in 1949/50 this group accounted for only 15.9 per cent of all personal incomes, by 1959/60 the share of post-tax income of the bottom 30 per cent was only 14.5 per cent. In 1964/5 the share of the bottom 30 per cent was 14.8 per cent – still less than it had been before the Second

Table 6.2   Wages, earnings and prices, 1948–65 (1948 = 100)

	Wages	Earnings	Retail prices	Real wages	Real earnings
1948	100	100	100	100	100
1949	102	104	103	100	102
1950	105	109	106	99	103
1951	113	120	116	98	103
1952	122	130	126	97	103
1953	128	137	130	98	106
1954	134	146	132	101	110
1955	143	159	138	103	115
1956	154	172	145	106	118
1957	162	181	151	107	120
1958	168	187	155	108	121
1959	172	192	156	110	123
1960	177	204	157	112	129
1961	184	218	163	113	134
1962	191	225	170	112	133
1963	198	235	174	114	135
1964	207	255	179	116	143
1965	216	276	188	115	147

Source: C. H. Feinstein, *National Income, Output and Expenditure of the United Kingdom* (1972), Table 65, T140, recalculated 1948 = 100. Columns (4) and (5) calculated from columns (1)–(3).

World War.[676] As Townsend argued, in comparison with the period of wartime egalitarianism, in the 1950s and 1960s 'there was some reversion to former inequalities, slow at first but probably quite fast by the middle and late 1950s'.[677]

Nevertheless, rising real incomes, smaller families and the increasing proportion of women who were in employment maintained the prosperity of most Britons in the 1950s. But it is important to remember how it started. The drab 'age of austerity' lasted well into the early 1950s, with petrol, clothes and many foodstuffs still rationed.[678] Harold Macmillan's exhortation that 'You've never had it so good', may have, in fact, been intended as a warning about inflation by the Conservative Prime Minister, but is also an appropriate epithet for living standards at the end of the decade.[679] Yet it would have seemed out of place as a description of the early 1950s, despite the fact that real improvements had been made when compared with pre-war standards of living.

6.3   Food, Nutrition and the 'Human Needs' Index, 1950–9

The National Food Survey, begun in 1940, was widened in 1950 to provide coverage of all classes on a national basis. Previously, it had been restricted to a survey of the diet of the working classes.[680] By the late 1950s, 2500–3000 households were providing weekly details of expenditure and consumption of food.[681] In Table 6.3 expenditure on different food types for 1955–6 is compared with expenditure in 1936–7. As Carr-Saunders *et al.* note, 'the increased proportion spent on meat and

Table 6.3   Percentage food expenditure, Great Britain 1936–7 and 1955–6

Food groups	Oct. 1936–Mar. 1937	Oct. 1955–Mar. 1956
Milk, eggs and cheese	18	18
Meat and fish	30	32
Fruit and vegetables	14	16
Cereals, fats, sugar and preserves	27	26
Other foods and beverages	11	8
All foods	100	100

Source: *Domestic Food Consumption and Expenditure*, 7 (1955–6). 1936–7 data from W. Crawford and H. Broadley, *The People's Food* (1938) reported in A. M. Carr-Saunders, D. Caradog Jones and C. A. Moser, *A Survey of Social Conditions in England and Wales* (1958), Table 15.2, p. 207.

fish and on fruit and vegetables are the only changes of any magnitude and even these are small'.[682]

In terms of the nutritional content of household diets, the average energy value per head was 2641 kcal and 77 g of protein, with little variation between town and country.[683] Notice that these *average* values are not very different from those in poor labourers' diets analysed prior to, and immediately after, the First World War. Moreover, the 1955 average diet easily met the 1950 BMA recommendations for minerals and vitamins.

The National Food Survey data only provide grouped data on family structure, and while it was possible to calculate food expenditure per head for different household types, it was not possible to relate this to household income, only income of household head. Nevertheless, during the 1950s, Schultz found significantly less variability in food expenditure per head across the income range than was evident in the interwar data. The lowest income group in 1959 (representing about 11 per cent of the population) spent about 80 per cent of the expenditure per head of the highest income group (the top 12.5 per cent of the population). In the 1930s, food expenditure per head of the bottom 10 per cent was only 30 per cent of the highest income group.[684]

Differences in the *pattern* of food consumption by social class were substantial, however, although these divisions may also be due to differences in demographic structure.[685] Unsurprisingly, households at the top of the social scale consumed significantly more fruit, milk and cream, meat and fish and eggs than the general average. Other groups of food increased in relative importance as income declined. The maximum consumption of cheap high carbohydrate food, such as white bread, potatoes and oatmeal, and margarine and prepared fish was in the lowest income groups.

The income consumption gradients for these foods did not translate into nutritional differentials by income class, however, as Table 6.4 shows. With the exception of iron intakes, average diets per capita all satisfied the 1950 BMA recommendations, irrespective of social class. Compared with the 1930s, the reduction in the class differential of the nutritional adequacy of diets was clearly considerable and was a continuation of the levelling that started during the war.[686] This is the single most important feature of these data. On the basis of a comparison of the National Food Survey data with Boyd-Orr's analysis, Schultz claimed that:

The consumption as well as the price patterns of the post-war surveys indicates that, on the whole, the families of all the income groups

Table 6.4 Nutritional content of average diets by social class, relative to 1950 BMA recommendations, Great Britain 1955 (BMA recommendations 1950 = 100)

	A1	A2	B	C	D1	D2	OAP	All classes
Energy value	113	109	105	103	103	109	107	105
Total protein	115	107	102	100	104	113	112	103
Calcium	121	114	107	107	108	114	112	108
Iron	116	113	111	109	105	96	90	109
Vitamin A	235	198	184	167	159	147	133	176
Vitamin B1	137	132	126	121	123	127	121	124
Riboflavin	132	120	110	103	104	112	110	108
Nicotinic acid	152	140	132	127	133	140	133	131
Vitamin C	291	265	240	220	214	209	174	231

Key: Social class A1 head of household weekly income £24 or more, A2 £15–24, B £9–15, C £6–9, D1 with earners, excluding OAP, less than £6, D2 without earners, excluding OAP, less than £6, OAP less than £6 weekly.

Source: A. M. Carr-Saunders, D. Caradog Jones and C. A. Moser, *A Survey of Social Conditions in England and Wales* (1958), Table 15.7, p. 215.

disposed of sufficient money to buy the type of diet that they pre-ferred, and that the pre-war danger of malnutrition through poverty no longer threatened large sections of the population.[687]

This improvement in nutrition was reflected in other health indicators too. For example, infant mortality rates continued to fall sharply in early post-war Britain, from 34.5 per 1000 in 1948 to 18.3 per 1000 in 1968.[688]

While this improvement in nutrition and health was widespread, the 1955 National Food Survey data do reveal a growing gap between the consumption of households with no, or few, children and large households with four or more children. The diets for these larger families, with four or more children, which accounted for 2 per cent of household types, were not adequate when judged against the 1950 BMA standard, particularly with respect to protein and calcium intakes.[689] Families with three children were marginally deficient, on average (accounting for 3.8 per cent of household types). Lambert, in a critical study of the National Food Survey findings, demonstrated how in 1960 'families with three or more children or with children and adolescents [were] still at risk – and not just the families in the lowest income groups'.[690] In comparison with the BMA standard, he argued that the families' diets of households with three children were marginal with respect to energy provision, protein and calcium intakes. Those with adolescents and children were also marginal for riboflavin intakes.[691]

As we saw in Chapter 5, the Oxford Institute of Statistics constructed a 'Human Needs' index from 1941 onwards, based on information on food prices from market stalls and shops in working-class districts. Originally this inquiry was based on Oxford, but gradually it was expanded to cover a number of Midland towns and London. This was used to construct a 'Human Needs' index based on the cost of providing a diet for a representative family, of two adults and three schoolchildren, that satisfied the nutritional assumptions embodied in the poverty line used by Rowntree in his second social survey of York in 1936.[692] During the 1940s, the change in cost of this 'Human Needs' diet exceeded that of the official Ministry of Labour cost of living index. This was partly because subsidies were targeted at the items that comprised the official index, thus artificially holding down apparent increases in retail food prices, and partly because rationing meant that certain parts of Rowntree's 1936 diet could not be satisfied in wartime and substitutes proved relatively expensive.

During the 1950s, these biannual surveys in the spring and autumn continued and the geographical coverage of the surveys increased. In the late 1950s, information on food prices was being collected from London, Reading, Oxford, Newbury, Birmingham, Banbury and Abingdon.[693] This 'constant nutrition' index allowed for the substitution of foodstuffs that had become relatively expensive with cheaper items, subject to (at least) meeting BMA nutritional intakes for the reference family. However, the index also reflected changes in nutritional knowledge since 1936, as by the early 1950s the benefit of reduced meat consumption and increased milk consumption had been recognised.[694] This diet was not least-cost in the mathematical sense, but designed to produce a low-cost diet 'without compelling people to eat strange dishes to which they might object'.[695]

The nutritional composition of the 'Human Needs' diet is shown in relation to the BMA standard in Table 6.5. This standard remained unchanged during the 1950s and with the exception of calcium intakes, the 'Human Needs' diet was more generous with respect to mineral and vitamin requirements than contemporary recommended dietary allowances. Of course, the diet that was devised to satisfy this standard also changed from survey to survey, depending on fluctuations in relative prices.

Table 6.5   The nutritional composition of the 'Human Needs' diet (equivalent male adults per day)

	BMA	'Human Needs' (autumn 1953)
kcal	3000	3100
Protein (g)	70	84
Calcium (g)	0.8	0.7
Iron (g)	10	13
Vitamin A (IU)	3000	3400
Vitamin B (mg)	0.9	1.6
Vitamin C (mg)	30	60

Source: *Bulletin of Oxford Institute of Statistics* (1954), Table IV, p. 135.

The cost of this 'Human Needs' diet, and how it changed during the decade, is given in Table 6.6. Unlike the situation in the 1940s where movements in the official cost of living index and the 'Human Needs' index diverge, during the 1950s there is much closer correspondence between these two series.[696] Indeed, by 1956, the overall increase in the 'Human Needs' index since 1936 was only marginally greater than the official cost of living index – 308 compared with 300 (1936 = 100).[697] According to Schultz, this gradual convergence of the cost of living index and the 'Human Needs' index from 1949, reflected the 'revival of the free market' as de-rationing reawakened competition among retailers, which tended to 'loosen up the general price structure'.[698]

Table 6.6   The cost of the 'Human Needs' diet, for 2 adults and 3 children, 1950–9

Year	'Human Needs'	Year	'Human Needs'
1950/i	51s 3d	1955/i	63s
1950/ii	50s 5$\frac{1}{2}$d	1955/ii	68s 8$\frac{1}{2}$d
1951/i	49s 11d	1956/i	71s 11$\frac{1}{2}$d
1951/ii	55s 7d	1956/ii	69s 7$\frac{1}{2}$d
1952/i	61s 4d	1957/i	69s 9d
1952/ii	63s 7$\frac{1}{4}$d	1957/ii	70s 5$\frac{1}{2}$d
1953/i	65s 3d	1958/i	74s 5d
1953/ii	63s	1958/ii	73s 11d
1954/i	63s 7d	1959/i	77s
1954/ii	62s 6d	1959/ii	77s 1d

Source: *Bulletin of the Oxford Institute of Statistics* (various issues, year refers to first and second half (i) and (ii)).

In the spring of 1953, the 'Human Needs' cost of 65s 3d amounted to
about one-third of average earnings of workers in manufacturing (about
193s per week), once family allowances and social insurance contributions are taken into account (deducting 6s social insurance and adding
16s family allowance). At the same date, in comparison with a family on
National Assistance, the 'Human Needs' diet represented about two-thirds
of net income, excluding rent (102s per week).[699]

Schulz also investigated changes in the cost of 'Human Needs' relative
to National Assistance scales between 1935 and 1953 for reference families
of different structures, ranging from an adult couple to a couple with
five children.[700] Using Rowntree's 1937 'Human Needs' poverty scale
between 1935 and 1941 and the Institute's own 'Human Needs' index
thereafter, Schulz found that prior to 1941, very little surplus income
would have remained for small households (of two or three persons),
and in the case of larger households receiving unemployment assistance,
they would not have sufficient income to satisfy their 'human needs'.
During the war, however, the real value of assistance incomes increased
and rose further in 1947. By 1952 Schulz claimed that

> even the family wholly dependent on assistance could count on an
> income that, as Mr Rowntree suggested in 1937, should enable a man
> to marry, live in a decent house, and bring up a family . . . in a state of
> physical efficiency, while allowing a reasonable margin for contingencies
> and recreation.[701]

In comparison, average earners' income was always sufficient to provide for 'human needs', even in the cases of large families.[702] By 1953,
in the case of households with two adults and five children, the real
value of surplus income (over and above that necessary to satisfy
'human needs' for housing, food, fuel and light), was ten times its 1935
value. The increase was less spectacular for other household structures
(25 per cent for a couple, 50 per cent for a couple with one child and
150 per cent for a couple with three children).[703] But taken in conjunction with the findings for the behaviour of assistance incomes relative
to the 'human needs' index, Schulz concluded that, 'poverty, in the
sense in which the term was understood before the war, has been abolished for families of the types considered'.[704] During the 1950s,
Schulz's analysis in the *Bulletin* argued strongly in support of the
position adopted by Rowntree and Lavers, that poverty had been
abolished.

6.4   Rowntree's Third Survey of York

The interwar desire for empirical poverty inquiry dissipated with the coming of peace and construction of the welfare state. In fact, only one survey was carried out in the immediate post-war period and that was Rowntree's third social survey of York in 1950. Rowntree and Lavers's *Poverty and the Welfare State*, first published in 1951, attempted to replicate Rowntree's second social survey of York in 1936, by applying the revised 'Human Needs' dietary standard at 1950 prices, with some minor modifications.[705] Other items of minimum needs expenditure were more substantially revised.[706] Rowntree and Lavers calculated that a reference family of two adults and three school-age children required an income of £5 0s 2d net of rent and rates and insurance to avoid primary poverty, compared with 43s 6d in 1936.[707]

Rowntree and Lavers reached two important conclusions. First, the percentage in poverty in York declined dramatically between 1936 and 1950. In 1950 Rowntree and Lavers found that 2.77 per cent of individuals, comprising 4.64 per cent of working-class households, were in poverty.[708] This compares with 31.1 per cent of working-class individuals in poverty in 1936. Second, this dramatic reduction in primary poverty, over the course of the Second World War, was primarily the result of the introduction of the Beveridge welfare state. Rowntree and Lavers concluded that if welfare legislation had remained unaltered, poverty among individuals would have been reduced from 31.1 to 22.18 per cent. Further, the effect of food subsidies was to reduce measured poverty from 13.74 to 2.77 per cent.[709]

Are these two claims reasonable? Had poverty dimished to such a startling extent? And what role had the state played in the reduction of poverty? Rowntree's third survey of York was an attempt to replicate his previous survey to ascertain what change had occurred in the incidence of an *unchanged definition of poverty*. Rowntree, who was 80 years old at the time, was assisted by Lavers and largely followed the methodology of the previous survey. One important difference, however, was the abandonment of universal household visits to every working-class family in York (earning less than £550 per annum), in favour of a one in nine sample.[710] According to Atkinson *et al.*, following their reinvestigation of Rowntree and Lavers's inquiry based on the surviving original returns, 'there was considerable departure from the original 1 in 9 sample [and] the quality of the information leaves quite a lot to be desired'.[711]

As Hatton and Bailey point out, although it is never explicitly stated that the 1950 poverty line was intended to be identical to that employed in 1936, it is the clear implication of Rowntree and Lavers's stated purpose.[712] For Rowntree's usual reference family of two adults and three children, the 1950 poverty line was slightly more generous for food and personal sundries, the clothing allowance for adult males was increased, while for women and children it was reduced. This is also true for poverty-line expenditure on household sundries.

The overall impact of these changes is not that great, but they serve to lower the poverty line, compared with repricing the 1936 poverty line, by about 5 per cent. Other things being equal, this should have meant that Rowntree and Lavers found more people in poverty than otherwise they would have done. But the effect of the minor revisions to the poverty line was not the same across all household types. For small families and single individuals, the poverty line was higher than the 1936 scale.[713] According to Hatton and Bailey, the overall impact of these slight changes in definition was to impart 'some downward bias to the calculations'.

Table 6.7 compares Rowntree's 1950 *Welfare State* standard with his 1936 'Human Needs standard'. This requires us to reprice Rowntree's 1936 standard at 1950 prices, but this is not a trivial exercise. The true extent of price inflation during the war is not reflected in the official cost of living index, as we saw in Chapter 5. There are two problems with the official cost of living index. First, it was, itself, an instrument of anti-inflation policy. Wartime subsidies and price controls were particularly directed at items that were included in the official index in an attempt to limit the perception of rising prices so as to dampen down wage inflationary pressure. Second, the official index used expenditure weights that did not adequately capture the expenditure patterns of working-class people at this time, as they dated to investigations of expenditure carried out before the First World War. The Ministry of Labour did carry out a survey of 10,800 working-class family budgets in 1937–8 for the purpose of revising the weighting and coverage of the official index, but the official index was not updated as war intervened.

The official cost of living index was revised in June 1947 and after this date it probably captures the extent of prices changes faced by working people fairly accurately. Between 1938 and the middle of 1947, the official series will not do. As we saw in Chapter 5, both Seers and Allen constructed alternative cost of living indices for this period, that are themselves very similar, which suggest that the rise in prices was roughly

Table 6.7 Rowntree's Welfare State (WS) poverty line, excluding rent, compared with his 'Human Needs' (HN) at 1950 prices[a]

	Rowntree: WS at 1950 prices		Rowntree: HN at 1950 prices using:	
	Employed	Unemployed	Official COL index	Revised COL index
Man (of working age)	36s 1d	37s 11d	36s 4d	44s $4\frac{1}{2}$ d
Woman (of working age)	31s 1d	33s 2d	27s $11\frac{1}{2}$ d	34s $1\frac{1}{2}$ d
Couple	57s 2d	56s 2d	44s $2\frac{1}{4}$ d	53s $11\frac{3}{4}$ d
Couple plus 1 child	71s 11d	70s 11d	55s $10\frac{3}{4}$ d	68s 3d
Couple plus 2 children	86s 4d	85s 4d	61s 9d	75s 5d
Couple plus 3 children	100s 2d	99s 2d	64s $6\frac{1}{2}$ d	78s 10d
Couple plus 4 children	114s 2d	113s 2d	73s $0\frac{3}{4}$ d	89s 3d
Retired man	Not specified	Not specified	24s $4\frac{1}{4}$ d	38s $11\frac{3}{4}$ d
Retired woman	Not specified	Not specified	19s $11\frac{1}{2}$ d	24s $4\frac{1}{2}$ d
Retired couple	Not specified	Not specified	35s 8d	43s $6\frac{1}{2}$ d

[a] Notes on retail price indices used to revalue Rowntree's 'Human Needs' poverty line: Official COL index. 1938–May 1947, *Abstract of British Historical Statistics*, Table 89. Interim official index June 1947–1950 (average of June and December), A. L. Bowley, 'Index Numbers of the Cost of Living', *Journal of the Royal Statistical Society* (1952), Table 7, p. 505. Revised COL index, 1938–May 1947. R. G. Allen as reported in Bowley, 'Index Numbers of the Cost of Living', Table 6, p. 504, linked to the interim official series in June 1947 (as above).

Source: B. S. Rowntree and G. R. Lavers, *Poverty and the Welfare State* (1951), p. 28 and author's calculations.

double that indicated by the official series. The series produced by Allen, who was himself a member of the Cost of Living Advisory Committee, has been used to give the revised estimates of revaluing Rowntree's 'Human Needs' scale at 1950 prices reported in Table 6.7.[714]

In comparison with Rowntree's 'Human Needs' poverty line, Rowntree and Lavers's *Welfare State* standard varied by household composition, as Table 6.7 shows.[715] Once due allowance is taken of the change in prices between 1936 and 1950, the 'Human Needs' scale is greater for single people than Rowntree's *Welfare State* standard (compare Table 6.7 column 4 with column 2), about the same for a couple and a couple with one child, but significantly less for couples with two or more children. Notice, too, the difference between the values of Rowntree's 'Human Needs' standard in 1950, depending on whether the official or a revised retail price index is used in the calculation (column 3 compared with 4).

From a careful comparison of the surviving schedules of the survey, however, Hatton and Bailey conclude that Rowntree and Lavers's errors in measurement of income and their inconsistent allocation of households to income classes, were empirically more important. These errors had a marked downward impact on Rowntree and Lavers's results, since 'they should have found some 11.8 per cent of working-class households in poverty rather than 4.6 per cent'.[716] As they point out, had the reduction in poverty, as defined and intended to be measured by Rowntree, been accurately reported in *Poverty and the Welfare State* (from 31.1 to 11.8 per cent), there would have been less scope for the apparently self-satisfied conclusion that poverty had been eliminated, though clearly a substantial reduction would still have been seen to have occurred. Moreover, its 'rediscovery' in the early 1960s would have been less surprising.

Rowntree and Lavers also overestimated significantly the role of the state in the reduction of poverty. This was because they only considered a subset of welfare benefits that had altered significantly with the introduction of the Beveridge welfare state (such as child allowances, retirement and widows' pensions), which had a high incidence among survey households. In addition, Hatton and Bailey claim that Rowntree and Lavers also failed to take account of changing real values of benefits. The net effect of these two errors was to dramatically exaggerate the impact of welfare provision on the reduction of poverty. Had this counterfactual calculation been performed properly, the impact of the Beveridge welfare state was to reduce poverty by 9.8 per cent, half that suggested by Rowntree and Lavers. Though still not insignificant, when food subsidies are ignored, the impact of social security payments by themselves was to reduce poverty by 'a mere 3.7 percentage points'.[717] On the basis of these calculations, Hatton and Bailey conclude reasonably 'that poverty in the early 1950s had been obscured rather than eliminated'.[718]

It is also possible to compare Rowntree's *Welfare State* poverty line with Beveridge's 1942 proposals. This involves revaluing Beveridge's 1938 recommendations at 1950 prices, using the same procedure as used to compare Rowntree's 'Human Needs' and *Welfare State* poverty standards. These calculations are set out in Table 6.8. As can be seen, Rowntree's *Welfare State* poverty line is greater than Beveridge's recommendations for every household type where direct comparison is possible.

Since Beveridge's proposals formed the basis of the benefit levels adopted in the 1946 and 1948 Acts, this comparison reveals that, even if all household units were prevented from falling below Beveridge's

Table 6.8 Beveridge's recommendations at 1938 and 1950 prices, excluding rent (shillings per week)

| | Beveridge 1938 | Beveridge 1950 prices: | | Rowntree: WS at 1950 prices: unemployed |
		Official COL index	Revised COL index	
Man (of working age)	12s 6d	18s 9$\frac{3}{4}$d	23s	37s 11d
Woman (of working age)	11s 6d	17s 3$\frac{3}{4}$d	21s 2d	33s 2d
Couple	22s	33s 1$\frac{3}{4}$d	40s 5$\frac{3}{4}$d	56s 2d
Couple plus 1 child	29s	43s 8$\frac{1}{4}$d	53s 4$\frac{1}{4}$d	70s 11d
Couple plus 2 children	36s	54s 2$\frac{3}{4}$d	66s 3d	85s 4d
Couple plus 3 children	43s	64s 9$\frac{1}{4}$d	79s 1$\frac{1}{2}$d	99s 2d
Couple plus 4 children	50s	75s 4d	92s	113s 2d
Retired man	11s 10d	17s 10d	21s 9$\frac{1}{2}$d	Not specified
Retired woman	11s 4d	17s 0$\frac{3}{4}$d	20s 10$\frac{1}{4}$d	Not specified
Retired couple	21s 2d	31s 10$\frac{1}{2}$d	39s 10$\frac{1}{4}$d	Not specified

Source: Calculated by author.

standard (which was not the case), Rowntree should still have found a significant amount of poverty in York, since his welfare state poverty standard was more generous than was Beveridge's recommendations. In this context, it is also instructive to examine Rowntree's conclusions on the changing cause of poverty. Table 6.9 reports Rowntree's analysis of the percentage cause of poverty at the two survey dates before and after the Second World War.

Table 6.9 Causes of poverty in York, 1936 and 1950

Cause of poverty	Percentage 1936	Percentage 1950
Unemployment of chief wage earner	28.6	Nil
Inadequate wages of earners in regular employment	32.8	1.0
Inadequate earnings of other workers	9.5	Nil
Old age	14.7	68.1
Death of chief wage earner	7.8	6.4
Sickness	4.1	21.3
Miscellaneous	2.5	3.2

Source: B. S. Rowntree and G. R. Lavers, *Poverty and the Welfare State* (1951) p. 35.

Unemployment, which was the chief cause of poverty in investigations carried out during the 1930s, accounted for nil poverty in 1950. Inadequate wages by 1950 were also an insignificant cause of poverty by 1950. The most important cause by far – accounting for over two-thirds of poverty in 1950 – was old age. Part of the reason why Rowntree and Lavers identified a high proportion of the elderly in poverty was because their poverty standard was significantly greater for retired couples than post-war state provision. Atkinson *et al.* estimate that 14.4 per cent of the working-class population of York had resources below the National Assistance scale and over half of these had less than 80 per cent of the National Assistance scale. Many of these were elderly people.[719]

6.5   Old Age and Poverty

Townsend and Wedderburn write that ' Suddenly, in the late forties and fifties, or so it may seem, to the historian of the written and spoken word, the problems of old age were discovered.'[720] However, as we saw in Chapter 1, Rowntree had found that old age was an important explanation for poverty at the turn of the twentieth century. For a number of reasons the extent and nature of the problem of poverty in old age were different in the early 1960s compared with what it had been in 1901. First, there were more old people: both in absolute terms and, as Table 6.10 shows, as a proportion of the population.[721] Second, while many old people who lived outside of institutions in 1900 lived with relatives and non-relatives, a much greater proportion lived alone in the 1960s. In a detailed survey of all of the houses in four streets in York, Rowntree found that one in ten lived alone, nearly one in four people over the age of 60 lived with non-relatives and the remainder lived with relatives of

Table 6.10   Proportion of the population over the age of 65, 1901–61

	Men	Women	Both
1901	4.2	5.1	4.7
1931	6.7	8.1	7.4
1961	9.4	14.3	11.9

Source: Jeremy Tunstall, *Old and Alone: a Sociological Study of Old People* (1966), p. 2 (derived from census returns).

Table 6.11 Household composition of old people in Britain, 1900 and 1962 (%)

	People aged 65 and over in Britain, 1962	People aged 60 and over in York, 1900
Living alone	22.2	10
With spouse only	32.8	19
Married child	11.9	26
Unmarried child	20.1	–
Sibling	6.7	13
Grandchildren	0.9	–
Other relatives	1.8	23
Non-relatives	3.6	–
Total	100	100
Number	2500	31

Source: Jeremy Tunstall, *Old and Alone: a Sociological Study of Old People* (1966), p. 59 (derived from Rowntree, *Poverty: a Study of Town Life* and Townsend and Wedderburn, *The Aged and the Welfare State*).

one kind or another. It is unfortunate that the sample size in the Rowntree inquiry is so small and, of course, it is possible that given this, the differences between the 1900 and 1962 samples do not indicate changes in the characteristics of the population. Nevertheless, as Table 6.11 shows, by 1962 the proportion living alone had doubled and the number living with non-relatives had declined to fairly trivial levels. Greater prosperity meant that more were able to maintain their own households into old age, at least until death of a spouse, if not beyond.

It is notable that one in eight old people in 1900 lived with grandchildren, whereas in 1962, this proportion was less than 1 per cent. It is likely that this is not a false inference. As Anderson points out, people lived longer by 1960, the age of marriage was slightly earlier, family size had fallen sharply in comparison with the turn of the century, and childbirth was more concentrated in a shorter number of years after marriage. Thus, there were fewer old people who had a child to share a home with and there was less opportunity for reciprocal caring arrangements across generations (care of parents by children and care of grandchildren by grandparents).[722]

Cole and Utting carried out the first empirical study of the material circumstances of old people at the end of the 1950s. Published in 1962, their *Economic Circumstances of Old People* reported the results of a small-scale survey based on 400 direct interviews with old people in Salisbury, Leicester, Hexham Rural District, Seaton Valley, Glasgow, Wimbledon and East Ham between July 1959 and March 1960.[723] They remind us that the term 'old' refers to a heterogeneous group of people with an age span of 30 years or more. Nevertheless, they highlight 'the stereotype of the problem of old age [as] a man or woman over 70, with failing health and difficulty in getting about, struggling to manage with inadequate income, living in an unsuitably large house and lonely and cut off from the world'.[724] About one-quarter of old people were keeping house alone, and there were significant differences between men and women; 70 per cent of the sample were either single or widowed and nearly one-third of all women were keeping house alone (32 per cent). In comparison only 13 per cent of men were in the same situation.

About 30 per cent of old people had no surviving children, but of those that did, roughly half of widows and widowers and 38 per cent of old-age couples were living with one of their children. Cole and Utting argue, however, that the majority of old people who were living with children had always done so (72 per cent of women and 80 per cent of men), and, in contrast to Wilmott and Young, they did not find much evidence of old people moving to live with children when widowed, or in circumstances of declining health.[725] The reasons given for such moves were generally related to emotional security or illness, rather than financial reasons.

The importance of family networks for old people's health was first revealed by Sheldon's 1945–7 study of the health of old people in Wolverhampton. Sheldon, who was Director of Medicine at the Royal Hospital Wolverhampton, found that many of those living alone were in close proximity to children who could provide help with shopping and provide meals.[726] Of those not living alone, with a spouse or a child, two out of five old people lived with siblings, though nearly one-third of old people in this category were living with people they were unrelated to. Just fewer than one in ten were living with grandchildren.[727]

By the end of the 1950s, Cole and Utting found that one-fifth of all men were still working full-time with a further 13 per cent working part-time, compared with 9 per cent of women in both categories. Nevertheless, the majority (60 per cent) of old people had income of less than £5 a week, compared with just under one-fifth of income units nationally (19 per cent). There were also fewer old people with incomes at the top of the distribution. This is not surprising because women especially were primarily dependent on state benefit (about one-third were solely dependent). This is because women were less likely to be working and fewer had occupational pensions. Of the quarter already receiving

National Assistance, there were at least as many below National Assistance threshold that were not receiving benefit.[728] Cole and Utting estimate
that in 1959–60 nearly 2.5 million old people were living near to the
poverty line as defined by National Assistance scales.

Townsend and Wedderburn (formerly Dorothy Cole) carried out
a larger-scale inquiry based on two separate random samples of people
65 and over, between May–July 1962 and November–December 1962.
In total 4067 people were interviewed. The sample had a similar age
and sex profile to the population.[729] *Aged and the Welfare State* was an
important study that largely confirmed the conclusions of Cole and
Utting's previous smaller-scale inquiry and enabled the authors to reach
wide-ranging conclusions concerning the relationship between old people,
their families and the state. They also revealed basic facts about the level
of material deprivation experienced by old people in the generally affluent
Britain of the early 1960s.

Townsend and Wedderburn found that basic amenities were lacking
in a high proportion of old people's homes; 27 per cent did not have
access to a fixed bath, with a further 4 per cent sharing a bath with
another household. One in 20 did not have sole use of a lavatory and
about another third only had access to an outside loo. Just over 6 per
cent had no sole use of inside lavatory, fixed bath or kitchen (estimated
equivalent to about 355,000 in the population). Old people living by
themselves had the worst level of provision, with only 40 per cent having
all three basic amenities (sole use of kitchen, sole use of fixed bath and
sole use of inside toilet), compared with 56 per cent of all old people.[730]

Rowntree tells us that in working-class districts of York in 1900, old
people were typically sharing one toilet between 10 people, living in
three households.[731] Despite the manifestly better condition of old
people in 1960s Britain, the extent of amenity deprivation revealed by
Townsend and Wedderburn rests uneasily juxtaposed with gilded
descriptions of 'golden years' or the 'long boom', that have been applied
to the period between the end of the Second World War and the end of
the 1960s. They cite, as a fairly typical example, the housing conditions
of the Shilwells. Mr Shilwell is 80 and his wife is 75 years old:

> Both are frail and he has severe bronchitis. They rent two rooms
> on the ground floor of an old house in a Tyneside city, which has no
> bathroom. The W.C. is in the back yard. They scarcely go out. He said,
> 'with my disability, it is becoming difficult to get to the front door.
> There's a long passage and two steps. And it's very damp indeed.'

They very much want a modern ground-floor home with a bath and indoor W.C.[732]

Wedderburn summarises the main findings with respect to the economic circumstances of old people.[733] First, for seven out of ten old people, income from the state was the main source of income and 30 per cent have no other income. Wedderburn writes that large numbers of old people had incomes close to the current retirement pension and 'This may be somewhat surprising because it is widely held that most old people have some other source of income with which to supplement their pension.'[734] Only about 10 per cent of old people continued to work and had income levels comparable those below retirement age. Second, the problem of inadequate income was greatest among old people who have never worked, like older women. Single and widowed women 'emerge as the largest problem group among the aged'. About 11 per cent of old people had incomes below the National Assistance scale and in general, the problem of inadequate income increased with age, partly because fewer of the very old would receive income from employment.[735]

In terms of the population, these sample estimates suggest that 1.5 million women and 0.25 million men had total weekly incomes of below £4 per week, and about 0.4 million couples had incomes below £6 per week.[736] The National Assistance scale in 1962 was about £3 15s per week (including rent) for a single person and £5 12s for a couple. In Townsend and Wedderburn's sample, the median income of single women was £3 14s per week. They write that:

so very nearly half of all single and widowed women had incomes below this subsistence level. A quarter of the single and widowed men were below it, and another quarter no more than fifth above it. Thirteen per cent of couples had incomes below this subsistence level and approximately another 18 per cent had incomes no more than a fifth above it.[737]

In comparison, median earnings were about £15 per week for adult male manual workers.

Although Townsend and Wedderburn did not collect expenditure data for old age households, the Ministry of Labour 1962 survey did. Of the lowest income group, those with weekly income below £4, the average expenditure on food was 31s 6d (though average total expenditure was 86s 9d). 'The data appear consistent with the figures from the National Food Survey for pensioner households which show a marked improvement in food consumption by pensioners over the period 1956–61.' The general rise in the nutritional status of pensioners might suggest the priority accorded to food expenditure by the old. Even among the lowest income groups of old people food expenditure was sufficient to buy a meat-based diet. Indeed, the National Food Survey data show that the diets of old people were improving, *relative to other groups*, throughout the 1950s, when judged against BMA recommendations, although Lambert has expressed some doubts about the reliability of the data.[738] But once the basic items of housing, food and heating had been paid for there was little left over for clothing or household goods. Single pensioners living alone would be significantly worse off than couples because housing, heating and other items of household expenditure are shared for little extra cost.

Tunstall reached similar conclusions from an interview-based study of 538 old people in Harrow, Northampton, Oldham and south Norfolk in 1963 and 1964.[739] About half of Tunstall's sample were receiving National Assistance and the median income was a little over £4 per week (compared with state retirement pension of £3 7s 6d), and he writes that there was 'obviously little to be spent on anything other than rent (or rates), food and fuel'. Nearly three in five 'isolated' old people reported 'special difficulty' finding enough to cover at least one basic expenditure, with two-thirds of these citing difficulty meeting the cost of fuel.[740]

Many of the retired in the 1950s would have been of prime working age during the Depression. This would help explain why in the 1950s about 30 per cent of old people had no assets at all and another 20 per cent had only trivial assets.[741] As one old person revealed, 'Never had a chance to save – I lay idle for many a year before the war.' And 'How could you save – it took all your time to live those days.'[742] Such was the disparity between those people within the labour force and those outside of it.

6.6   The Rediscovery of Poverty

Abel-Smith and Townsend's *The Poor and the Poorest* is usually seen as providing the first serious challenge to the belief that the Beveridge welfare state had abolished poverty in Britain for good. Published in 1965, the authors argued that despite the apparent prosperity of the

1950s, poverty increased during the decade. Their findings indicated that poverty was still widespread in the United Kingdom among particular types of households, particularly small and large households. Typically, these were the elderly and very large families, comprising six individuals or more.

It is often suggested that their 'rediscovery' of poverty was due to a change in definition, but this is only partly true.[743] While Abel-Smith and Townsend adopt a definition that is, for the first time, explicitly relative, previous work by Townsend and others had catalogued an alarming level of deprivation among Britain's old people. As we have seen, this included a lack of basic amenities and a level of income that provided only for bare necessities of consumption (food, shelter, fuel and light). Moreover, Lambert argued that when the National Food Survey data were analysed by family size, they showed increasing levels of dietary inadequacy during the 1950s.[744] This contention is supported by Wilkinson's analysis of trends in mortality by socio-economic class. He writes that 'By 1961 differentials had widened dramatically and the familiar gradient of death rates was firmly re-established.'[745] He attributes this change in the trend of relative mortality experience to the 'restoration of the market', following the ending of rationing and government controls.

In the *Poor and the Poorest*, Abel-Smith and Townsend used two Family Expenditure Surveys to infer changes in poverty. The first, carried out in 1953–4 by the Ministry of Labour, was the most extensive and was designed to provide information on expenditure weights to allow revision to the official cost of living index, which still used data from the 1937–8 working-class expenditure inquiry. The 1953–4 Household Expenditure Survey was based on 20,000 households, of whom about 13,000 kept detailed budgets. The 2.1 per cent below the National Assistance scale and 10.1 per cent below 140 per cent of the National Assistance scale in 1953–4. This large-scale inquiry was followed by regular, smaller, annual surveys. Abel-Smith and Townsend also analysed evidence from one of these surveys – the 1960 inquiry – which was based on about 5000 households, of whom about 3500 thousand kept budgets.[746]

On the basis of their analysis, Abel-Smith and Townsend estimated that approximately 7.5 million people in Britain in 1960 were in poverty or on the margins of poverty, or 17.9 per cent of households.[747] This was defined as 140 per cent of the then current National Assistance scale plus rent, although this multiple is regarded as rather arbitrary.[748] According to Abel-Smith and Townsend, the 7.5 million people living below 'a defined national assistance level of living', were composed of 35 per cent of households primarily dependent on pension, 23 per cent primarily dependent on state benefit and 41 per cent dependent on earnings.[749] In comparison, in 1953–4, they found 10.1 per cent of households had 'low levels of living'. They attribute this increase partly to demographic factors (relatively more old people in the population and an increase in the proportion of large families) and an increase in the numbers of 'chronic sick' dependent for long periods on sickness benefit. They also do not exclude the possibility that the incomes of the poor did not grow as fast as average incomes.[750]

The 7.5 million people with a low level of living included 2.25 million children and 3 million old people in low-income households in 1960.[751] Abel-Smith and Townsend provide no further breakdown of the causes of poverty in 1960.[752] Timed to coincide with the publication of the *Poor and the Poorest*, the Child Poverty Action Group (CPAG) was launched in December 1965.[753] Although the authors of the *Poor and the Poorest* provided the 'primary initiative' for the CPAG, there is surprisingly little discussion of child poverty in the *Poor and the Poorest*, outside of the final short section dealing with 'implications for policy'. Nevertheless, according to Banting, 'the CPAG campaign made an impact throughout the political world, and family poverty attained an almost immediate salience'.[754] Glennerster's recent assessment is that the press and television coverage resulting from the creation of the CPAG 'forced child poverty back on to the political agenda for the first time since the 1940s'.[755]

Their poverty study was also important for its definite rejection of early twentieth-century methodology. Abel-Smith and Townsend argued that the approach normally identified with Rowntree was conceptually flawed – principally because of the arbitrary nature of the judgement surrounding the definition of subsistence needs, though this fact had been recognised by Bowley in the 1920s. Indeed, as Lowe points out, the concept of relative poverty was not new in social investigation and stretched back to Adam Smith's work in the 1770s.[756]

What Abel-Smith and Townsend reject, though not as explicitly, was a justification for the 'subsistence' poverty-line approach that was based on examining changes in the number of people in poverty over time.[757] It is clear that they believed the changes living standards brought about by the introduction of new products, such as electricity, and changing cultural expectations of poverty, undermined the efficacy of this approach. Instead, they argued that poverty was an entirely relative concept – even over the relatively short run of a decade or so. They write that 'The approach which we have adopted follows from the principle that the minimum level of living regarded as acceptable by a society increases with rising prosperity.'[758]

Gough and Stark, who analyse the proportion of low-income families in the 1950s and 1960s, provided an alternative conceptualisation and reach rather different conclusions from Abel-Smith and Townsend. They adopt two different definitions of low incomes. The first was based on actual National Assistance rates in each year (or this rate plus 20 or 40 per cent), the second used 1948 National Assistance rates scaled by the average increase in income per head since that year.[759] Between 1949 and 1963, National Assistance rates increased much faster than average income per head (153 per cent compared with 120 per cent).[760] This led to an increased divergence between Gough and Stark's two measures, with the lower figure resulting from the application of the second definition. This can be seen from Table 6.12.

It is clear that defining 'low incomes' on the basis of contemporaneous National Assistance scales (definition 1), provides limited evidence for a decline in poverty during the 1950s and early 1960s. This is especially true if National Assistance rates are increased by 40 per cent to take account of special cases. In contrast, basing the definition of 'low income' on the 1948 National Assistance scale multiplied by the growth in average incomes (definition 2), suggests a declining proportion of low-income households – though, again, the decrease is significantly less marked if the National Assistance scale plus 40 per cent is used. Gough and Stark demonstrate that the highest proportions of low-income households were to be found among single-person households and households with two adults and four or more children.[761]

Table 6.12 Proportions and numbers of low-income households, 1954–63 (%; millions of units in parentheses)[a]

	Definition 1	Definition 1, plus 40%	Definition 2	Definition 2, plus 40%
1954	16.7 (4.30)	25.9	16.5 (4.24)	20.6
1959	12.3 (3.16)	22.4	10.9 (2.82)	15.7
1963	13.9 (3.70)	25.4	9.3 (2.48)	15.6

[a] Numbers rounded by author. Proportions and number of people on 'low incomes' differ from these figures.

Source: Extracted from I. Gough and T. Stark, 'Low Incomes in the United Kingdom, 1954, 1959 and 1963', Manchester School (1968), Tables II and III, p. 178.

6.7   Changes in Poverty

Using Family Expenditure Survey data (FES) for the period 1953/4–73, Fiegehen *et al.* evaluated changes in both 'absolute' and relative poverty.[762] Table 6.13 reports their calculations for changes in real income, based on the transformation of the FES data to an equivalent adult couple basis. From these data, Fiegehen *et al.* derive a frequency distribution of equivalent incomes for each household type, so as to generate a composite distribution for all household structures.[763] From Table 6.12 it can be seen that the real gross incomes of the fifth percentile households increased by 63 per cent between 1953/4 and 1971 and by 76 per cent if 1973 is taken as the terminal date instead. For the tenth percentile, the increases are slightly lower. If individuals are considered rather than households, the increases are 55 per cent for both percentiles 1953/4–71 and about 75 per cent between 1953/4 and 1973. Fiegehen *et al.* attribute these changes to increases in economic growth, rather than to a redistribution of income. In comparison with median income, they write that,

> When measured by equivalent net income, the relative living standards of the poor appear to have remained approximately constant between 1953/4 and 1971, at about 49 per cent of the median for the 5th percentile and about 58 per cent for the 10th percentile.[764]

Table 6.13   Real household incomes of the poor 1953/4–73 (equivalent gross incomes at 1971 prices)

	1953/4	*1963*	*1967*	*1971*	*1973*	*Per cent increase*	
						1953/4–71	*1953/4–73*
Households: 5th percentile	7.04	9.04	10.99	11.45	12.40	63	76
Households: 10th percentile	8.61	11.26	13.04	13.25	14.71	54	71
Individuals: 5th percentile	7.63	9.63	11.18	11.80	13.25	55	74
Individuals: 10th percentile	9.10	11.98	13.43	14.10	15.95	55	75

Source: Extracted from G. C. Fiegehen, P. S. Lansley and A. D. Smith, *Poverty and Progress in Britain 1953–73* (CUP, 1977), Table 3.3, p. 26.

Table 6.14 Numbers and proportions of people in 'absolute' poverty, 1953/4–73 (1953/4 National Assistance scale)

	Poverty standard (£/week)	Households (percentage)	Individuals (percentage)	Individuals (millions)
1953/4	3.84	6.5	4.8	2.4
1963	5.07	2.5	1.4	0.8
1967	5.86	0.9	0.9	0.5
1971	7.51	0.5	0.5	0.3
1973	8.78	0.3	0.2	0.1

Source: Extracted from G. C. Fiegehen, P. S. Lansley and A. D. Smith, *Poverty and Progress in Britain 1953–73* (CUP, 1977), Table 3.4, p. 27.

Overall, they conclude that the increase in the real incomes of the poor is the consequence of a general improvement in living standards.

If the 1953/4 National Assistance scale is taken as an income measure of subsistence, and is revalued using the official retail price index, the numbers in 'absolute' poverty decreased dramatically over the same period, as Table 6.14 reveals. The number of individuals falling below this standard fell from 2.4 million in 1953/4 to 0.1 million in 1973. This represented about 4.8 and 0.2 per cent of individuals, respectively and 6.5 and 0.3 per cent of households at the same dates. Alternatively, if the 1971 supplementary benefit scale is taken as the appropriate poverty scale, then the numbers and proportions in poverty greatly increase, because benefits were worth considerably more in real terms in 1971 than they were in 1953/4. Nevertheless, the data still show a significant reduction in poverty. Using the 1971 supplementary benefit level as the standard, held constant in real terms, the number of individuals in poverty fell from 10.6 million in 1953/4 (which is 21 per cent of all individuals and 22.5 per cent of households) to 1.3 million in 1973 (2.3 per cent of all individuals and 3.5 per cent of households).[765]

Of course, it is also possible to calculate the number and proportion of individuals and households falling below contemporaneous indicators of poverty. These are reported in Table 6.15, where for each year, poverty is assessed by the current National Assistance or supplementary benefit scale (plus 30 per cent for rent and other discretionary benefits). This is conceptually identical to Abel-Smith and Townsend's definition of relative poverty, although they used 140 per cent of the benefit scale, rather than 130 per cent. This table appears to indicate that the number and proportion of individuals and households falling below the

Table 6.15   Numbers and proportions of people in relative poverty, 1953/4–73 (current benefit scale plus 30 %)

	Poverty standard (£/week)	Households (percentage)	Individuals (percentage)	Individuals (millions)
1953/4	3.84	6.5	4.8	2.4
1963	6.63	6.8	5.5	3.0
1967	8.78	5.8	5.3	2.9
1971	11.40	4.9	4.2	2.3
1973	14.17	4.3	3.0	1.7

Source: Extracted from G. C. Fiegehen, P. S. Lansley and A. D. Smith, *Poverty and Progress in Britain 1953–73* (CUP, 1977), Table 3.6, p. 29.

contemporaneous benefit level increased until the 1960s and then fell moderately quickly from the end of the 1960s until 1973. However, it is worth noting Fiegehen *et al.*'s caution that this method is 'unsuitable for tracing changes to poverty over time, since the changes revealed may owe as much to modifications of the standards as they do to developments in the nature and extent of poverty'.[766]

Fiegehen *et al.* conclude that the numbers in 'absolute' poverty declined sharply over the course of these two decades, to about a 'tenth, or even a twentieth, of its original level'.[767] But the extent of relative poverty 'probably changed little', which suggests that the decline in absolute poverty is the result of a general improvement in living standards rather than an improvement in the 'relative living standards of the poor'.[768]

For the period between 1961–3 and 1974–6, Beckerman and Clark reached similar conclusions. On a simple headcount measure of poverty, using the contemporaneous supplementary benefit scale as the poverty standard, poverty was 4.8 per cent at both dates. Adjusting for within-year inflation increased measured poverty, nearly doubling it to 8.1 per cent in 1974–6. However, they argue that this increase in the incidence of poverty was partly the consequence of an increase in the proportion of old people in the population (who have a higher incidence of poverty), coupled with an increase in the pensioner poverty line relative to net disposable income.[769]

Beckerman and Clark argue that state benefits were particularly efficacious in reducing the poverty gap during this period. Income maintenance expenditure increased from 6.5 per cent of GDP to 8.0 per cent between these dates (which was partly a consequence of the doubling of unemployment). Although poverty was still widespread, state support affected the extent to which sections of the population were below the poverty line.[770] Although no comparable analysis exists for the interwar period, it seems clear that unemployment provision operated in a similar way in interwar Britain.

Summary

Despite full employment and a growth of average real earnings of nearly 2.5 per cent per annum, poverty was not eradicated in Britain during the 1950s. This was not just because the definition of poverty changed from a relative one, based on the cost of items necessary for subsistence (with or without an extra allowance for social participation), to an alternative relative conception of poverty based on contemporaneous state benefit scales. It was also because Rowntree seriously miscalculated the extent of poverty in York after the Second World War and had wrongly attributed its eradication to the social policies of the 1945 Labour government, who implemented (with some modification) Beveridge's 1942 recommendations.

The causes of poverty *had* changed, however. Unemployment was no longer a significant factor in the period 1945–60. There was evidence of severe material deprivation among old people, who were of prime working age during the interwar Depression and had little opportunity to accumulate saving for their retirement. Moreover, National Assistance scales for the elderly were considerably below 'basic needs' definitions of poverty and many failed to apply for National Assistance in any case. Old age constituted the largest single cause of poverty in Britain at this time. Explicitly relative definitions of poverty also found that children from large families experienced 'low levels of living'. Even though large family households accounted for a relatively small proportion of household types, the proportion of these increased during the 1950s and early 1960s. Indeed, there is some evidence to suggest that although the class gradients in the nutritional adequacy of diets had all but disappeared, the diets of families with three or more children were not meeting contemporaneous dietary standards.

7

CONCLUDING REMARKS

Was poverty less in 1960 than 1900? There are compelling reasons to believe so. Average weekly earnings increased nearly tenfold between 1900 and 1960, double the increase in consumer prices, and the state had taken considerable responsibility for citizens' welfare by the latter date.[771] Of course, this conclusion implies that the term 'poverty' equates with the inability of individuals or families to attain certain basic needs. Once the definition of poverty moves away from this narrow definition, it is not as obvious that poverty was less in 1960 than it had been in 1900, though I would wish to support this contention as well.

Keeping the same standard and examining the way that poverty has changed over time would seem a logical way of addressing how many people were in poverty in 1960, compared with 1900. Using Rowntree's original primary poverty measure, repriced at 1960 prices, would give an answer to this question, but it is not one that many would find acceptable. For while an unchanged poverty standard might be useful for gauging short-run changes, such as whether there were fewer people in poverty before or after the First World War, the poverty measure itself fails to take account of changing cultural norms and rising expectations resulting from increases in living standards. It is for this reason, after all, that Rowntree revised his primary poverty-line measure in 1936.

If it is accepted that all measures of poverty are relative, including those that have been interpreted as measuring some 'absolute' standard, then it is clear that poverty at any date would need to be judged relative to a standard viewed at the time as appropriate. This is what lay behind Abel-Smith and Townsend's desire in the *Poor and the Poorest* to measure changes in poverty relative to contemporaneous measures of adequacy,

186

defined as the current scale of social payment. Another way of addressing the question would be to adopt a measure that was constant in relation to income. It has been argued through this book that rises in income (including more continuous income from full employment), as well as changes in state provision, have been responsible for reducing poverty. In a nutshell, this is why the periods of war stand out as being particularly significant.

Piachaud formalised this idea by suggesting that changes in poverty over time could be investigated by using a constant relative poverty measure, 'if it remains constant to prevailing living standards'.[772] The measure of income suggested by Piachaud was personal disposable income per capita (hereafter income per capita). Comparing poverty standards with income per capita allows a judgement to be made whether the relative poverty measure has increased faster or more slowly than the general increase in incomes. If it has, and poverty remains unchanged or has increased, then part of this increase in measured poverty is due to the relative poverty measure not being held constant.

Piachaud's results, for the first 60 years of the twentieth century, are set out in Tables 7.1 and 7.2. From these tables it can be seen that the poverty level relative to per capita income varies by household type, as might be expected. However, with the exception of Rowntree's 1936 'Human Needs' scale, these poverty scales represent a remarkably constant percentage of income per capita. This would suggest that Rowntree's finding that roughly 10 per cent of the population of York were in primary poverty is comparable with Abel-Smith and Townsend's claim that 2.1 per cent of the population lived below the National Assistance scale in 1953. In other words, the reduction in poverty during the first 50 years of the century was a genuine reduction in relative

Table 7.1   Poverty level, 1899–1960 (£ per week)[a]

	Single adult non-pensioner	Single pensioner	Adult couple	Couple and one child	Couple and three children
1899 Rowntree	0.275	0.275	0.46	0.60	0.88
1936 Rowntree	1.01	0.69	1.38	1.75	2.02
1953 Abel-Smith	1.75	1.75	2.95	3.63	4.98
1960 Abel-Smith	2.50	2.50	4.25	5.20	7.10

[a] It appears that these figures exclude rent.

Table 7.2   Poverty levels as percentage of personal disposable income per capita[a]

	Single adult non-pensioner	Single pensioner	Adult couple	Couple and one child	Couple and three children
1899 Rowntree	36	36	60	78	114
1936 Rowntree	59	40	81	102	118
1953 Abel-Smith	38	38	64	79	109
1960 Abel-Smith	37	37	63	77	105

[a] For 1899 and 1936, Piachaud used consumer expenditure per capita.
Source: Piachaud, 'Poverty in Britain', Table 1, p. 339.

poverty and not the result of using different poverty scales (relative to changes in per capita income, that is).

The exception to this general conclusion is the result of Rowntree's 1936 poverty survey. This poverty scale represents a significantly greater proportion of per capita income, for all household types, than Rowntree's earlier standard or the 1953 National Assistance scale. Although Piachaud does not consider Bowley's poverty standard, for a family of two adults and three children, it is clear that Bowley's standard represents a smaller proportion of 1936 income per capita than Rowntree's 1899 primary poverty line (relative to 1899 income per capita).[773] In consequence, if we are interested in how poverty changed over time, Bowley's standard it is likely to underestimate poverty relative to Rowntree's 1899 standard or the 1953 National Assistance scale.

What factors explain the reduction in poverty in the first half of the twentieth century? Before the First World War the most important causes of poverty were low and irregular wages. The earnings of a significant proportion of wage earners were such that it was not possible to support a household above the level at which contemporaries defined as the poverty line. This, coupled with large family size, almost guaranteed a period in which many working-class families would experience hard times. When children were young, or when they were older and they were not bringing in any income, the economic position of the household was especially vulnerable to illness, loss of employment, or death of a family member. These events could easily force the family into dire straits and even utter destitution if the cause continued unabated. As family size continued to fall, and married women's labour force participation increased, the grinding poverty associated with too many mouths to feed on too few resources gradually assumed less importance.

In addition, at the end of their lives, many old people would end up in poverty. In fact, this is one of the constant themes that emerge from the analysis presented in this book. Old age is identified consistently as an important cause of poverty, and as other causes of poverty ceased to be as important, the relative importance of poverty among the elderly increases. Despite non-contributory pensions in 1911, contributory pensions from 1925 and the Beveridge reforms of the 1940s, old age meant poverty for a significant proportion of those over retirement age, once they withdrew from the labour force. This was for a variety of different reasons, but initially benefit levels in old age were only paid at 70 years of age and the pension was below subsistence. The position of old people improved somewhat when contributory pensions were introduced at age 65, coupled with the ameliorating effect of falling prices. It is not until after the Second World War, however, that the evidence of poverty surveys suggests that old people generally had sufficient income to satisfy their basic material needs, though many did not receive the state benefits that they were entitled to. What they lacked, often, was anything extra that would allow for social participation. This was increasingly a problem because fewer of Britain's elderly were living with their family and increasing numbers were living alone.

Unemployment is only a major cause of poverty during the interwar period. Prior to the First World War, unemployment played a contributory role – sometimes a crucial role – but it is only during the 1920s and 1930s that persistent joblessness becomes the most important cause of poverty. In the years after the Second World War, until the middle of the 1960s at least, it is fair to say that unemployment is almost irrelevant. This conclusion is, of course, heavily dependent on the chosen period of this investigation. Taking a perspective of twentieth-century history, it is the full employment period of the post-Second World War boom that stands out as being unusual, not the joblessness of the 1930s. However, what set the 1930s apart from the 1920s and probably the years before the First World War, was an increase in the duration of unemployment. The precise impact that this had on health may never be known. Certainly, the lack of good longitudinal data does not make enquiry any easier, but it appears from the Pilgrim Trust's work that the relative impact of unemployment on skilled workers may, if anything, have been worse than its impact on the unskilled.

The argument advanced here is that state assistance for the unemployed during the Depression, in terms of unemployment benefits and increasingly generous poor relief, aided by a fall in consumer prices, helped prevent there being serious health consequences. Indeed, it is the 30-year period between 1920 and about 1950 that stands out as one in which the role of the state in alleviating poverty was seemingly at its greatest.

NOTES

1   Quoted in Charles Smith, *Britain's Food Supplies in Peace and War* (1940), p. 271.
2   Wilfred Beckerman and Stephen Clark, *Poverty and Social Security in Britain since 1961* (1982), p. 1.
3   See Vic George and Irving Howards, *Poverty Amidst Affluence* (1991), pp. 1–22.
4   These tend to be very low and quite controversial. See, for example, A. S. Truswell, 'Minimal Estimates of Needs and Recommended Intakes of Nutrients', in J. Yudkin (ed.), *The Diet of Man: Needs and Wants* (London, 1978), pp. 4–19.
5   Martin Rein, 'Problems in the Definition and Measurement of Poverty', in Peter Townsend (ed.), *The Concept of Poverty* (1970).
6   P. Townsend and D. Wedderburn, *The Aged and the Welfare State* (1970), Ch. 4.
7   See, for example, the description of Rowntree's 'Human Needs' standard in John Veit-Wilson, 'Muddle or Mendacity? The Beveridge Committee and the Poverty Line', in John Hills, John Ditch and Howard Glennerster, *Beveridge and Social Security* (1994).
8   Following Piachaud, George and Howards postulate a further division between subsistence and social participation, namely 'social coping', but this further refinement has not been followed here, as it does not appear to have great heuristic merit. George and Howards, *Poverty Amidst Affluence*.
9   David Piachaud, 'Poverty in Britain 1899 to 1983', *Journal of Social Policy*, 17 (1988).
10 Jonathan Bradshaw, Deborah Mitchell and Jane Morgan, 'Evaluating Adequacy: the Potential of Budgetary Standards', *Journal of Social Policy*, 16, 2 (1987), p. 167.
11 Bradshaw *et al.*, 'Evaluating Adequacy', p. 167.
12 Peter Townsend, *Poverty in the United Kingdom* (1979).
13 Amartya Sen, 'Issues in the Measurement of Poverty', *Scandinavian Journal of Economics*, 81 (1979), p. 289.
14 Bradshaw *et al.*, 'Evaluating Adequacy', p. 167.
15 An exception to this general statement is Beckerman and Clark, *Poverty and Social Security in Britain since 1961*. But as the title implies, Beckerman and Clark are largely concerned with poverty in the period following the time span of this study.
16 Amartya Sen, *Poverty and Famines* (1981), p. 33.
17 A. D. K. Owen, *A Survey of the Standard of Living in Sheffield* (1933). The data are insufficiently disaggregated to calculate the income gap, however. And even if it were possible, income gap measures of poverty are insensitive to intra-poor

transfers of income, as long as nobody moves out of poverty as a result. See Sen, *Poverty and Famines*, p. 33.

18 Jose Harris, *William Beveridge* (1997), p. 382.

19 John Boyd Orr, *Food Health and Income* (1936).

20 Sen, *Poverty and Famines*, pp. 27–8.

21 J. Stern, 'The Relationship between Unemployment, Morbidity and Mortality in Britain', *Population Studies*, 37 (1983).

22 Noel Whiteside, 'Counting the Cost: Sickness and Disability among Working People in an Era of Industrial Recession, 1920–39', *Economic History Review* (May 1987).

23 Readers requiring a fuller discussion of the development of welfare policies should consult Pat Thane's *The Foundation of the Welfare State* (2000), or Derek Fraser's *The Evolution of the Welfare State* (2002) for the period before the Second World War. For the post-war period, readers are referred to Howard Glennerster's *British Social Policy since 1945* (1995) or Rodney Lowe's *The Welfare State in Britain since 1945* (1993).

24 Not because these are unimportant, but because there are already good books that cover this material. For example, David Vincent, *Poor Citizens* (1991).

25 N. F. R. Crafts, 'Patterns of Development in Nineteenth Century Europe', *Oxford Economic Papers*, 36 (1984) and *British Economic Growth During the Industrial Revolution* (1985).

26 W. Ashworth, *An Economic History of England 1870–1939* (1960), p. 3.

27 A. H. Halsey, *Change in British Society*, 4th edn (1995), Table 2.1, pp. 40–1.

28 Note that this contrasts with Rowntree's implied estimate of the size of the working class in 1900. He thought that the non-servant-keeping class accounted for about two-thirds of the population of York. *Poverty: A Study in Town Life*, pp. 14 and 26.

29 The Hamilton Committee carried out a survey of representative areas within 28 poor law unions in England and Wales to ascertain the likely demand for old age pensions. The range in the proportion of old people in urban areas was 3.3–3.5 per cent compared with 7.6 per cent in some rural areas. Cited in Pat Thane, *Old Age in English History* (2000), pp. 211–12.

30 Karel Williams, *From Pauperism to Poverty* (1981), Table 4.5, p. 161.

31 Derek Fraser, *The Evolution of the Welfare State*, 2nd edn (1984), p. 103.

32 Fraser, *The Evolution of the Welfare State*, pp. 130–1.

33 Fraser, *The Evolution of the Welfare State*, p. 108.

34 *The Minority Report of the Poor Law Commission, Part I, Summary and Conclusions* (1909), pp. 574–5.

35 Pat Thane, *The Foundations of the Welfare State*, 2nd edn (1996), pp. 81–3.

36 Williams, *From Pauperism to Poverty*, p. 91.

37 From 1911, however, all poor law unions were able to offer unemployed men and their families out relief on the basis of a 'labour test'.

38 Thane, *The Foundations of the Welfare State*, pp. 33–4.

39 The totals include casuals and the insane.

40 Williams, *From Pauperism to Poverty*, p. 129.

41 A. L. Bowley and A. R. Burnett-Hurst, *Livelihood and Poverty* (1915), pp. 39–40.

42 This is especially true of the rural surveys. In Corsley, 15 families in the village were in receipt of relief during 1904–5. Many old people of Corsley refused to apply for relief because of independence of spirit and self-sacrifice of their children who supported them in old age. Maud F. Davies, *Life in an English Village*

(1909), p. 189. In Ridgmount, 25 families were in receipt of relief. P. H. Mann, 'Life in an Agricultural Village in England', *Sociological Papers* (1904), p. 178. In Dundee, 132 families (just over 4 per cent) were receiving out relief. These were widows, old people and invalids and received amounts varying between 1s 6d and 10s per week, which were 'insufficient for maintenance'. Dundee Social Union, *Report on Housing and Industrial Conditions* (Dundee, 1905), p. 28.

43 *How the Destitute Live* (Liberal Christian League, 1912), p. 37.
44 *How the Destitute Live*, pp. 18–19.
45 *How the Destitute Live*, p. 34.
46 W. H. Beveridge, *Unemployment: a Problem of Industry* (1909 and 1930), p. 261.
47 Beveridge, *Unemployment*, pp. 257–61.
48 Thane, *Foundations of the Welfare State*, pp. 69–90.
49 Social reformers and investigators were influential in framing both pieces of legislation. Booth and Cadbury acted as advisors on pensions and the unemployment insurance scheme owes much to Beveridge and his emphasis on the cyclical and seasonal nature of unemployment. Indeed, the scheme was to be administered by labour exchanges, which he had also played an important role in setting up in 1909.
50 Thane, *Old Age in English History*, pp. 226–8.
51 A. L. Bowley, *Wages and Income since 1860* (Cambridge, 1937 and references therein) and G. H. Wood, 'Real Wages and the Standard of Comfort since 1850', *Journal of the Royal Statistical Society* (1909), pp. 91–103.
52 Bowley, *Wages and Income since 1860*, Table VII, p. 30.
53 T. R. Gourvish, 'The Standard of Living', in A. O'Day, *The Edwardian Age* (1979), provides a useful review.
54 See also I. Gazeley, 'The Cost of Living for Urban Workers', *Economic History Review* (1989).
55 See E. H. Hunt, *Regional Wage Variations in Britain, 1850–1914* (Oxford, 1973) and Gourvish, 'The Standard of Living' for a survey. Also G. J. Barnsby, 'The Standard of Living in the Black Country during the Nineteenth Century', *Economic History Review* (1971), E. Hopkins, 'Small Town Aristocrat of Labour and their Standards of Living, 1840–1914', *Economic History Review* (1975), S. Pollard, 'Real Earnings in Sheffield, 1851–1914', *Yorkshire Bulletin of Economic and Social Research*, 9 (1957), S. Pollard, 'Wages and Earnings in the Sheffield Trades, 1851–1914', *Yorkshire Bulletin of Economic and Social Research*, 6 (1954) and A. A. Hall, 'Wages, Earnings and Real Earnings in Teeside', *International Review of Social History*, XXVI, 2 (1981).
56 H. Phelps Brown, *The Inequality of Pay* (1977), Table 3.1, p. 71.
57 J. G. Williamson, 'The Structure of Pay in Britain, 1710–1911', *Research in Economic History*, 7 (1982), Table 2, p. 15 and Table 3, p. 17. See also *Did British Capitalism Breed Inequality?* (1985), Tables 3.6 and 3.8, pp. 48–9.
58 W. A. Mackenzie, 'Changes in the Standard of Living in the United Kingdom, 1860–1914', *Economica*, No. 3 (1921), p. 213.
59 P. Snowden, *The Living Wage* (1912), p. 28. The difference possibly reflects Bowley's inclusion of mining and agriculture in the 1906 census data. Snowden reminds us that these figures refer to full-time earnings and do not take account of loss of earnings due to short time or unemployment.
60 Bowley, *Wages and Incomes since 1860*, p. 51.

61   E. Cadbury, Cecile M. Matheson and G. Shann, *Women's Work and Wages*, 2nd edn (1908), p. 128.

62   Cadbury *et al.*, *Women's Work and Wages*, pp. 210 and 214.

63   Cadbury *et al.*, *Women's Work and Wages*, p. 220.

64   E. Roberts, 'Working-class Standards of Living in Three Lancashire Towns, 1890–1914', *International Review of Social History* (1982), pp. 48–9.

65   E. Roberts, *Women's Work, 1840–1940* (CUP, 1995), p. 37.

66   Roberts, *Women's Work*, p. 15.

67   Roberts, 'Working-class Standards of Living', p. 54.

68   E. G. Howarth and M. Wilson, *West Ham: a Study in Social and Industrial Problems* (1907), p. 269. Usually tailoring or dressmaking done at home. Their survey included 516 households in which women or girls were so engaged. In just over half of these the husbands were engaged in 'regular employment'.

69   Angela John, 'Introduction', in Angela John (ed.), *Unequal Opportunities: Women's Employment in England 1800–1918* (1986), pp. 3–5 and Appendix B, pp. 36–7.

70   Roberts, *Women's Work*, Table 3.1, p. 36.

71   Cadbury *et al.*, *Women's Work and Wages*, pp. 171–4.

72   Roberts, *Women's Work*, p. 40.

73   Thane, *Foundations of the Welfare State*, p. 40.

74   Mackenzie, 'Changes in the Standard of Living in the United Kingdom', p. 227.

75   Cd 2337 (1905) B.P.P. *Consumption and the Cost of Food in Workmen's Families in Urban Districts of the United Kingdom*, p. 9.

76   Cd 1761 (1903) B.P.P. *Consumption of Food and Cost of Living of Working Classes in the United Kingdom and Certain Foreign Countries*, p. 211.

77   Eleanor Rathbone, *How the Casual Labourer Lives*, Report of the Liverpool Joint Research Committee on Domestic Conditions and Expenditure of the Families of Certain Liverpool Labourers (Liverpool, 1909), p. xxv.

78   See S. J. Prais and H. S. Houthakker, *The Analysis of Family Budgets* (Cambridge, 1971).

79   Rathbone, *How the Casual Labourer Lives*, p. xiv.

80   Cd 3864 (1908) B.P.P. *Cost of Living of the Working Classes. Report of an Enquiry by the Board of Trade into Working-Class Rents, Housing and Retail Prices Together with Standard Rates of Wages Prevailing in Certain Occupations in Principal Industrial Towns in the United Kingdom*, pp. xxxi–xxxii.

81   Cd 6955 (1912–13) B.P.P. *Cost of Living of the Working Classes. Report of an Enquiry by the Board of Trade into Working-Class Rents and Retail Prices Together with the Rates of Wages in Certain Occupations in Industrial Towns in the United Kingdom.*

82   Earlier eighteenth-century examples would include F. M. Eden, *The State of the Poor* (London, 1797) and D. Davies, *The Case of Labourers in Husbandry* (Bath, 1795).

83   M.Bulmer, K. Bales and K. Kish Sklar, 'The Social Survey in Historical Perspective', in M. Bulmer, K. Bales and K. Kish Sklar (eds), *The Social Survey in Historical Perspective* (1991), p. 1.

84   An early empirical inquiry is W. Neild, 'Comparative Statement of the Income and Expenditure of Certain Families of the Working-Classes in Manchester and Dukfield, in the Years 1836 and 1841', *Journal of the Statistical Society*, IV (1841), pp. 330–4. This provides a contrast with the impressionistic study by Henry Mayhew undertaken a little later in *London Labour and London Poor*, 3 vols (London, 1851–52) and *London Labour and the London Poor*, 4 vols (London, 1861–62).

85 Bulmer *et al.*, 'The Social Survey in Historical Perspective', p. 19.

86 See Andrew Mearns, 'The Bitter Cry of Outcast London' in Peter Keating (ed.), *Into Unknown England* (1976), pp. 91–111 and Bulmer *et al.*, 'The Social Survey in Historical Perspective'.

87 Bulmer *et al.*, 'The Social Survey in Historical Perspective', p. 19. Further analysis of the evolution of Booth's ideas can be found in Jane Lewis, 'Social Facts, Social Theory and Social Change: the Ideas of Booth in Relation to Those of Beatrice Webb, Octavia Hill and Helen Bosanquet', in David Englander and Rosemary O'Day (eds), *Retrieved Riches: Social Investigation in Britain 1840–1914* (1995).

88 See Jose Harris, *Unemployment and Politics* (1972 and 1984), pp. 7–50 for a detailed account of contemporary investigation of the late Victorian and Edwardian labour market.

89 E. P. Hennock, 'Concepts of Poverty in the British Social Surveys from Charles Booth to Arthur Bowley', in Bulmer *et al.*, *The Social Survey in Historical Perspective* (1991), p. 189.

90 Jose Harris, *Private Lives, Public Spirit: Britain 1870–1914* (1993), p. 204.

91 Thane, *Foundations of the Welfare State*, pp. 37–45 and Bulmer *et al.*, 'The Social Survey in Historical Perspective', p. 23.

92 See G. R. Searle, 'Critics of Edwardian Society: the Case of the Radical Right', in Alan O'Day (ed.), *The Edwardian Age* (1979).

93 Hennock, 'Concepts of Poverty', p. 201.

94 Joanna Bourke, *Dismembering the Male* (1996), pp. 13–14.

95 Harris, *Unemployment and Politics*, p. 141.

96 Thane, *Foundations of the Welfare State*, pp. 64–5 and cited in Harris, *Unemployment and Politics*, p. 141.

97 Williams, *From Pauperism to Poverty*, p. 355.

98 Snowden, *The Living Wage*, pp. 44–5.

99 Asa Briggs, *Social Thought and Social Action: a Study of the Work of Seebohm Rowntree* (1961), p. 25.

100 Briggs, *Social Thought and Social Action*, p. 26.

101 Briggs, *Social Thought and Social Action*, p. 25.

102 Williams, *From Pauperism to Poverty*, pp. 346–9.

103 Rowntree, *Poverty*, pp. 111–18.

104 Rowntree, *Poverty*, pp. 111 and 117.

105 For recent contributions, see Hennock, 'Concepts of Poverty', and J. H. Veit-Wilson, 'Paradigms of Poverty: a Rehabilitation of B. S. Rowntree', in David Englander and Rosemary O'Day (eds), *Retrieved Riches: Social Investigation in Britain 1840–1914* (1995).

106 Veit-Wilson, 'Paradigms of Poverty', pp. 203–7.

107 Hennock, 'Concepts of Poverty', p. 205.

108 Hennock, 'Concepts of Poverty', p. 195.

109 Veit-Wilson, 'Paradigms of Poverty', pp. 203–7.

110 Much of the following argument is based upon I. S. Gazeley and A. Newell, 'Rowntree Revisited: Poverty in Britain, 1900', *Explorations in Economic History*, 37 (2000).

111 Rowntree, *Poverty*, pp. 99–106.

112 Veit-Wilson, 'Paradigms of Poverty', p. 212.

113 See for example M. Rein, 'Problems in the Definition and Measurement of Poverty', in P. Townsend (ed.), *The Concept of Poverty* (1971), pp. 44–63.

114 P. Townsend, quoted in Rein, 'Problems', p. 57.

115 Rowntree's diets are in excess of mathematical least cost by about 200 per cent, though the extent varies with household composition – I. S. Gazeley, D.Phil. thesis, 'The Standard of Living of the Working-Classes, 1881–1912' (1985), Table 13, p. 349.

116 Williams, *From Pauperism to Poverty*, pp. 357–8.

117 See Veit-Wilson, 'Paradigms of Poverty', p. 202.

118 Veit-Wilson, 'Paradigms of Poverty', pp. 213–16 and Veit-Wilson, 'Condemned to Deprivation? Beveridge's Responsibility for the Invisibility of Poverty', in John Hills, John Ditch and Howard Glenneste (eds), *Beveridge and Social Security* (1994).

119 Briggs, *Social Thought and Social Action*, p. 30.

120 Cited in Briggs, *Social Thought and Social Action*, p. 33.

121 Rowntree, *Poverty*, p. 122.

122 Rowntree *Poverty*, p. 122.

123 C. Booth, *Life and Labour of the People of London* (1889), pp. 132 and 138. Booth gives few details of non-food equivalence, and food equivalent scales are noted for representative families only. In Llewelyn Smith's *New Survey*, a table of dietary equivalent scales for Booth is given and described as 'rough estimates' (Vol. iii, p. 433). Linsley and Linsley have interpreted these scales as all expenditure 'equivalent scales', and, from the piecemeal evidence recorded in Booth's survey, they might be right. *Economic History Review* (1993), p. 90. If interpreted in this fashion, the equivalent scales look remarkably like Bowley's 'new standard'.

124 Rowntree, *Poverty*, p. 136. As other writers have noted, Rowntree's analysis is permeated by contradiction and inconsistency at various points in the text. See Veit-Wilson, 'Paradigms of Poverty', p. 204.

125 Rowntree's subsequent tables refer to families with a notional number of 'school children'. Rowntree, *Poverty*, p. 137.

126 I. Gazeley and A. Newell, 'Rowntree Revisited: Poverty in Britain, 1900', *Explorations in Economic History*, 37 (2000).

127 Rowntree, *Poverty*, p. 138.

128 Rowntree, *Poverty*, p. 141. Men and women at 6d per day, children of 12 at 6d per day, children of 2 yrs 4d per day (average primary poverty cost of clothing for children 5d per day).

129 Rowntree, *Poverty*, p. 141. Fuel at 1s 10d per week and sundries at 2d per capita per week.

130 Rowntree found that 1465 families (7230 individuals) were living below his primary poverty-line income.

131 Gazeley and Newell, 'Rowntree Revisited', pp. 184–7.

132 Bowley and Burnett-Hurst, *Livelihood and Poverty*, pp. 9–11.

133 Hennock, 'Concepts of Poverty', p. 207.

134 Bowley and Burnett-Hurst, *Livelihood and Poverty*, pp. 16 and 46.

135 Bowley and Burnett-Hurst, *Livelihood and Poverty*, p. 36.

136 Bowley and Burnett-Hurst, *Livelihood and Poverty*, p. 80 and Hennock, 'Concepts of Poverty', p. 207. As Hennock points out, Bowley recognised that Rowntree's minimum needs measure for rent and sundries was socially determined, and

modified Rowntree's food component to reflect conventional standards of consumption.

137 Bowley and Burnett-Hurst, *Livelihood and Poverty*, p. 91. His equivalent scale was: boys 14–18 and girls 14–16 were 0.75, children 5–14 were 0.5 and infants under 5 were 0.25 adult equivalent.

138 The minimum food needs of adults and children in Bowley's 'new standard' are: males 18 yrs and over 1.0; female 18 yrs and over 0.8; males 16–18 yrs 0.85; female 16–18 yrs 0.8; males 14–16 yrs 0.85; females 14–16 yrs 0.7; children 5–14 yrs 0.5; children 0–5 yrs 0.33; old aged 0.6. Bowley and Burnett-Hurst, *Livelihood and Poverty*, p. 80.

139 Bowley and Burnett-Hurst, *Livelihood and Poverty*, p. 12. The population of Northampton was 90,064, Warrington 72,100 and Reading 87,693. Stanley was significantly smaller, with a population of 23,294 in 1911.

140 Bowley and Burnett-Hurst, *Livelihood and Poverty*, p. 41.

141 Bowley and Burnett-Hurst, *Livelihood and Poverty*, p. 34.

142 Note that the figures for Stanley are based on very small absolute numbers as only 12 out of 203 working-class households were in primary poverty.

143 Bowley and Burnett-Hurst, *Livelihood and Poverty*, pp. 30–1.

144 Sara Horrell and Deborah Oxley, 'Crust or Crumb?: Intra-household Resource Allocation and Male Breadwinning in Late Victorian Britain', *Economic History Review*, LII, 3 (1999), p. 500. Based on the analysis of the United States Commissioner of Labour household budgets for 1890–91.

145 Horrell and Oxley, 'Crust or Crumb?', p. 507.

146 Rowntree, *Poverty*, p. 178.

147 Pilgrim Trust, *Men without Work* (1938), pp. 102–3.

148 Dundee Social Union, *Report on Housing and Industrial Conditions* (Dundee, 1905) pp. 24–5.

149 Dundee Social Union, *Report on Housing and Industrial Conditions*. Calculated from Table A, p. 26.

150 Angela John, 'Introduction', in *At the Works* (Virago, 1985), pp. xi–xiii.

151 John, 'Introduction', pp. ix–x.

152 John, 'Introduction', p. x.

153 John, 'Introduction', p. xii.

154 Florence Bell, *At the Works* (Virago, 1985), p. 47.

155 Bell, *At the Works*, p. 51.

156 Bell, *At the Works*, p. 50.

157 Bell, *At the Works*, p. 51.

158 Bell, *At the Works*, p. 52.

159 Sally Alexander, 'Introduction', in *Round About a Pound a Week* (Virago, 1979).

160 Maud Pember Reeves, *Round About a Pound a Week* (Virago, 1979), p. 9.

161 A. E. Dingle, 'Drink and Working-Class Living Standards in Britain, 1870–1914', *Economic History Review* (1975), p. 609. Figures refer to average consumption per year.

162 Pember Reeves, *Round About a Pound a Week*, p. 66.

163 Pember Reeves, *Round About a Pound a Week*, p. 68.

164 Robert Roberts, *The Classic Slum* (1973), p. 104.

165 Bell, *At the Works*, p. 77.

166 Bell, *At the Works*, pp. 83–4.

167   Eleanor Rathbone, *How the Casual Labourer Lives* (Liverpool, 1909), p. xv.

168   Pat Thane, *Old Age in English History* (2000), p. 292.

169   Bell, *At the Works*, p. 47.

170   W. H. Beveridge, *Unemployment: a Problem of Industry* (1909 and 1930), p. 68.

171   Beveridge, *Unemployment*, p. 75.

172   Beveridge, *Unemployment*, p. 76.

173   B. S. Rowntree and B. Lasker, *Unemployment: a Social Study* (1911).

174   Rowntree and Lasker, *Unemployment*, p. viii.

175   Rowntree and Lasker, *Unemployment*, p. x. The categories were: under 19 years old, regular workers, casual workers, building trade workers, 'workshy' and women and girls. A typical 'character report', provided by a teacher, on one unemployed youth was: 'Thriftless family. Father dead. Mother drinks. Bad school attendance. Often in rags and underfed. Normal intelligence.' Rowntree and Lasker, *Unemployment*, p. 6.

176   Rowntree and Lasker, *Unemployment*, p. 68.

177   Rowntree and Lasker, *Unemployment*, pp. 62 and 66.

178   Rowntree and Lasker, *Unemployment*, p. 61.

179   Rowntree and Lasker, *Unemployment*, p. 224.

180   Pember Reeves, *Round About a Pound a Week*, p. 210.

181   See T. C. Barker, D. J. Oddy and J. Yudkin, *The Dietary Surveys of Dr Edward Smith* (1970).

182   N. Paton, J. C. Dunlop and E. Inglis, *On the Dietaries of the Labouring Classes of the City of Edinburgh* (1901), p. 2, A. E. Carver, *An Investigation of the Dietary of the Labouring Classes of Birmingham* (1913), p. 7 and D. E. Lindsay, *Report upon the Study of the Diet of the Labouring Classes in the City of Glasgow, 1911–12* (1913), pp. 30–1.

183   Lindsay included five Jewish and three Italian families in her survey. Lindsay, *Report*, pp. 23–6.

184   The method adopted by Rowntree and Bowley is identical to the dietary surveys up to the point of comparing family diet with a recommended dietary allowance and then costing a diet that would satisfy this standard. Rowntree and Bowley go further by incorporating the cost of this diet into a poverty line.

185   Lindsay, *Report*, p. 10.

186   See, for example, A. S. Truswell, 'Minimal Estimates of Needs and Recommended Intakes of Nutrients', in J. Yudkin (ed.), *The Diet of Man: Needs and Wants* (1978), pp. 4–19.

187   *Energy and Protein Requirements*. Report of the Joint Expert Committee of the Food and Agriculture Organization of the United Nations and the World Health Organization *ad hoc* committee, Technical Report series, No. 522 (1973), p. 73.

188   D. S. Miller, 'Nutritional Surveys', in D. J. Oddy and D. S. Miller (eds), *The Making of the Modern British Diet* (1976), p. 208.

189   A. E. Carver, *Investigation*, pp. 7–8.

190   In the Edinburgh and Glasgow studies, families were required to store food waste, which was subsequently analysed by the investigators.

191   Booth, *Life and Labour*, Table 2, p. 156. It may not be possible to generalise these results to areas outside of London, however. Cd 2337 reports the analysis of 1994 working-class budgets and shows that workers' families in London and the

suburbs spent consistently higher amounts on 'meals out' than in other regions. *Second Series of Memoranda, Statistical Tables and Charts*, PP LXXXIV (1905), pp. 21–5.

192   W. H. Chaloner, 'Trends in Fish Consumption', in T. C. Barker, J. C. McKenzie and J. Yudkin (eds), *Our Changing Fare* (1966), pp. 109–10.

193   See J. Treble, *Urban Poverty in Britain* (1979), p. 195.

194   Dingle, 'Drink and Working-Class Living Standards in Britain', p. 614.

195   Paton *et al*. applied a standard of 130 g of protein, 100 g of fat and 500 g of carbohydrate per man-day (p. 9); Lindsay used a standard of 120 g protein, 100 g of fat and 500 g of carbohydrate per man-day (p. 6); while Carver's was 62 g of protein, 110 g fat and 425 g carbohydrate (p. 36).

196   J. C. Drummond and A. Wilbraham, *The Englishman's Food* (1957), p. 403.

197   W. A. Mackenzie, 'Changes in the Standard of Living in the United Kingdom, 1860–1914', *Economica*, No. 3 (1921), pp. 223–7. It may be that Mackenzie's estimates need revision given the recent revisions made to the data on wages and prices for this period.

198   Mackenzie, 'Changes in the Standard of Living in the United Kingdom', p. 226.

199   D. Oddy, in D. Oddy and D. S. Miller (eds), *The Making of the Modern British Diet* (1976), p. 225. See also D. J. Oddy, 'Working-Class Diets in Late Nineteenth-Century Britain', *Economic History Review* (1970), pp. 321–2.

200   P. E. Dewey, 'Nutrition and Living Standards in Wartime Britain', in R. Wall and J. M. Winter (eds), *The Upheaval of War* (1988), p. 198, Table 6.1.

201   Oddy's estimates do not appear wholly reliable. Budget studies for the period typically only record expenditure on food items. Oddy transformed these figures into quantities by deflating the expenditure figures by the relevant prevailing price. He used the same price for each article of food for all years 1887–1912, at a time when the prices of food were changing quite rapidly. His average price is liable to underestimate food quantities (and hence per capita nutrient consumption) when food prices were falling (in the late nineteenth century) and overestimate food quantities when food prices were rising (towards the end of the period). See I. S. Gazeley, D. Phil. thesis, 'Standard of Living of the Working Classes 1881–1912: the Cost of Living and the Analysis of Family Budgets' (Oxford, 1985), pp. 299–300.

202   B. S. Rowntree, *Poverty* (Macmillan, 1904), p. 135 and Report of the Inter-Departmental Committee on Physical Deterioration PP 1904 (Cd 2175) XXXII, quoted in J. Burnett, *Plenty and Want* (1966), p. 272.

203   Paton *et al.*, *On the Dietaries*, pp. 70–3.

204   Lindsay, *Report*, p. 33.

205   Elizabeth Roberts, 'Working-Class Standards of Living in Barrow and Lancaster, 1890–1914', *Economic History Review* (1977), p. 315.

206   Pember Reeves, *Round About a Pound a Week*, p. 97.

207   *How the Casual Labourer Lives*. Report of the Liverpool Joint Research Committee on the Domestic Condition and Expenditure of the Families of Certain Liverpool Labourers (Liverpool, 1909), pp. 44–5 (written by Eleanor Rathbone). This menu is reproduced in Treble, *Urban Poverty in Britain* (1979), p. 153 and in W. H. B. Court, *British Economic History 1870–1914* (1965), p. 312.

208   Burnett, *Plenty and Want*, p. 272.

209   Paton *et al.*, *On the Dietaries*, p. 79, Lindsay, *Report*, pp. 27–9 and Carver, *An Investigation*, pp. 38–45.

210 Paton *et al.*, *On the Dietaries*, pp. 78–9.

211 Pember Reeves, *Round About a Pound a Week*, p. 145.

212 Oddy, in Oddy and Miller (eds), *The Making of the Modern British Diet*, p. 226.

213 See, for example, *Recommended Intakes of Nutrients for the United Kingdom*. Department of Health and Social Security: Reports on Health and Medical Subjects No.120 (HMSO, 1969) and *Recommended Dietary Allowances* (National Research Council, 1980), p. 23.

214 Dorothy Hollingsworth, 'Developments Leading to Present-day Nutritional Knowledge', in Oddy and Miller (eds), *The Making of the Modern British Diet*, pp. 192–3.

215 Roberts, 'Working-Class Standards of Living', p. 310.

216 Roberts, 'Working-Class Standards of Living', pp. 314–15.

217 P. H. Mann, 'Life in an Agricultural Village in England', *Sociological Papers* (1904).

218 Mann, 'Life in an Agricultural Village', pp. 170–1. Mann's calculations included income from 'harvest payments' and food grown on allotments; 25 families were in receipt of poor relief in January 1904.

219 Mann, 'Life in an Agricultural Village', pp. 176 and 185.

220 Mann, 'Life in an Agricultural Village', p. 178.

221 Mann, 'Life in an Agricultural Village', p. 192.

222 Mann, 'Life in an Agricultural Village', p. 193.

223 Maud F. Davies, *Life in an English Village* (1909), p. 132.

224 Davies, *Life in an English Village*, p. 136.

225 Davies, *Life in an English Village*, pp. 117–18.

226 Davies, *Life in an English Village*, pp. 120–1.

227 Davies, *Life in an English Village*, p. 138.

228 Davies, *Life in an English Village*, p. 139.

229 Davies, *Life in an English Village*, p. 141.

230 Davies, *Life in an English Village*, p. 142.

231 Davies, *Life in an English Village*, p. 145.

232 Davies, *Life in an English Village*, p. 147.

233 Davies, *Life in an English Village*, pp. 193–4.

234 Davies, *Life in an English Village*, p. 195.

235 Davies, *Life in an English Village*, pp. 151–4.

236 Davies, *Life in an English Village*, p. 153.

237 Davies, *Life in an English Village*, p. 289.

238 B. S. Rowntree and M. Kendall, *How the Labourer Lives: a Study of the Rural Labour Problem* (1913), p. 38.

239 Rowntree and Kendall, *How the Labourer Lives*, p. 297.

240 Rowntree and Kendall, *How the Labourer Lives*, pp. 36–7.

241 *Earnings and Hours of Labour in 1907* (Cd 5460).

242 Rowntree and Kendall, *How the Labourer Lives*, pp. 23–4. Of the total of 457,639 agricultural labourers in England and Wales surveyed, the frequency distribution of earnings (including perquisites) was 7.7 per cent with earnings less than 16s per week; 16.7 per cent between 16s and 17s; 21.2 per cent between 17s and 18s; 44.1 per cent between 18s and 20s and 9.5 per cent over 20s. Table p. 25.

243 Roughly 40 per cent had incomes less than 17s per week compared with 24 per cent in the 1907 earnings inquiry. Calculated from Rowntree and Kendall, *How the Labourer Lives*, Table 25 and frequency distribution given on p. 298.

244 Rowntree and Kendall, *How the Labourer Lives*, pp. 27–30. Although Rowntree and Kendall state that they use Atwater's equivalence scale, this was also for Rowntree's York survey. In the 1901 study Rowntree actually used an equivalence scale that valued all schoolchildren's food needs as equal to 0.75 of an adult. It seems likely that this procedure was also followed by Rowntree and Kendall.

245 Rowntree and Kendall, *How the Labourer Lives*, p. 31.

246 Rowntree and Kendall, *How the Labourer Lives*, pp. 31–2.

247 Calculated from table of 'Household Budgets of Agricultural Labourers during Typical Weeks in 1912–13.' Rowntree and Kendall, *How the Labourer Lives*, facing p. 36 and pp. 299–303.

248 Lindsay, *Report*, p. 34.

249 Rowntree and Kendall, *How the Labourer Lives*, p. 142.

250 Rowntree and Kendall, *How the Labourer Lives*, pp. 163, 180, 206 and 308–9.

251 Rowntree and Kendall, *How the Labourer Lives*, p. 213.

252 Robert Roberts, *The Classic Slum* (Pelican Books, 1973), p. 109.

253 Pember Reeves, *Round About a Pound a Week*, p. 97.

254 Roberts, *The Classic Slum*, p. 105.

255 Rowntree and Kendall, *How the Labourer Lives*, pp. 60, 135, 146, 245 and 264.

256 Rowntree and Kendall, *How the Labourer Lives*, pp. 50 and 54.

257 Rowntree and Kendall, *How the Labourer Lives*, p. 74.

258 Rowntree and Kendall, *How the Labourer Lives*, pp. 312–13.

259 George Newman, *Infant Mortality: a Social Problem* (1906), quoted in Lindsay, *Report*, pp. 30–1.

260 Cited in Helen Jones, *Health and Society in Twentieth Century Britain* (1994), p. 7.

261 T. McKeown, *The Modern Rise of Population* (1976), pp. 28–9.

262 Jane Lewis, 'Restructuring Women's Experience of Home and Family', in Jane Lewis (ed.), *Labour and Love: Women's Experience of Home and Family, 1850–1940* (1986), p. 3.

263 Louise Tilly and Joan Scott, *Women, Work and the Family* (1978), p. 173.

264 B. Woolf, 'Studies on Infant Mortality, Part II. Social Aetiology of Stillbirths and Infant Deaths in County Boroughs of England and Wales', *British Journal of Social Medicine* (1974), pp. 119–24 and Carol Dyhouse, 'Working Class Mothers and Infant Mortality in England 1895–1914', *Journal of Social History*, 12 (1978).

265 J. M. Winter, 'The Decline of Mortality in Britain, 1870–1950', in T. Barker and M. Drake (eds), *Population and Society in Britain 1850–1980* (1982), p. 105.

266 M. W. Beaver, 'Population, Infant Mortality and Milk', *Population Studies* (1975), p. 245.

267 Dyhouse, 'Working Class Mothers', p. 255.

268 R. Titmuss, *Birth, Poverty and Wealth* (1943), pp. 22–6.

269 For a review, see Winter, 'The Decline of Mortality in Britain'.

270 McKeown, *The Modern Rise of Population*, Table 6.1, p. 120.

271 Dyhouse, 'Working Class Mothers', p. 251.

272 Cd 3864 (1908) B.P.P. *Cost of Living of the Working Classes*, Appendix II, pp. 592–3.

273 Bowley and Burnett-Hurst, *Livelihood and Poverty*, Table II, p. 21.

274 T. R. Marr, *Housing Conditions in Manchester and Salford* (1904), Table to face p. 58.

275   E. G. Howarth and M. Wilson, *West Ham: a Study in Social and Industrial Problems* (1907), p. 22.

276   Beaver, 'Population, Infant Mortality and Milk', pp. 250–1.

277   Beaver, 'Population, Infant Mortality and Milk', p. 244.

278   J. C. Drummond and A. Wilbraham, *The Englishman's Food* (1957), p. 529 quoted in J. M. Winter, 'The Impact of the First World War on Civilian Health in Britain', *Economic History Review*, 20 (1977), p. 488.

279   J. M. Winter. *The Great War and the British People* (1985).

280   Winter, 'The Impact of the First World War', p. 492.

281   See also J. M. Winter, 'Aspects of the Impact of the First World War on Infant Mortality in Britain', *Journal of European Economic History*, 11, 3 (1982).

282   Winter, 'The Impact of the First World War', p. 494.

283   Winter, 'Aspects of the Impact of the First World War', pp. 728–30.

284   Winter, 'The Impact of the First World War', p. 500.

285   Winter, 'The Impact of the First World War', p. 500.

286   Linda Bryder, 'The First World War: Healthy or Hungry?', *History Workshop*, 24 (Autumn 1987) and reply by Winter, 'Public Health and the Political Economy of War, 1914–18', *History Workshop*, 26 (1988).

287   Bryder, 'The First World War: Healthy or Hungry?', pp. 144–5. Bryder argues that there is good evidence to suggest that maternal mortality is positively correlated with medical intervention until the mid-1930s, rather than nutrition.

288   B. Harris, 'The Height of Schoolchildren in Britain 1900–50', in J. Komlos (ed.), *Stature, Living Standards and Economic Development* (1994), p. 33.

289   C. H. Feinstein, *National Income, Output and Expenditure of the U.K since 1870* (1972) T141. Average weekly wages are based on Bowley 1914–20, average weekly earnings are based on (interpolated) Bowley 1914–20, retail prices are Abstract of Labour Statistics 1914–36.

290   A. L. Bowley, *Wages and Prices 1914–20* (1921).

291   Feinstein's index for the period 1914–24 is Bowley's wage index. The earnings series was interpolated using Bowley's wage index and Chapman's wage-bill estimates for 1924 in conjunction with new earnings estimates 1914–20. Dowie provides a careful analysis of some of the problems with Bowley's indices of wages, *Economic History Review* (1975), pp. 448–50. Gazeley investigated the reliability of the expenditure weights used in the official cost of living index in 'Prices in Interwar Britain', *Explorations in Economic History*, 31 (1994), Table 3, p. 204.

292   J. A. Dowie, '1919–20 is in Need of Attention', *Economic History Review* (1975), pp. 439–40. This is slightly higher than Bowley's estimate of about 10 per cent. According to Dowie, 97 per cent of all changes in hours worked occurred in these two years, with 95 per cent taking place in 1919.

293   Dowie argues that hourly rates rose by about 15 per cent by December 1920. Dowie, '1990–20 is in Need of Attention', pp. 440–1.

294   Dowie, '1990–20 is in Need of Attention', pp. 440–1.

295   P. E. Dewey, 'Nutrition and Living Standards in Wartime Britain' in R. Wall and J. M. Winter (eds), *The Upheaval of War* (1988), Table 6.1, p. 198.

296   Dewey, 'Nutrition and Living Standards in Wartime Britain', Table 6.8, p. 208.

297   Dewey, 'Nutrition and Living Standards in Wartime Britain', p. 204.

298   A. L. Bowley and Margaret Hogg, *Has Poverty Diminished?* (1925), p. 1.

299   Bowley and Hogg, *Has Poverty Diminished?* p. 3.
300   David Coleman and John Salt, *The British Population* (1992), Table 3.1, pp. 90–1.
301   Although female participation did increase to about 0.46 during the war, this
      was an entirely transitory increase as participation rates were only marginally
      greater in 1931 than in 1911. E. Roberts, *Women's Work, 1840–1940* (CUP,
      1995), p. 11 and Coleman and Salt, *The British Population*, Table 2.1, p. 41.
302   See, for example, N. Branson and M. Heinemann, *Britain in the 1930s* (1976),
      p. 138.
303   I. Gazeley, 'Prices in Interwar Britain', *Explorations in Economic History* (1994).
304   A. Chapman, *Wages and Salaries in the United Kingdom, 1920–38* (CUP, 1953),
      pp. 84–6 and M. Thomas, 'Wage Behaviour in Inter-War Britain: a Sceptical
      Enquiry', in G. Grantham and M. Mackinnon (eds), *Labour Market Evolution*
      (1997).
305   Ramsbottom uses the monthly returns collected by the Ministry of Labour,
      published in the *Gazette*. The aggregate index for the manufacturing sector is
      compiled as a weighted average of the industry wage series taking as weights
      (1) total industrial earnings in 1924 and (2) the total industrial earnings in 1934
      (which is in turn derived from information on earnings in 1930). These indices
      were published in the *JRSS* 1935, 1938 and 1939. Although Ramsbottom's
      series is by far the most comprehensive wage-rate index, it has a number of
      limitations: (i) the published series gives only the value of the wage index at June
      and December of each year; (ii) although Ramsbottom used over 900 wage
      records, the occupational and geographical coverage varies enormously for
      different industries and the weighting of occupation/regions for each industry is
      not known; (iii) occupational specific rates are not given, unlike some of the
      series used by Bowley and the *Gazette* which provide data on rates of wages for
      occupations within particular industries. *Journal of the Royal Statistical Society*,
      1935 and 1938; Chapman, *Wages and Salaries in the United Kingdom*. These esti-
      mates are derived from data on the total wage bill and numbers employed in
      each industry. There is no separate information on earnings of particular
      groups within industries, though inter-industry comparisons are possible as
      is a comparison of the movement of average salaries per head and average
      wages per head. Chapman makes use of the Ministry of Labour's interwar earn-
      ings inquiries in conjunction with time series estimates of wages. Inevitably,
      however, there was a significant need for interpolation.
306   See A. L. Bowley, *Wages and Income since 1850* (1937), pp. 100–6 for a full discussion.
307   1924 published June 1926–September 1927, 1928 published October–December
      1929, 1931 published January–March 1933, 1935 published February–July
      1937.
308   The 1924 inquiry was actually conducted in four separate weeks in January,
      April, July and October 1924. The reports published in 1926 and 1927 present
      separate details of earnings in these four weeks as well as average figures. The
      1928 inquiry is restricted to one week in October 1928 and makes compari-
      son with the October figures for 1924. The 1931 and 1935 surveys collected
      information on earnings and hours for one week in October, but also data on
      numbers employed for a different week in October and the total wage bill for
      1930. This information was required to complement the census of production.
      See *Gazette*, January 1933, p. 8.

309 *Gazette*, January 1933, p. 8. All the interwar inquiries are based on 'manufactur-
     ing' only. In terms of employment, several important industries are excluded,
     including agriculture, coal mining, railway service, shipping, port transport
     and dock labour, distributive trades, catering, entertainment, commerce and
     banking and domestic service.

310 Increases (decreases) in earnings within an industry could be due to a number
     of causes: (i) increases (decreases) in wage rates; (ii) longer (shorter) working
     hours; (iii) more (less) overtime at enhanced hourly rate; (iv) changes in the age
     composition of the workforce; (v) changes in gender composition; (vi) changes
     in skill mix; (vii) changes in method of payment (the extension of payment by
     results tends to increase earnings, for example). With these data, it would then
     be possible to compare earnings data with the disaggregated wage-rate data for
     each industry so as to ascertain the extent of earnings drift. The Ministry of
     Labour are clearly aware of these factors and from July 1941 indicate that
     the published earnings figures by industry should not be taken as indications
     of wage rates. Moreover, in each inquiry they also attempt to investigate the
     extent to which, at an aggregate level, the increase in wartime earnings was due
     to increases in wage rates and other causes. *Gazette*, November 1941, p. 214.
     Clearly, if the intention is to undertake an economy-wide comparison, earnings
     data for each industry must be appropriately weighted, though this does not
     concern us here. See Bowley, *Wages and Incomes in the United Kingdom since 1860*,
     pp. 100–6 for a full discussion and evaluation of alternative weighting schemes
     for the results of the interwar surveys. It is worth noting that the Ministry were
     aware that part of the explanation for the aggregate increase in average earnings
     was due to increases in the relative numbers employed in industries in which
     wages were relatively high (especially munitions). *Gazette*, June 1942, p. 119.

311 Bowley, *Wages and Incomes in the United Kingdom since 1860*, pp. 101–3.

312 In comparison, the 1906 census distinguishes between earnings for a 'normal'
     week and actual earnings. The 1906 census also provides details of the distribu-
     tion of earnings for each industry. See Bowley, *Wages and Incomes in the United
     Kingdom since 1860*, p. 101.

313 *Gazette*, January 1933, p. 10.

314 According to the October 1924 inquiry, there was on average no short-time
     working in general engineering and vehicles and only a little in shipbuilding.
     Gazette, September 1926, p. 324. Although there was a substantial amount of
     short-time working also taking place in 1935, it was generally of shorter dur-
     ation and compensated by a large part of the workforce working overtime. In
     shipbuilding, for example, 23.4 per cent of workpeople were on short time (of
     average duration of 7.7 hours), but 32.1 per cent were on overtime (of average
     duration of 6.3 hours). *Gazette*, April 1937, p. 135.

315 This may have been because of the impact short-time working had on women's
     earnings in textiles in 1924. See G. Rottier, 'The Evolution of Wage Differentials:
     a Study of British Data', in J. T. Dunlop (ed.), *The Theory of Wage Determination*
     (1966), p. 239.

316 See Rottier, 'The Evolution of Wage Differentials', p. 239 and Table 2, p. 241.

317 D. Sells, *British Wage Boards* (1939), p. 26.

318 See, for example, G. D. H. Cole, *The Payment of Wages* (1928) and D. J. Robertson,
     Factory Wage Structures and National Agreements (1960).

319 As Knowles and Hill remind us, however, the piece-rates percentage only applied to basic rates, and not to national bonuses. Moreover, piece-rate workers' national bonus was 2s below time-workers' national bonus between 1927 and 1943 and 8s less between 1943 and 1950. K. G. J. C. Knowles and T. P. Hill, 'The Structure of Engineering Earnings', *Bulletin of the Oxford University Institute of Statistics*, 16, 9 & 10 (Sept. and October 1954), p. 281.

320 Whitely Councils were the Ministry of Labour's attempt to stimulate industrial devolution. At their peak there were 106 Whitely Councils covering about 3 million workers. See R. Lowe, *The Ministry of Labour* (1986), p. 92.

321 D. J. Robertson, *The Economics of Wages* (1961), p. 68.

322 R. Lowe, *Adjusting to Democracy* (1986), p. 99.

323 Sells, *British Wage Boards*, pp. 48–9. The 2.7 million workers covered by statutory wage fixing were estimated as 1.136 million Trade Board workers (*Gazette*, 1935, p. 127), 0.742 million agricultural workers, 0.2 million in road haulage, 0.615 million underground coal miners (*Gazette*, Oct. 1923, p. 383). A full list of Trades Boards industries is given in Sells, *British Wage Boards*, p. 188.

324 K. Knowles and D. Robertson, D. 'Wages of Skilled and Unskilled Workers, 1880–1950', *The Bulletin of Oxford University Institute of Statistics* (1951).

325 K. G. J. C. Knowles and D. J. Robertson, 'Differences between the Wages of Skilled and Unskilled Workers, 1880–1950', *The Bulletin of the Oxford University Institute of Statistics* (1951).

326 D. J. Robertson, *Factory Wage Structures and National Agreements* (CUP, 1960), p. 172.

327 D. J. Robertson, *The Economics of Wages and the Distribution of Income* (Macmillan, 1961), p. 72.

328 G. Routh, *Occupation and Pay in Great Britain 1906–79* (Macmillan, 1980), p. 185.

329 D. N. Paton and L. Findlay, *Poverty, Nutrition and Growth*, Medical Research Council Special Report, No. 101 (1926), pp. 17–19.

330 Paton and Findlay, *Poverty, Nutrition and Growth*, pp. 145–205.

331 Paton and Findlay, *Poverty, Nutrition and Growth*, Table 127, p. 186.

332 Paton and Findlay, *Poverty, Nutrition and Growth*, Table 127, p. 186 and discussion, pp. 301–5.

333 A. B. Hill, 'A Physiological and Economic Study of the Diets of Workers in Rural Areas as Compared with Those of Workers Resident in Urban Districts', *Journal of Hygiene*, XVIV (October 1925), pp. 195–221.

334 G. C. M. M'Gongile and J. Kirby, *Poverty and Public Health* (1936), Table 16, p. 120.

335 M'Gongile and Kirby, *Poverty and Public Health*, Tables 17 and 18, p. 124.

336 M'Gongile and Kirby, *Poverty and Public Health*, p. 128.

337 H. L. Beales and R. S. Lambert (eds), *Memoirs of the Unemployed* (1973), pp. 263–70.

338 Cited in Pilgrim Trust, *Men without Work* (1938), p. 135.

339 Cited in Pilgrim Trust, *Men without Work*, p. 140.

340 Cited in Dorothy Hollingswood, in J. C. Drummond and Anne Wilbraham (eds), *The Englishman's Food*, revised edition (1991), p. 446.

341 John Boyd Orr, *Food, Health and Income* (revised 1937), p. 18.

342 Boyd Orr, *Food, Health and Income*, Table IV, p. 27. Group II was 10–15s, Group III 15–20s, Group IV 20–30s, and Group V 30–45s.

343 Boyd Orr, *Food, Health and Income*, p. 55.

344 Boyd Orr, *Food, Health and Income*, p. 55.

345 Ministry of Health Advisory Committee on Nutrition, First Report 1937, cited in Boyd Orr, *Food, Health and Income*, pp. 5–6.

346 Cited in Boyd Orr, *Food, Health and Income*, pp. 6–7.

347 Boyd Orr, *Food, Health and Income*, p. 7.

348 Boyd Orr, *Food, Health and Income*, p. 38.

349 Boyd Orr, *Food, Health and Income*, p. 39.

350 Bowley and Hogg, *Has Poverty Diminished?*, pp. 13–14 and Bowley, *Wages and Income in the United Kingdom since 1860*, p. 61.

351 Bowley and Hogg, *Has Poverty Diminished?*, p. 14.

352 Bowley and Hogg, *Has Poverty Diminished?*, p. 27. The sample in Northampton was 1 in 17, Warrington was 1 in 13 and Reading 1 in 18.

353 Bowley and Burnett-Hurst, *Livelihood and Poverty*, p. 42.

354 Bowley and Hogg, *Has Poverty Diminished?*, Table F, p. 19.

355 Bowley and Hogg, *Has Poverty Diminished?*, p. 20.

356 Bowley and Hogg, *Has Poverty Diminished?*, p. 23.

357 A. L. Bowley, 'The Poverty Line', in H. Llewelyn-Smith *et al.*, *The New Survey of London Life and Labour*: Vol III *Survey of Social Conditions (I) Eastern Are*a (1932), pp. 70–2.

358 Cited in C. A. Lindsey and C. L. Lindsey, 'Booth, Rowntree and Llewelyn-Smith: a Reassessment of Interwar Poverty', *Economic History Review* (1993), p. 89.

359 Lindsey and Lindsey, 'Booth, Rowntree and Llewelyn-Smith', pp. 89–100.

360 Bowley, 'The Poverty Line', p. 70.

361 Bowley, 'The Poverty Line', p. 70.

362 Bowley, 'The Poverty Line', pp. 70–1. See also the discussion in Bowley, *Wages and Income in the United Kingdom since 1860*, pp. 55–7.

363 Bowley, 'The Poverty Line', pp. 70–1. Though note Lindsey and Lindsey's criticism of this calculation. They argue that an appropriate repricing of Booth's poverty line would produce a figure nearer 35s at 1928 [*sic*] prices. Lindsey and Lindsey, 'Booth, Rowntree and Llewelyn-Smith', pp. 89–91.

364 B. S. Rowntree, *Poverty: a Study of Town Life* (Macmillan, 1902), Introduction, p. viii.

365 For a comparison, see A. D. K. Owen, *A Survey of the Standard of Living in Sheffield* (1933), pp. 14–15.

366 A. L. Bowley, 'The Extent and Causes of Poverty', in H. Llewelyn-Smith *et al.*, *The New Survey of London Life and Labour*: Vol. III *Survey of Social Conditions (I) Eastern Are*a (1932), p. 80.

367 Bowley, 'The Extent and Causes of Poverty', p. 82.

368 Pat Thane, *Old Age in English History* (2000), p. 304.

369 H. Llewelyn-Smith *et al.*, *The New Survey of London Life and Labour*: Vol. VI *Survey of Social Conditions (2) Western Area* (1935), p. 93.

370 William Beveridge, 'Unemployment and its Treatment', in H. Llewelyn-Smith *et al.*, *The New Survey of London Life and Labour*: Vol. 1: *Forty Years of Change* (1930), Table IV, p. 357.

371 Beveridge, 'Unemployment and its Treatment', pp. 350–1.

372 D. Caradog Jones (ed.), *Social Survey of Merseyside*, Vol. 1 (1934), p. 157. The modifications made to the Bowley standard were an additional dress allowance of $4\frac{1}{2}$d for all females over 16 and reduced clothing allowance for people

over 65 years (1s 2½ d rather than 1s 5d). Jones modified Bowley's clothing
standard because it had originally been devised by Rowntree for *Poverty* in
1899.

373 Jones, *Social Survey of Merseyside*, Vol. 1, p. 150.
374 The survey of Liverpool was carried out in the autumn of 1929, while Bootle was
surveyed in the spring of 1930 and Birkenhead and Wallasey in the summer of
1930. Unemployment increased sharply between the autumn of 1929 and the
summer of 1930 (by 27 per cent in Bootle, 23 per cent in Birkenhead and 12.5
per cent in Wallasey). Jones maintains that the proportion of families in poverty
in districts other than Liverpool would have been reduced by about 20 per cent,
had the entire survey been carried out in the autumn of 1929. Jones, *Social
Survey of Merseyside*, Vol. 1, pp. 160–1.
375 Jones, *Social Survey of Merseyside*, Vol. 1, p. 148.
376 Jones, *Social Survey of Merseyside*, Vol. 1, p. 111.
377 Jones, *Social Survey of Merseyside*, Vol. 1, p. 186.
378 Jones, *Social Survey of Merseyside*, Vol. 1, p. 147.
379 Jones, *Social Survey of Merseyside*, Vol. 1, pp. 162–70.
380 Calculated from Table IV, Jones, *Social Survey of Merseyside*, Vol. 1, p. 174.
381 Owen, *A Survey of the Standard of Living in Sheffield*.
382 Owen, *A Survey of the Standard of Living in Sheffield*, p. 22.
383 Owen, *A Survey of the Standard of Living in Sheffield*, p. 21.
384 Owen, *A Survey of the Standard of Living in Sheffield*, p. 24.
385 Owen, *A Survey of the Standard of Living in Sheffield*, p. 28, Table 11.
386 Owen, *A Survey of the Standard of Living in Sheffield*, p. 42.
387 P. Ford, *Work and Wealth in a Modern Port* (1934). Unlike most other social investigators, Ford makes little of the poverty-line income for a 'reference family',
seemingly because this household type accounts for only 6 per cent of working-
class families in his sample (pp. 91–2).
388 Ford, *Work and Wealth in a Modern Port*, p. 116.
389 Ford, *Work and Wealth in a Modern Port*. The modifications were a reduction in
the clothing allowance from 60s per annum to 30s per annum and a reduction
in the fuel allowance from 3s to 2s 6d per week. Bowley's equivalence scale was
also adjusted so that youths aged 16–18 were 0.85 of an adult male rather than
0.8 (p. 118).
390 Ford, *Work and Wealth in a Modern Port*, p. 118.
391 Ford, *Work and Wealth in a Modern Port*, p. 119.
392 Ford, *Work and Wealth in a Modern Port*, p. 136.
393 Ford, *Work and Wealth in a Modern Port*, p. 147.
394 H. Tout, *The Standard of Living in Bristol* (1937), p. 51.
395 Tout, *The Standard of Living in Bristol*, pp. 12 and 23.
396 R. F. George, 'A New Calculation of the Poverty Line', *Journal of the Royal Statistical
Society*, part I (1937), pp. 74–95.
397 George, 'A New Calculation', p. 74.
398 George, 'A New Calculation', p. 74.
399 George, 'A New Calculation', pp. 77–8.
400 George, 'A New Calculation', pp. 84–90.
401 B. S. Rowntree, *Poverty and Progress* (1941), pp. v–vi.
402 Rowntree, *Poverty and Progress*, p. v.

403 Rowntree, *Poverty and Progress*, p. vi.

404 B. S. Rowntree, *The Human Needs of Labour* (revised 1937), p. 59.

405 Rowntree, *The Human Needs of Labour*, pp. 67–9 and 79–80.

406 Rowntree, *The Human Needs of Labour*, p. 65.

407 Rowntree, *The Human Needs of Labour*, pp. 83–4.

408 Rowntree, *The Human Needs of Labour*, p. 92.

409 Rowntree, *The Human Needs of Labour*, p. 95.

410 Rowntree, *The Human Needs of Labour*, p. 97.

411 Rowntree, *The Human Needs of Labour*, pp. 98–9.

412 B. S. Rowntree, *The Responsibility of Women Workers for Dependants* (Clarendon Press, 1921). The cities covered were Newcastle, Middlesborough, Hull, Sheffield, Leeds, Oldham, Manchester, Derby, Nottingham, Birmingham and Leicester.

413 Rowntree, *The Human Needs of Labour*, pp. 104–5.

414 Rowntree, *The Human Needs of Labour*, pp. 108–10.

415 Rowntree, *The Human Needs of Labour*, p. 111.

416 Rowntree, *Poverty and Progress*, p. 34.

417 Rowntree, *Poverty and Progress*, p. 461.

418 Rowntree, *Poverty and Progress*, p. 108.

419 Rowntree, *Poverty and Progress*, p. 454.

420 Rowntree, *Poverty and Progress*, p. 452.

421 Rowntree, *Poverty and Progress*, p. 45.

422 The proportion of the population of York over 65 years had increased from 4.65 per cent in 1899 to 7.35 per cent in 1936. Thane, *Old Age in English History*, p. 306.

423 Cited in Thane, *Old Age in English History*, p. 305.

424 Coleman and Salt, *The British Population*, Table 6.2, p. 221.

425 Rowntree, *Poverty and Progress*, p. 465.

426 Rowntree, *Poverty and Progress*, p. 286.

427 Rowntree, *Poverty and Progress*, p. 468.

428 Rowntree, *Poverty and Progress*, p. 469.

429 See S. G. Jones, *Workers at Play: a Social and Economic History of Leisure 1918–39* (1986), A. Davies, *Leisure, Gender and Poverty* (1992) and D. Fowler, *The First Teenagers: the Lifestyle of Young Wage-Earners in Interwar Britain* (1995).

430 Tout, *The Standard of Living in Bristol*, pp. 16 and 25, Table II. Tout's poverty line used the 1933 BMA recommended diet, not George's modified diet.

431 Tout, *The Standard of Living in Bristol*, p. 56.

432 Timothy Hatton and Roy Bailey, 'Poverty and the Welfare State in Interwar London', in Clara Eugenia Nunez (ed.), *The Microeconomic Analysis of the Household Labour Market, 1880–39* (1998), p. 139.

433 Hatton and Bailey, 'Poverty and the Welfare State in Interwar London', p. 140.

434 Hatton and Bailey, 'Poverty and the Welfare State in Interwar London', p. 140.

435 A. M. Carr-Saunders and D. Caradog Jones, *A Survey of the Social Structure of England and Wales*, 2nd edn (1937), pp. 178–9.

436 Rowntree, *Human Needs of Labour*, pp. 71–2.

437 Ellen Wilkinson, *The Town That Was Murdered* (Gollancz, 1939), p. 209.

438 Quoted in A. Deacon, 'Unemployment and Politics in Britain since 1945', in B. Showler and A. Sinfield (eds), *The Workless State: Studies in Unemployment* (1981), p. 77.

439   This section draws on material by I. S. Gazeley and P. Thane, 'Patterns of
      Visibility: Unemployment in Britain during the Nineteenth and Twentieth
      Centuries', in Gail Lewis (ed.), *Forming Nation, Framing Welfare* (Routledge, 1998).

440   Alan Booth and Sean Glynn, 'Unemployment in the Interwar Period: a Multiple
      Problem', *Journal of Contemporary History* (1975), p. 611.

441   See Mark Thomas, 'Unemployment in Interwar Britain', in B. Eichengreen and
      T. J. Hatton (eds), *Interwar Unemployment in International Perspective* (1988) who
      provides a succinct review of the way in which the Ministry of Labour collected
      unemployment data.

442   W. R. Garside, *British Unemployment, 1919–1939* (Cambridge, 1990), p. 4.

443   Booth and Glynn, 'Unemployment in the Interwar Period', p. 612.

444   See Booth and Glynn, 'Unemployment in the Interwar Period', pp. 615–18 for
      a discussion of possible shortcomings, and Barry Eichengreen, 'Unemployment
      in Interwar Britain: Dole or Doledrums?', *Oxford Economic Papers*, 39 (1987),
      p. 598 for a discussion of the recording of juvenile unemployment in the
      census.

445   W. R. Garside, *British Unemployment, 1919–1939* (Cambridge, 1990), p. 6.

446   See Wilkinson, *The Town that was Murdered*.

447   Hilda Jennings, *Brynmawr: a Study of a Distressed Area* (1934), p. 3. Two-thirds of
      all insured employment were in these trades in 1933.

448   Jennings, *Brynmawr*, p. 138. The figures provided by Jennings are not easy to
      interpret. They are undated, but relate to some period between September
      1929 and August 1932 when the survey was carried out. In July 1932 there were
      1669 wholly unemployed men and 252 temporarily stopped. It would seem
      likely, therefore, that the sample represents about 70 per cent of the wholly
      unemployed population of Brynmawr.

449   Thomas, 'Unemployment in Interwar Britain', p. 98.

450   Thomas, 'Unemployment in Interwar Britain', p. 98.

451   Thomas, 'Unemployment in Interwar Britain', pp. 104–5

452   W. Beveridge, *Full Employment in a Free Society* (1944), p. 66.

453   Beveridge, *Full Employment in a Free Society*, p. 66.

454   Pilgrim Trust, *Men without Work* (1938), p. 6.

455   Pilgrim Trust, *Men without Work*, p. 7.

456   Pilgrim Trust, *Men without Work*, p. 7.

457   N. F. R. Crafts, 'Long-Term Unemployment in Britain in the 1930s', *Economic
      History Review*, 40 (1987), pp. 418–20.

458   Crafts, 'Long-Term Unemployment in Britain in the 1930s', Table 1, p. 420.

459   Eichengreen, 'Unemployment in Interwar Britain', p. 598.

460   Barry Eichengreen, 'Juvenile Unemployment in 20th Century Britain: the
      Emergence of a Problem', *Social Research*, 54 (1987), pp. 273–302.

461   Cited in Thomas, 'Unemployment in Interwar Britain', p. 118.

462   Eichengreen, 'Unemployment in Interwar Britain', pp. 616–17.

463   Thomas, 'Unemployment in Interwar Britain', p. 115.

464   Eichengreen, 'Unemployment in Interwar Britain', p. 59.

465   A. Deacon, *In Search of the Scrounger* (1976), p. 9.

466   The Pilgrim Trust, *Men without Work*, p. 133 cited in J. Stern, 'The Relationship
      between Unemployment, Morbidity and Mortality in Britain', *Population Studies*,
      37 (1983), p. 65.

467 A discussion of the empirical difficulties of establishing causality in this context can be found in Stern, 'The Relationship between Unemployment, Morbidity and Mortality in Britain'.

468 This latter view is associated with the lifelong work of Marie Jahoda, who argues that work has both a manifest function (financial reward) and five latent functions: providing people with a time structure to their lives, giving them the opportunity for social contact outside the home, linking an individual to goals and purposes, conferring a sense of status and identity and providing regular enforced activity. Unemployment is seen as destructive primarily because of the absence of these latent functions. M. Jahoda, 'The Impact of Unemployment in the 1930s and 1970s', *Bulletin of the British Psychological Society* (1979) cited in D. Fryer, 'Monmouthshire and Marienthal: Sociographies of Two Unemployed Communities', in D. Fryer and P. Ullah, *Unemployed People: Social and Psychological Perspectives* (1988), p. 88.

469 E. Wright Bakke, *The Unemployed Man: A Social Study* (1933), p. 71.

470 Wright Bakke, *The Unemployed Man*, pp. 73–4.

471 Wright Bakke, *The Unemployed Man*, p. 71.

472 Pilgrim Trust, *Men without Work*, pp. 26–36.

473 Pilgrim Trust, *Men without Work*, pp. 175–6.

474 James Halliday, 'Psychoneurosis as a Cause of Incapacity among Insured Persons', Supplement to the *British Medical Journal*, 1 (1935), cited in Bernard Harris, 'Unemployment, Insurance and Health in Interwar Britain', in B. Eichengreen and T. J. Hatton (eds), *Interwar Unemployment in International Perspective* (1988), p. 154. Halliday's results are also discussed in the Pilgrim Trust, *Men without Work*, pp. 136–7.

475 Jahoda was responsible for seminal research into the psychological impact of unemployment in Marienthal in 1933. This was a textile town in Austria, where employment was almost totally dependent on one factory, which was closed in 1933. See Marie Jahoda, *Employment and Unemployment: a Social–Psychological Analysis* (1982), p. 6.

476 Pilgrim Trust, *Men without Work*, pp. 354–70.

477 Marie Jahoda, 'Unemployed Men at Work', in D. Fryer and P. Ullah, *Unemployed People: Social and Psychological Perspectives* (1987), p. 1.

478 Jahoda, 'Unemployed Men at Work', pp. 22–3.

479 Fryer, 'Monmouthshire and Marienthal', p. 77.

480 Jahoda, 'Unemployed Men at Work', p. 64.

481 Fryer, 'Monmouthshire and Marienthal', p. 85.

482 H. L. Beales and R. S. Lambert, *Memoirs of the Unemployed* (1973), pp. 25–6.

483 P. Eisenberg and P. F. Lazarsfeld, 'The Psychological Effects of Unemployment', *Psychological Bulletin*, 35 (June 1938), cited in P. Kelvin and J. Jarrett, *Unemployment: Its Social–Psychological Effects* (1985), p. 20. See also R. McKibbin, 'The Social Psychology of Unemployment in Interwar Britain', in P. J. Waller (ed.), *Politics and Social Change in Modern Britain* (1987), p. 161.

484 Catherine Marsh, 'Unemployment in Britain', in Duncan Gallie (ed.), *Employment in Britain* (1988), p. 361. See also Jean Hartley and David Fryer, 'The Psychology of Unemployment: a Critical Appraisal', *Progress in Applied Social Psychology*, 2 (1984), pp. 7–9.

485 McKibbin, 'The Social Psychology of Unemployment in Interwar Britain', pp. 181–2.

486   Thomas, 'Unemployment in Interwar Britain', p. 135.
487   D. K. Benjamin and L. A. Kochin, 'Searching for an Explanation of Interwar Unemployment', *Journal of Political Economy* (1979).
488   Cited in Noel Whiteside, 'Counting the Cost: Sickness and Disability among Working People in an Era of Industrial Recession, 1920–39', *Economic History Review* (May 1987), p. 230.
489   Pilgrim Trust, *Men without Work*, p. 142.
490   Whiteside, 'Counting the Cost', p. 245.
491   H. W. Singer, 'Unemployment and Health', Pilgrim Trust unemployment interim paper No. 4 (London, Pilgrim Trust, 1937).
492   Pilgrim Trust, *Men without Work*, pp. 140–1.
493   J. Stern, 'The Relationship between Unemployment, Morbidity and Mortality in Britain', *Population Studies*, 37 (1983), p. 68.
494   M. H. Brenner, 'Mortality and the National Economy: a Review and the Experience of England and Wales, 1936–76', *Lancet*, 15 September (1979).
495   Stern, 'The Relationship between Unemployment, Morbidity and Mortality in Britain', pp. 61–74 and Adam Wagstaff, 'Time Series Analysis of the Relationship between Unemployment and Mortality: a Survey of Econometric Critiques and Replications of Brenner's Studies', *Social Science Medicine*, 21, 9 (1985), pp. 985–96.
496   For a review of the evidence for the early 1980s see P. Warr, *Work, Unemployment and Mental Health* (1987) and Richard Smith, *Unemployment and Health* (1987).
497   Cited in Charles Webster, 'Healthy or Hungry Thirties?', *History Workshop Journal* (1982), p. 113.
498   Webster, 'Healthy or Hungry Thirties?', p. 114.
499   Cited in Webster, 'Healthy or Hungry Thirties?', p. 114–15.
500   Harris, 'Unemployment, Insurance and Health in Interwar Britain', p. 161.
501   Webster, 'Healthy or Hungry Thirties?', pp. 114 and 118–19.
502   Harris, 'Unemployment, Insurance and Health in Interwar Britain', p. 154.
503   J. M. Winter, 'Infant Mortality, Maternal Mortality and Public Health in Britain in the 1930s', *Journal of European Economic History*, 8 (1979), p. 443.
504   Winter, 'Infant Mortality, Maternal Mortality, and Public Health in Britain in the 1930s', p. 443.
505   Harris, 'Unemployment, Insurance and Health in Inter-war Britain', p. 176. Note that Harris reaches this conclusion despite finding an inverse correlation between umemployment and the height of schoolchildren in these areas.
506   Webster, 'Healthy or Hungry Thirties?', p. 116.
507   E. R. Pamuk, 'Social Class Inequality in Mortality from 1921–1971 in England and Wales', *Population Studies* (1985), p. 39.
508   Richard Wilkinson, 'Class Mortality Differentials, Income Distribution and Trends in Poverty 1921–81', *Journal of Social Policy*, 18, 3 (1988), p. 325.
509   Pilgrim Trust, *Men without Work*, p. 101.
510   Pilgrim Trust, *Men without Work*, pp. 109–10.
511   Pilgrim Trust, *Men without Work*, p. 111.
512   Pilgrim Trust, *Men without Work*, p. 112.
513   Margery Spring Rice, *Working Class Wives* (Penguin, 1939 and Virago, 1981), p. 106.
514   See Winter, 'Infant Mortality, Maternal Mortality and Public Health in Britain in the 1930s', S. Rowbotham, *Hidden from History* (1973) and D. Beddoe, *Back to Home and Duty* (1989).

515   J. M. Munro Kerr, *Maternal Mortality and Morbidity: a Study of their Problems* (Edinburgh, 1933), pp. 32–3, Table XII.

516   Harris, 'Unemployment, Insurance and Health in Interwar Britain', p. 166.

517   I. Loudon, *Death in Childbirth* (1992), pp. 542–5. Maternal mortality varied between 4.41 and 4.81 per 1000 between 1897 and 1902. In 1933 and 1934 rates were 4.51 and 4.60 per 1000.

518   *Final Report of the Departmental Committee on Maternal Mortality and Morbidity*, Ministry of Health (1932), p. 25.

519   *Final Report of the Departmental Committee on Maternal Mortality and Morbidity*, cited in Spring Rice, *Working Class Wives*, p. 21.

520   Harris, 'Unemployment, Insurance and Health in Interwar Britain', p. 166.

521   Cited in R. Titmuss, *Poverty and Population* (1938), p. 139.

522   Though considerably less than Rowntree's 'Human Needs' standard of 43s 6d plus rent.

523   Alan Deacon, *In Search of the Scrounger: the Administration of Unemployment Insurance in Britain 1920–31*, Occasional Papers on Social Administration No. 60 (1976), p. 9.

524   A. M. Carr-Saunders and D. Caradog Jones, *A Survey of the Social Structure of England and Wales* (1937), p. 183.

525   B. Gilbert, *British Social Policy 1914–39* (1970), p. 216. Cited in Wilkinson, 'Class Mortality Differentials, Income Distribution and Trends in Poverty 1921–81', p. 327.

526   Deacon, *In Search of the Scrounger*, p. 21.

527   Deacon, *In Search of the Scrounger*, pp. 23 and 26.

528   Gilbert, *British Social Policy 1914–39*, pp. 90–1.

529   Deacon, *In Search of the Scrounger*, p. 41 and Appendix 2.

530   Deacon, *In Search of the Scrounger*, p. 55.

531   Deacon, *In Search of the Scrounger*, p. 61.

532   *First Report of the Royal Commission on Unemployment Insurance*, June 1931, Cmd 3872, pp. 50–1.

533   E. M. Burns, *British Unemployment Programmes* (1941), p. 104.

534   Interested readers should refer to R. Skidelsky, *Politicians and the Slump* (1969) and Gilbert, *British Social Policy, 1914–39*.

535   Garside, *British Unemployment, 1919–39*, pp. 66–7.

536   Alan Deacon and Jonathan Bradshaw, *Reserved for the Poor: the Means Test in British Social Policy* (1983), p. 17.

537   Garside, *British Unemployment, 1919–39*, pp. 66–7.

538   Deacon and Bradshaw, *Reserved for the Poor*, p. 21.

539   Garside, *British Unemployment, 1919–39*, pp. 71–3.

540   Garside, *British Unemployment, 1919–39*, Table 9, p. 78.

541   Deacon and Bradshaw, *Reserved for the Poor*, p. 25.

542   W. Beveridge, *Full Employment in a Free Society* (1944), p. 196, Table 20.

543   The Churchill government attempted to encourage, cajole, coerce and then conscript women into the labour market in ever-increasing numbers. In the first three years of the war, women workers partly replaced conscripted males until the peak of wartime mobilisation in 1943, when about 2 million additional women were employed in industry. See Penny Summerfield, *Women Workers and the Second World War* (1984).

544   According to Parker, this was due to bad weather, the cessation of building work, and contraction in the leisure and catering industries. Although

unemployment was growing, the number of long-term unemployed fell by 86,000. H. M. D. Parker, *Manpower* (HMSO, 1957), p. 73.

545 M. M. Potsan, *British War Production* (HMSO, 1952) p. 97.

546 Parker, *Manpower*, pp. 87–96.

547 K. Middlemass, *Politics in Industrial Society* (1979).

548 See P. Dewey, *War and Progress* (1997), pp. 300–1.

549 P. Townsend, *Poverty in the United Kingdom* (1970), p. 116.

550 J. F. Wright, 'Real Wage Resistance: Eighty Years of the British Cost of Living', *Oxford Economic Papers*, 36 (November 1984), Supplement, p. 164.

551 The weights used in the official cost of living index were: 0.6 food, 0.16 rent, 0.12 clothing, 0.08 fuel and light and 0.04 for other items. The constituents of these categories were typically quite limited. See I. Gazeley, 'Prices in Interwar Britain', *Explorations in Economic History*, 31 (1994).

552 J. L. Nicholson, 'Employment and National Income during the War', *Bulletin of the Oxford Institute of Statistics*, 7, 4 (1945), Table V, p. 238.

553 A. Calder, *The People's War* (1969), pp. 238–40.

554 Calder, *The People's War*, p. 240.

555 Gazeley, 'Prices in Interwar Britain', pp. 196–7.

556 Quoted in Nicholson, 'Employment and National Income during the War', p. 236.

557 *Gazette*, 'Enquiry into Working Class Family Budgets' (October 1937), p. 378.

558 *Gazette*, 'Weekly Expenditure of Working-Class Households in the United Kingdom in 1937–38' (December 1940), pp. 300–5.

559 White Paper on *National Income and Expenditure*, Cmd 7099 (1947).

560 D. Seers, 'The Increase in Working Class Cost of Living since before the War', *Bulletin of the Oxford Institute of Statistics*, 10,4 (1948), pp. 140–61 and 'The Cost of Living, 1938–48', *Bulletin of the Oxford Institute of Statistics*, 11,4 (1949), pp. 127–47. R. G. D. Allen, *Bulletin of the London and Cambridge Economic Service* (11 August 1947), p. 75 and (18 February 1948), pp. 18–19.

561 Seers also reminds us that we need to be careful with the interpretation of these series, because 'the working-classes are prevented by rationing from buying in 1947 what they bought in 1937–8'. Making allowances for changes in quality and constrained choices through rationing, the increases in the working-class cost of living between 1938 and June 1947 was more likely about 67 per cent, than the 61.5 per cent indicated in Table 5.1. Seers, 'The Increase in Working Class Cost of Living since before the War', pp. 144–5.

562 Seers, 'The Increase in Working Class Cost of Living since before the War', p. 143. See also D. Seers, *The Levelling of Incomes since 1938* (Oxford University Institute of Statistics, n.d.), pp. 18–30.

563 In 1954, there were 1.054 million adult male workers employed in federated engineering firms, about half the number in the industry. Non-federated firms, while not being party to wage agreements in the industry, would certainly have to observe them, since they constitute 'recognised terms and conditions'. D. J. Robertson, *Factory Wage Structures and National Agreements* (1960), p. 12.

564 G. Routh, *Occupation and Pay in Great Britain, 1906–79* (1980), p. 201.

565 K. Knowles and D. Robertson, 'Wages of Skilled and Unskilled Workers, 1880–1950', *The Bulletin of Oxford University Institute of Statistics* (1951).

566 Seers, *The Levelling of Incomes since 1938*, p. 54.

567 Townsend, *Poverty in the United Kingdom*, pp. 117–18.

568 *Royal Commission on the Distribution of Income and Wealth*, Report No. 1 (Diamond Report) (1975) Cmd 6171, Table 10, p. 36.

569 Report of the Food (Defence Plans) Department (1938) quoted in *How Britain was Fed in Wartime* (HMSO, 1946), p. 42.

570 Ina Zweiniger-Bargielowska, *Austerity in Britain* (2000), p. 36.

571 R. J. Hammond, *Food*: Vol.1 *The Growth of Policy* (HMSO, 1951), pp. 220–1.

572 *The Urban Working Class Household Diet, 1940–49* (HMSO, 1951).

573 *First Report of the National Food Survey Committee* (HMSO, 1951). Discussed in T. Schulz, 'Working-class Food Consumption', *Bulletin of the Oxford Institute of Statistics*, 14, 2 (1952), pp. 34–5.

574 John Boyd Orr was possibly the most important. See, for example, John Orr and David Lubbock, *Feeding the People in War-time* (1940) and his Fabian Society pamphlet *Nutrition in War* (1940).

575 *How Britain was Fed in Wartime*, Appendix D.

576 Calder, *The People's War*, p. 72. Calder points out that the bacon ration was actually greater than average pre-war consumption.

577 Calder, *The People's War*, pp. 239–40.

578 Calder, *The People's War*, p. 276.

579 Calder, *The People's War*, p. 276.

580 *How Britain was Fed in Wartime*, p. 42.

581 *How Britain was Fed in Wartime*, p. 43.

582 *How Britain was Fed in Wartime*, p. 43.

583 Zweiniger-Bargielowska, *Austerity in Britain*, p. 33.

584 Report of the Chief Medical Officer of the Board of Education (1937–8), quoted in Charles Smith, *Britain's Food Supplies in Peace and War* (1940), p. 275.

585 *How Britain Was Fed in Wartime*, pp. 43 and 46.

586 *How Britain Was Fed in Wartime*, pp. 43–4.

587 Zweiniger-Bargielowska, *Austerity in Britain*, p. 33.

588 Hammond, *Food*: Vol.1 *The Growth of Policy*, pp. 259–60.

589 Orr and Lubbock, *Feeding the People in War-time*, p. 49.

590 *How Britain Was Fed in Wartime*, p. 47 and Appendix D, p. 62.

591 Zweiniger-Bargielowska, *Austerity in Britain*, pp. 32–3.

592 Zweiniger-Bargielowska, *Austerity in Britain*, pp. 37–8.

593 Zweiniger-Bargielowska, *Austerity in Britain*, pp. 36–7.

594 Ministry of Food, *The Urban Working-Class Household Diet 1940–49* (1951), pp. 58–9 quoted in Zweiniger-Bargielowska, *Austerity in Britain*, p. 37.

595 *How Britain Was Fed in Wartime*, p. 49.

596 *How Britain Was Fed in Wartime*, p. 49.

597 Zweiniger-Bargielowska, *Austerity in Britain*, p. 39.

598 T. Schulz, 'Working-class Food Consumption', *Bulletin of the Oxford Institute of Statistics*, 14,2 (1952), p. 35. Between 1942 and 1947, between 151 and 226 families recorded food consumption. In 1948 and 1949 the number was 65 and 64 respectively, but these two surveys were based on recorded expenditure over a four-week period. Table II, p. 36. This article also presents a comparison of the results of the Institute of Statistics food consumption inquiries with those carried out by the Ministry of Food.

599 In the 1949 survey, this applied to only 41 of the 64 households. T. Schulz, 'Family Expenditure in 1949' (Part I and Part II), *Bulletin of the Oxford Institute of Statistics* (1951), p. 132.

600 Schulz, 'Working-class Food Consumption' pp. 35–6.

601 Schulz, 'Family Expenditure in 1949', pp. 128–50.

602 Schulz, 'Family Expenditure in 1949', p. 140. Most of these surveys are concerned with interpreting year-on-year changes in the pattern of family expenditure, but this is problematic because the sample is small, income data are incomplete and household structure varies between years.

603 The Institute also calculated another price index, an 'inexpensive diet', which is a hybrid cost of living index and 'human needs' index. But the movement in cost of the 'inexpensive diet' is reasonably similar to the 'human needs' index and since it does not add any analytical insight it has been ignored here. See T. Schulz, 'The Cost of Inexpensive Nutrition before and after the War', *Bulletin of the Oxford Institute of Statistics* (1952), pp. 231–44.

604 T. Schulz, 'Human Needs Diets from 1936 to 1949', *Bulletin of the Oxford Institute of Statistics*, 11 (1949), pp. 308–9.

605 These changes did create some problems of comparability. For a full discussion, see Schulz, 'Human Needs Diets from 1936 to 1949', p. 307.

606 Rowntree's diet was rich in vitamin A (due to the inclusion of a large amount of liver); the Institute's diet was rich in calcium (because of a generous milk allowance).

607 Note that the equivalence scale used for the construction of the 'human needs' diet was different from the equivalence scale used to investigate changes in working-class food consumption. See Schulz, 'Family Expenditure in 1949', p. 130 for the latter.

608 Schulz, 'Human Needs Diets from 1936 to 1949', Table II, pp. 313 and 324.

609 At first sight it might seem odd that during the war, and immediate post-war period, the increase in the cost of a human needs diet was greater than the increase in prices measured by a cost of living index. After all, food policy was ostensibly directed towards securing 'fair shares for all' through rationing and subsidy. The explanation for this, according to Schulz, was because 'people [did] not receive "according to their needs" but rather – as far as the broad groupings for the purpose of rationing permit – in *proportion* to their needs'. T. Schulz, *Bulletin of the Oxford Institute of Statistics* (1953), p. 421.

610 T. Schulz, 'Human Needs' Cost of Living for a Single Person', *Bulletin of the Oxford Institute of Statistics*, 5, 9 (1943). Male energy needs were assumed to be 3000 kcal per day, while females' needs were 2500 kcal per day. Males also had a higher protein allowance than females (70 g rather than 60 g) and a higher vitamin B allowance (0.90 rather than 0.75 mg).

611 T. Schulz, 'Human Needs Cost of Living for a Single Person', *Bulletin of the Oxford Institute of Statistics*, 12, 6 (1950), p. 166.

612 Liverpool University, *The Cost of Living of Representative Working-Class Families* (University Press, Liverpool, 1941), p. 5.

613 Liverpool University, *The Cost of Living of Representative Working-Class Families*, p. 10. It is noted that the price increases for the diets for all three household types are significantly in excess of the 48 per cent increase in prices suggested by the Ministry of Labour food index between 1933 and October 1940 (between 63 and 80 per cent).

614 Liverpool University, *The Cost of Living of Representative Working-Class Families*, pp. 12–13. The cost of subsidised milk was also deducted from the 'Human Needs' standard (but not the Merseyside poverty line).

615   Liverpool University, *The Cost of Living of Representative Working-Class Families*, p. 16.
616   Thane, *Old Age in English History*, p. 354.
617   Thane, *Old Age in English History*, p. 359.
618   R. Titmuss, *Problems of Social Policy* (HMSO, 1950), p. 115.
619   According to Titmuss, 13 per cent of Newcastle and 20 per cent of Manchester children arrived with inadequate footwear. *Problems of Social Policy*, p. 115.
620   Titmuss, *Problems of Social Policy*, p. 116.
621   Titmuss, *Problems of Social Policy*, p. 120.
622   Mass Observation, *Evacuation* (University of Sussex, 1987), p. 5.
623   Titmuss, *Problems of Social Policy*, p. 125.
624   Medical officer, 1 February 1941, cited in Titmuss, *Problems of Social Policy*, p. 127. See also John Macnicol, 'The Evacuation of School Children', in H. L. Smith (ed.), *War and Social Change* (1986), pp. 19–21.
625   Macnicol, 'The Evacuation of School Children', p. 21, and Titmuss, *Problems of Social Policy*, pp. 128–31.
626   Titmuss, *Problems of Social Policy*, notes to pp. 131–2.
627   Titmuss, *Problems of Social Policy*, p. 508.
628   Macnicol, 'The Evacuation of School Children', p. 22.
629   Though even in this case, sick civilians paid the price. Titmuss, *Problems of Social Policy*, p. 490.
630   Howard Glennerster and Martin Evans, 'Beveridge and his Assumptive Worlds: the Incompatibilities of a Flawed Design', in John Hills, John Ditch and Howard Glennerster, *Beveridge and Social Security* (1994), p. 59.
631   Thane, *Old Age in English History*, pp. 354 and 363.
632   The Beveridge Report was published just after the victory at El Alamein and the Allied invasion of North Africa and just before the Soviet victory at Stalingrad.
633   J. Tomlinson, *Employment Policy: the Crucial Years* (1987), pp. 71–2.
634   Coleman and Salt, *The British Population*, Table 6.2, p. 221.
635   Thane, *The Foundation of the Welfare State*, p. 228.
636   Dilnot et al., *The Reform of Social Security*, pp. 10–11.
637   Jane Lewis, *Women in England 1870–1950* (1984), pp. 48–9.
638   John Clarke, Allan Cochrane and Carol Smart, *Ideologies of Welfare* (1987), pp. 100–9.
639   Hills, Ditch and Glennerster, *Beveridge and Social Security*, p. 3.
640   Glennerster and Evans, 'Beveridge and his Assumptive Worlds', p. 57.
641   Glennerster and Evans, 'Beveridge and his Assumptive Worlds', p. 57.
642   Dilnot et al., *Reform of Social Security*, p. 31.
643   John Veit-Wilson, 'Condemned to Deprivation? Beveridge's Responsibility for the Invisibility of Poverty?', in John Hills, John Ditch and Howard Glennerster, *Beveridge and Social Security* (1994).
644   Glennerster and Evans, 'Beveridge and his Assumptive Worlds', p. 61.
645   J. Harris, *William Beveridge* (1997), p. 382.
646   Harris, *William Beveridge*, pp. 381–2.
647   W. Beveridge, *Social Insurance and Allied Services* (November 1942), Cmd 6404, p. 19.
648   Beveridge, *Social Insurance and Allied Services*, Table IV, p. 78 and Harris, *William Beveridge*, p. 386.
649   Beveridge, *Social Insurance and Allied Services*, p. 79.

650 Beveridge, *Social Insurance and Allied Services*, pp. 79–81.
651 Veit-Wilson, 'Condemned to Deprivation?', p. 101.
652 Harris, *William Beveridge*, p. 382.
653 Beveridge, *Social Insurance and Allied Services*, pp. 84–5.
654 Beveridge, *Social Insurance and Allied Services*, p. 85.
655 Beveridge, *Social Insurance and Allied Services*, pp. 85–7.
656 Beveridge, *Social Insurance and Allied Services*, pp. 87–8.
657 Beveridge, *Social Insurance and Allied Services*, p. 89.
658 Beveridge, *Social Insurance and Allied Services*, p. 90.
659 Beveridge, *Social Insurance and Allied Services*, para 369, p. 141.
660 Beveridge, *Social Insurance and Allied Services*, para 371, pp. 141–2.
661 Beveridge, *Social Insurance and Allied Services*, para 372, p. 142.
662 Veit-Wilson argues that this was simply a heuristic device to guard against criticism
    suggesting his standard was too generous. 'Paradigms of Poverty: a Rehabilita-
    tion of B. S. Rowntree', in David Englander and Rosemary O'Day (eds), *Social
    Investigation in Britain 1840–1914* (1995), pp. 213–14.
663 See also calculations at 1971 prices by G. C. Fiegehen, P. S. Lansley and
    A. D. Smith, *Poverty and Progress in Britain 1953–73* (CUP, 1977), p. 134 that
    make the same point.
664 Thane, *Foundations of the Welfare State*, p. 238.
665 Titmuss, *Problems of Social Policy*, p. 506 cited in Peter Hennessy, *Never Again,
    Britain 1945–51* (1992), p. 70.
666 See, for example, Harris, *William Beveridge*, pp. 478–98 and Lowe, *The Welfare
    State in Britain since 1945*, pp. 125–35.
667 Kenneth O. Morgan, *The People's Peace* (1990), pp. 154–94.
668 Timothy J. Hatton and Roy E. Bailey, 'Seebohm Rowntree and the Post-war
    Poverty Puzzle', *Economic History Review*, LIII, 3 (2000), p. 517.
669 Keith Banting, *Poverty, Politics and Policy: Britain in the 1960s* (1979), p. 70.
670 Coleman and Salt, *The British Population*, Table 3.1, p. 371.
671 Lowe, *The Welfare State since 1945*, p. 74.
672 Michael Anderson, 'The Emergence of the Modern Life Cycle in Britain', *Social
    History* (1985).
673 Coleman and Salt, *The British Population*, Table 3.1, p. 221.
674 C. H. Feinstein, *National Income, Output and Expenditure of the United Kingdom*
    (1972), Table 57, T126.
675 Jim Tomlinson, *Employment Policy, The Crucial Years 1939–55* (1987), pp. 45–64.
676 *Royal Commission on Income and Wealth Report No. 1* (Diamond Report) (1975),
    Cmnd 6171, Table 10, p. 36.
677 P. Townsend, *Poverty in the United Kingdom* (1970), p. 116.
678 Paul Addison, *Now the War is Over* (1985), pp. 26–8.
679 Morgan, *The People's Peace*, p. 176.
680 Ministry of Food, *The Urban Working-Class Household Diet 1940–49* (1951).
681 A. M. Carr-Saunders, D. Caradog Jones and C. A. Moser, *A Survey of Social
    Conditions in England and Wales* (1958), p. 206.
682 Carr-Saunders *et al.*, *A Survey of Social Conditions in England and Wales*, p. 207.
683 Carr-Saunders *et al.*, *A Survey of Social Conditions in England and Wales*, pp. 209–12,
    Table 15.4. Average rural diets provided 2748 kcal per capita, whereas urban
    diets provided 2616 kcal.

684 T. Schultz, 'Income, Family Structure and Food Expenditure before and after the War', *Bulletin of the Oxford Institute of Statistics*, 24 (1962), p. 466.

685 Schultz maintains that differences in expenditure per head on food were 'on the whole concomitants of differences in family structure rather than in family income'. Schultz, 'Income, Family Structure and Food Expenditure before and after the War', p. 467.

686 Zweiniger-Bargielowska, *Austerity in Britain*, pp. 44–5.

687 Schultz, 'Income, Family Structure and Food Expenditure before and after the War', p. 457.

688 Townsend, *Poverty in the United Kingdom*, pp. 170–1.

689 Carr-Saunders *et al.*, *A Survey of Social Conditions in England and Wales*, pp. 217–18. See also the discussion in Townsend, *Poverty in the United Kingdom*, pp. 168–70.

690 Royston Lambert, *Nutrition in Britain 1950–60*, Occasional papers on social administration No. 6 (1964), p. 16.

691 Lambert, *Nutrition in Britain 1950–60*, Table 5, p. 17.

692 There were some minor differences between Rowntree's diet and those adopted by Schultz. See *Bulletin of the Oxford Institute of Statistics* (1953), p. 426.

693 T. Schulz, *Bulletin of the Oxford Institute of Statistics* (1958), p. 107.

694 T. Schulz, *Bulletin of the Oxford Institute of Statistics* (1953), p. 422.

695 T. Schulz, *Bulletin of the Oxford Institute of Statistics* (1952), p. 177.

696 T. Schulz, *Bulletin of the Oxford Institute of Statistics* (1954), p. 130.

697 T. Schulz, *Bulletin of the Oxford Institute of Statistics* (1958), p. 110.

698 T. Schulz, *Bulletin of the Oxford Institute of Statistics* (1954), p. 368 and (1952), p. 423.

699 *Bulletin of the Oxford Institute of Statistics* (1953), pp. 434–5.

700 T. Schultz, 'The Means of Subsistence', *Bulletin of the Oxford Institute of Statistics* (1955).

701 Schultz, 'The Means of Subsistence', p. 231.

702 Based on recosting average consumption from the 1937–8 working-class expenditure survey. Schultz, 'The Means of Subsistence', pp. 216–25.

703 Schultz, 'The Means of Subsistence', p. 231.

704 Schultz, 'The Means of Subsistence', p. 232.

705 The same diet was used except for the replacement of white flour for wholemeal flour; fresh milk for skimmed condensed milk and increased sugar content (to replace the sugar in condensed milk). Further changes resulted from rationing. The amount of cheese, bacon and cooking fat were reduced and margarine increased. Free school milk was included for schoolchildren. Note that Rowntree and Lavers's 1950 diets were still based on the BMA 1933 nutritional recommendations. B. S. Rowntree and G. R. Lavers, *Poverty and the Welfare State* (1951), pp. 8–9.

706 Poverty-line clothing and household expenditure was based on evidence from a new inquiry; 29 women provided details of expenditure on women and children's clothing and household sundries. Rowntree and Lavers took the average of the lowest three cases as their poverty-line minimum. This was 5s 2d a week for women's clothing, 5s 6d for children's clothing and 6s for household sundries. Rowntree and Lavers, *Poverty and the Welfare State*, pp. 13–15. A similar inquiry was undertaken with 32 men to ascertain expenditure on men's clothing and fuel and light. Again, the poverty-line figure was based upon

the average of the three lowest cases, viz 6s 1d per week for men's clothing and 7s 7d for fuel and light. Rowntree and Lavers, *Poverty and the Welfare State*, pp. 15–16.

707 Rowntree and Lavers, *Poverty and the Welfare State*, p. 28.
708 Rowntree and Lavers, *Poverty and the Welfare State*, p. 40.
709 Rowntree and Lavers, *Poverty and the Welfare State*, p. 40.
710 Rowntree and Lavers, *Poverty and the Welfare State*, pp. 1–2. Justified with reference to the results of a comparison of one in ten households compared with the entire sample from the 1936 survey.
711 A. B. Atkinson, A. K. Maynard and C. G. Trinder, 'National Assistance and Low Incomes in 1950', *Social Policy and Administration*, 15, 1 (Spring 1981), p. 21, and A. B. Atkinson *et al.*, 'Poverty in York; a Re-Analysis of Rowntree's 1950 Survey', *Bulletin of Economic Research*, 33 (1981), pp. 61–2.
712 Hatton and Bailey, 'Post War Poverty Puzzle', p. 522.
713 Hatton and Bailey, 'Post War Poverty Puzzle', pp. 525–6.
714 These calculations accord with Hatton and Bailey's calculations using Feinstein's cost of living index.
715 It is also necessary to adjust for the different way that unemployment insurance is treated between Rowntree's second and third surveys. In 1936, unemployment insurance is included in the poverty line as an item of expenditure, whereas in 1950 it is not – but is deducted from income instead. Rowntree and Lavers, *Poverty and the Welfare State*, p. 22.
716 Hatton and Bailey, 'Post War Poverty Puzzle', p. 536.
717 Hatton and Bailey, 'Post War Poverty Puzzle', p. 536.
718 Hatton and Bailey, 'Post War Poverty Puzzle', p. 536.
719 Atkinson *et al.*, 'National Assistance and Low Incomes in 1950', p. 24.
720 P. Townsend and D. Wedderburn, *The Aged and the Welfare State* (1970), p. 1.
721 In 1901 there were 1.52 million people over the age of 65 in England and Wales. Coleman and Salt, *The British Population*, p. 231.
722 Anderson, 'The Emergence of the Modern Life Cycle in Britain', p. 74.
723 Dorothy Cole and John Utting, *The Economic Circumstances of Old People* (1962), pp. 8–11. In fact, 1078 interviews were carried out, but most of the report was written on the basis of the first 400 of these. Old people living alone, or with wives only, and with an income of below £8 for single pensioners and £10 for couples, kept weekly records of expenditure.
724 Cole and Utting, *The Economic Circumstances of Old People*, p. 23.
725 Cole and Utting, *The Economic Circumstances of Old People*, pp. 25–7.
726 J. H. Sheldon, *The Social Medicine of Old Age* (Nuffield Foundation, 1949), cited in P. Thane, 'The Family Lives of Old People', in P. Johnson and P. Thane (eds), *Old Age From Antiquity to Post Modernity* (1998), pp. 181–2.
727 Cole and Utting, *The Economic Circumstances of Old People*, p. 29 and Table 12.
728 Cole and Utting, *The Economic Circumstances of Old People*, pp. 45–53.
729 Townsend and Wedderburn, *The Aged and the Welfare State*, pp. 3–4.
730 Townsend and Wedderburn, *The Aged and the Welfare State*, Table 33, p. 53.
731 Jeremy Tunstall, *Old and Alone: a Sociological Study of Old People* (1966), p. 60.
732 Townsend and Wedderburn, *The Aged and the Welfare State*, pp. 2 and 54.
733 Townsend and Wedderburn, *The Aged and the Welfare State*, Ch. 4. These conclusions were based on financial data provided by 3146 income units, p. 65.

734   Townsend and Wedderburn, *The Aged and the Welfare State*, Table 4, p. 74.
735   Townsend and Wedderburn, *The Aged and the Welfare State*, p. 65.
736   Townsend and Wedderburn, *The Aged and the Welfare State*, p. 76.
737   Townsend and Wedderburn, *The Aged and the Welfare State*, p. 76.
738   Lambert, *Nutrition in Britain 1950–60*, p. 13.
739   Tunstall, *Old and Alone*. The sample corresponded reasonably well with sex, marital status and demographic profile of old people in the 1961 population census (p. 5).
740   Tunstall, *Old and Alone*, p. 200. Tunstall defines social isolation in terms of contact with children, relatives and friends (p. 66).
741   Cole and Utting, *The Economic Circumstances of Old People*, p. 67.
742   Cole and Utting, *The Economic Circumstances of Old People*, p. 72.
743   For example, A. Deacon and J. Bradshaw, *Reserved for the Poor* (1983), p. 61.
744   Lambert, *Nutrition in Britain 1950–60*, p. 45.
745   Wilkinson, 'Class Mortality Differentials, Income Distribution and Trends in Poverty 1921–81', p. 329.
746   Brian Abel-Smith and Peter Townsend, *The Poor and the Poorest* (1965), p. 14.
747   Abel-Smith and Townsend, *The Poor and the Poorest*, p. 40.
748   Lowe, *The Welfare State in Britain since 1945*, p. 138.
749   Abel-Smith and Townsend, *The Poor and the Poorest*, p. 49.
750   Abel-Smith and Townsend, *The Poor and the Poorest*, p. 62.
751   Abel-Smith and Townsend, *The Poor and the Poorest*, p. 65.
752   Lowe provides a table in *The Welfare State in Britain since 1945* (Table 6.6, p. 154) purporting to show the breakdown in the cause of poverty in 1960, from Abel-Smith and Townsend. This information is not included in *The Poor and the Poorest*. Moreover, Lowe attributes 2.5 million in poverty to reasons of old age, whereas, in fact, in *The Poor and the Poorest*, Abel-Smith and Townsend's best estimate is around 3 million.
753   Banting, *Poverty, Politics and Policy*, pp. 70–2.
754   Banting, *Poverty, Politics and Policy*, p. 74.
755   Howard Glennerster, *British Social Policy since 1945* (1995), p. 117.
756   Lowe, *The Welfare State in Britain since 1945*, p. 136.
757   See, for example, the discussion of Rowntree's various poverty lines in Townsend, *Poverty in the United Kingdom*, pp. 160–1.
758   Abel-Smith and Townsend, *The Poor and the Poorest*, p. 19.
759   I. Gough and T. Stark, 'Low Incomes in the United Kingdom, 1954, 1959 and 1963', *Manchester School* (1968). The first definition included an allowance for rent (which varies with household structure) and corrected the distortion caused by the uneven rise in National Assistance rates by using the trend value. The second definition was based on the proportion equal to the 1948 National Assistance rate (plus rent) relative to average incomes for different household structures. In 1948 this proportion was 25 per cent for a single person, 53 per cent for a couple with two children and 66 per cent for a couple with four children. The 1948 low-income limits were then multiplied by the increase in average income at subsequent dates (pp. 175–6).
760   See Lowe, *The Welfare State in Britain since 1945*, Tables 6.4 and 6.5, pp. 152–3.
761   Gough and Stark, 'Low Incomes in the United Kingdom, 1954, 1959 and 1963', Table V1, p. 182.

762 G. C. Fiegehen, P. S. Lansley and A. D. Smith, *Poverty and Progress in Britain 1953–73* (CUP, 1977). The authors provide a full discussion of the difficulties associated with the use of the FES data for this purpose – especially the problems posed by the use of 'normal' rather than current income in the post-1960 surveys and the necessity of adjusting for family composition (pp. 20–6).

763 Fiegehen *et al.*, *Poverty and Progress in Britain 1953–73*, p. 22.

764 Fiegehen *et al.*, *Poverty and Progress in Britain 1953–73*, p. 29.

765 Fiegehen *et al.*, *Poverty and Progress in Britain 1953–73*, Table 3.4, p. 27. They calculate that 1953/4 benefits would have been worth £7.51 in 1971, whereas actual benefits were £11.40.

766 Fiegehen *et al.*, *Poverty and Progress in Britain 1953–73*, p. 30.

767 Fiegehen *et al.*, *Poverty and Progress in Britain 1953–73*, p. 28.

768 Fiegehen *et al.*, *Poverty and Progress in Britain 1953–73*, p. 31.

769 Wilfred Beckerman and Stephen Clark, *Poverty and Social Security in Britain since 1961* (1982), pp. 22–30.

770 Beckerman and Clark, *Poverty and Social Security in Britain since 1961*, pp. 43–4.

771 Feinstein's index of average weekly earnings was 95 in 1900 and 914 in 1960 (1913 = 100), which is an increase of about 9.6 times the average value for 1900. Retail prices increased by 4.7 times over the same period. Feinstein, *National Income, Expenditure and Output of the United Kingdom 1855–1965*, T140.

772 David Piachaud, 'Poverty in Britain 1899 to 1983', *Journal of Social Policy*, 17 (1988), p. 338.

773 Bowley's scale repriced to 1936 and excluding rent is 0.85 of average consumer expenditure per capita for a family of two adults and three children (calculated from Table 3.20).

BIBLIOGRAPHY

Abel-Smith, B. and Townsend, P. *The Poor and the Poorest* (Andover, Hants, 1965)

Addison, P. *The Road to 1945* (1975)

Addison, P. *Now the War is Over* (1985)

Alexander, S. 'Introduction', Pember Reeves, M. *Round About a Pound a Week* (Virago, 1979)

Allen, R. G. D. *Bulletin of the London and Cambridge Economic Service* (Cambridge, 1947)

Anderson, M. 'The Emergence of the Modern Life Cycle in Britain', *Social History* (1985)

Ashworth, W. *An Economic History of England 1870–1939* (1960)

Atkinson, A. B., Maynard, A. K., and Trinder, C. G. 'National Assistance and Low Incomes in 1950', *Social Policy and Administration*, 15, 1 (1981)

Atkinson, A. B. *et al*. 'Poverty in York; a Re-Analysis of Rowntree's 1950 Survey', *Bulletin of Economic Research*, 33 (1981)

Bakke, E. Wright, *The Unemployed Man: a Social Study* (1933)

Banting, K. *Poverty, Politics and Policy: Britain in the 1960s* (1979)

Barker, T. C. and Drake, M. (eds) *Population and Society in Britain 1850–1980* (1982)

Barker, T. C., McKenzie, J. C. and Yudkin, J. (eds) *Our Changing Fare* (1966)

Barker, T. C., Oddy, D. J. and Yudkin, J. *The Dietary Surveys of Dr Edward Smith* (Department of Nutrition, Queen Elizabeth College, University of London, 1970)

Barnsby, G. J. 'The Standard of Living in the Black Country during the Nineteenth Century', *Economic History Review* (1971)

Beales, H. L. and Lambert, R. S. (eds) *Memoirs of the Unemployed* (Gollancz, 1934 and Wakefield, Yorkshire, 1973)

Beaver, M. W. 'Population, Infant Mortality and Milk', *Population Studies* (1975)

Beckerman, W. and Clark, S. *Poverty and Social Security in Britain since 1961* (Oxford, 1982)

Beddoe, D. *Back to Home and Duty* (1989)

Bell, F. *At the Works: a Study of a Manufacturing Town* (Virago, 1985)

Benjamin, D. and Kochin, L. A. 'Searching for a Explanation of Interwar Unemployment', *Journal of Political Economy* (1979)

Beveridge, W. 'Unemployment and its Treatment', in Llewelyn-Smith, H. *et al*., *The New Survey of London Life and Labour*: Vol. 1: *Forty Years of Change* (1930)

Beveridge, W. *Full Employment in a Free Society* (1944)

Beveridge, W. *Social Insurance and Allied Services*, Cmd 6404 (1942)

Beveridge, W. *Unemployment: a Problem of Industry* (1909 and 1930)

Booth, B. and Glynn, S. 'Unemployment in the Interwar Period: a Multiple Problem', *Journal of Contemporary History* (1975)

Booth, C. *Life and Labour of the People of London* (1889–1903)

Bourke, J. *Dismembering the Male* (1996)

Bowley, A. L. 'Index Numbers of the Cost of Living', *Journal of the Royal Statistical Society* (1952)

Bowley, A. L. 'The Poverty Line' in Llewelyn-Smith, H. *et al.*, *The New Survey of London Life and Labour*: Vol. III *Survey of Social Conditions (I) Eastern Area* (1932)

Bowley, A. L. *Wages and Income since 1860* (Cambridge, 1937)

Bowley, A. L. *Wages and Prices, 1914–20* (Oxford, 1921)

Bowley, A. L. and Burnett-Hurst, A. R. *Livelihood and Poverty* (1915)

Bowley, A. L. and Hogg, M. *Has Poverty Diminished?* (1925)

Boyd Orr, J. *Food, Health and Income* (revised 1937)

Boyd Orr, J. *Nutrition in War* (1940)

Boyd Orr, J. and Lubbock, D. *Feeding the People in War-time* (1940)

Bradshaw, J., Mitchell, D. and Morgan, J. 'Evaluating Adequacy: the Potential of Budgetary Standards', *Journal of Social Policy*, 16, 2 (1987)

Branson, N. and Heinemann, M. *Britain in the 1930s* (1976)

Brenner, M. H. 'Mortality and the National Economy: a Review and the Experience of England and Wales, 1936–76', *Lancet*, 15 (1979)

Briggs, A. *Social Thought and Social Action: a Study of the Work of Seebohm Rowntree* (1961)

British Parliamentary Papers, Cd 1761 *Consumption of Food and Cost of Living of Working Classes in the United Kingdom and Certain Foreign Countries* (1903)

British Parliamentary Papers, Cd 2175 *Report of the Inter-Departmental Committee on Physical Deterioration* (1904)

British Parliamentary Papers, Cd 2337 *Consumption and the Cost of Food in Workmen's Families in Urban Districts of the United Kingdom* (1905)

British Parliamentary Papers, Cd 2337 *Second Series of Memoranda, Statistical Tables and Charts* (1905)

British Parliamentary Papers, Cd 3864 *Cost of Living of the Working Classes. Report of an Enquiry by the Board of Trade into Working-Class Rents, Housing and Retail Prices Together with Standard Rates of Wages Prevailing in Certain Occupations in Principal Industrial Towns in the United Kingdom* (1908)

British Parliamentary Papers, Cd 5460 *Earnings and Hours of Labour* (1907)

British Parliamentary Papers, Cd 6955 *Cost of Living of the Working Classes. Report of an Enquiry by the Board of Trade into Working-Class Rents and Retail Prices Together with the Rates of Wages in Certain Occupations in Industrial Towns in the United Kingdom* (1912–13)

British Parliamentary Papers, Cmd 3872 *First Report of the Royal Commission on Unemployment Insurance* (1931)

British Parliamentary Papers, Cmd 7099 *White Paper on National Income and Expenditure* (1947)

Brown, H. Phelps, *The Inequality of Pay* (Oxford, 1977)

Bryder, L. 'The First World War: Healthy or Hungry?' *History Workshop*, 24 (1987)

Bulmer, M., Bales, K. and Kish Sklar, K. *The Social Survey in Historical Perspective* (1992)

Burnett, J. *Plenty and Want* (1966)

Burns, E. M. *British Unemployment Programmes* (1941)

Cadbury, E., Matheson, Cecile M. and Shann, G. *Women's Work and Wages*, 2nd edn (1908)

Calder, A. *The People's War* (1969)

Carr-Saunders, A. M. and Caradog Jones, D. *A Survey of the Social Structure of England and Wales*, 2nd edn (Oxford, 1937)

Carr-Saunders, A. M., Caradog Jones, D. and Moser, C. A. *A Survey of Social Conditions in England and Wales*, 3rd edn (Oxford, 1958)

Carver, A. E. *An Investigation of the Dietary of the Labouring Classes of Birmingham* (Birmingham, 1913)

Chaloner, W. H. 'Trends in Fish Consumption', in Barker, T. C., McKenzie, J. C. and Yudkin, J. (eds) *Our Changing Fare* (1966)

Chapman, A. L. *Wages and Salaries in the United Kingdom, 1920–38* (Cambridge, 1953)

Clarke, J., Cochrane, A. and Smart, C. *Ideologies of Welfare* (1987)

Cole, D. and Utting, J. *The Economic Circumstances of Old People* (Welwyn, Herts, 1962)

Cole, G. D. H. *The Payment of Wages* (1928)

Coleman, D. and Salt, J. *The British Population* (Oxford, 1992)

Court, W. H. B. *British Economic History 1870–1914* (Cambridge, 1965)

Crafts, N. F. R. *British Economic Growth during the Industrial Revolution* (Oxford, 1985)

Crafts, N. F. R. 'Long-term Unemployment in Britain in the 1930s', *Economic History Review*, 40 (1987)

Crafts, N. F. R. 'Patterns of Development in Nineteenth Century Europe', *Oxford Economic Papers*, 36 (1984)

Davies, A. *Leisure, Gender and Poverty* (Buckingham, 1992)

Davies, D. *The Case of Labourers in Husbandry* (Bath, 1795)

Davies, M. F. *Life in an English Village* (1909)

Deacon, A. *In Search of the Scrounger: the Administration of Unemployment Insurance in Britain 1920–31*, Occasional Papers on Social Administration No. 60 (1976)

Deacon, A. 'Unemployment and Politics in Britain since 1945' in Showler, B. and Sinfield, A. (eds) *The Workless State: Studies in Unemployment* (Oxford, 1981)

Deacon, A. and Bradshaw, J. *Reserved for the Poor: the Means Test in British Social Policy* (Oxford, 1983)

Department of Health and Social Security, *Recommended Intakes of Nutrients for the United Kingdom*: Reports on Health and Medical Subjects No. 120 (HMSO, 1969)

Dewey, P. E. 'Nutrition and Living Standards in Wartime Britain', in Wall, R. and Winter, J. M. (eds) *The Upheaval of War* (1988)

Dewey, P. *War and Progress* (1997)

Dilnot, A. *et al. The Reform of Social Security* (Oxford, 1988)

Dingle, A. E. 'Drink and Working-Class Living Standards in Britain, 1870–1914', *Economic History Review* (1975)

Dowie, J. A. '1919–20 is in Need of Attention', *Economic History Review* (1975)

Drummond, J. C. and Wilbraham, A. *The Englishman's Food* (1957)

Dundee Social Union, *Report on Housing and Industrial Conditions* (Dundee, 1905)

Dyhouse, C. 'Working Class Mothers and Infant Mortality in England 1895–1914', *Journal of Social History* (1978)

Eden, F. M. *The State of the Poor* (1797)

Eichengreen, B. 'Juvenile Unemployment in 20th Century Britain: the Emergence of a Problem', *Social Research*, 54 (1987)

Eichengreen, B. 'Unemployment in Interwar Britain: Dole or Doledrums?' *Oxford Economic Papers*, 39 (1987)

Eisenberg, P. and Lazarsfeld, P. F. 'The Psychological Effects of Unemployment', *Psychological Bulletin*, 35 (1938)

Englander, D. and O'Day, R. (eds) *Retrieved Riches: Social Investigation in Britain 1840–1914* (Aldershot, 1995)

Feinstein, C. 'What Really Happened to Real Wages?: Trends in Wages, Prices, and Productivity in the United Kingdom, 1880–1913', *Economic History Review* (1990)

Feinstein, C. H. *National Income, Output and Expenditure of the U.K since 1870* (Cambridge, 1972)

Fiegehen, G. C., Lansley, P. S. and Smith, A. D. *Poverty and Progress in Britain 1953–73* (Cambridge, 1977)

First Report of the National Food Survey Committee (HMSO, 1951)

Ford, P. *Work and Wealth in a Modern Port* (1934)

Fowler, D. *The First Teenagers: the Lifestyle of Young Wage-Earners in Interwar Britain* (1995)

Fraser, D. *The Evolution of the Welfare State* (1984)

Fryer, D. 'Monmouthshire and Marienthal: Sociographies of Two Unemployed Communities', in Fryer, D. and Ullah, P. *Unemployed People: Social and Psychological Perspectives* (Milton Keynes, 1987)

Garside, W. R. *British Unemployment, 1919–1939* (Cambridge, 1990)

Gazeley, I. S. and Newell, A. 'Rowntree Revisited: Poverty in Britain, 1900', *Explorations in Economic History*, 37 (2000)

Gazeley, I. S. and Thane, P. 'Patterns of Visibility: Unemployment in Britain during the Nineteenth and Twentieth Centuries', in Lewis, Gail (ed.) *Forming Nation, Framing Welfare* (Routledge, 1998)

Gazeley, I. S. 'The Cost of Living for Urban Workers', *Economic History Review* (1989)

Gazeley, I. S. 'Prices in Interwar Britain', *Explorations in Economic History*, 31 (1994)

Gazeley, I. S. 'The Standard of Living of the Working Classes, 1881–1912', D.Phil. thesis (Oxford, 1985)

George, R. F. 'A New Calculation of the Poverty Line', *Journal of the Royal Statistical Society* (1937 part I)

George, V. and Howards, I. *Poverty amidst Affluence* (Aldershot, 1991)

Gilbert, B. *British Social Policy 1914–39* (1970)

Glennerster, H. *British Social Policy since 1945* (Oxford, 1995)

Glennerster, H. and Evans, M. 'Beveridge and his Assumptive Worlds: the Incompatibilities of a Flawed Design', in Hills, J., Ditch, J. and Glennerster, H. *Beveridge and Social Security* (Oxford, 1994)

Gough, I. and Stark, T. 'Low Incomes in the United Kingdom, 1954, 1959 and 1963', *Manchester School* (1968)

Gourvish, T. R. 'The Standard of Living', in O'Day, A. *The Edwardian Age* (1979)

Hall, A. A. 'Wages, Earnings and Real Earnings in Teeside', *International Review of Social History* (1981), Vol. XXVI, part 2

Halliday, J. 'Psychoneurosis as a Cause of Incapacity among Insured Persons', Supplement to the *British Medical Journal*, 1 (1935)

Halsey, A. H. *Change in British Society*, 4th edn (1995)

Hammond, R. J. *Food*: Vol. 1 *The Growth of Policy* (HMSO, 1951)

Harris, B. 'The Heights of Schoolchildren in Britain, 1900–1950', in Komlos, J. (ed.) *Stature, Living Standards and Economic Development* (Chicago, 1994)

Harris, B. 'Unemployment, Insurance and Health in Interwar Britain', in Eichengreen, B. and Hatton, T. J. (eds) *Interwar Unemployment in International Perspective* (Dordrecht, 1988)

Harris, J. *Private Lives, Public Spirit: Britain 1870–1914* (Oxford, 1993)

Harris, J. *Unemployment and Politics* (Oxford, 1972 and 1984)

Harris, J. *William Beveridge* (Oxford, 1997)

Hartley, J. and Fryer, D. 'The Psychology of Unemployment: a Critical Appraisal', *Progress in Applied Social Psychology*, 2 (1984)

Hatton, T. and Bailey, R. 'Poverty and the Welfare State in Interwar London', in Nunez, C. E. (ed.) *The Microeconomic Analysis of the Household Labour Market, 1880–39* (1998)

Hatton, T. J. and Bailey, R. E. 'Seebohm Rowntree and the Post-war Poverty Puzzle', *Economic History Review*, LIII, 3 (2000)

Hennessy, P. *Never Again, Britain 1945–51* (1992)

Hennock, E. P. 'Concepts of Poverty in the British Social Surveys from Charles Booth to Arthur Bowley', in M. Bulmer *et al.*, *The Social Survey in Historical Perspective* (Cambridge, 1992)

Hill, A. 'Physiological and Economic Study of the Diets of Workers in Rural Areas as Compared with those of Workers Resident in Urban Districts', *Journal of Hygiene*, XVIV (1925)

Hollingsworth, D. 'Developments Leading to Present-day Nutritional Knowledge', in Oddy, D. and Miller, D. S. (eds) *The Making of the Modern British Diet* (1976)

Hopkins, E. 'Small Town Aristocrat of Labour and their Standards of Living, 1840–1914', *Economic History Review* (1975)

Horrell, S. and Oxley, D. 'Crust or Crumb?: Intra-household Resource Allocation and Male Breadwinning in Late Victorian Britain', *Economic History Review*, LII, 3 (1999)

How Britain was Fed in Wartime (HMSO, 1946)

Howarth, E. G. and Wilson, M. *West Ham: a Study in Social and Industrial Problems* (1907)

Hunt, E. H. *Regional Wage Variations in Britain, 1850–1914* (Oxford, 1973)

Inman, P. *Labour in the Munitions Industries* (HMSO, 1957)

Jahoda, M. *Employment and Unemployment: a Social-Psychological Analysis* (Cambridge, 1982)

Jahoda, M. 'The Impact of Unemployment in the 1930s and 1970s', *Bulletin of the British Psychological Society* (1979)

Jahoda, M. 'Unemployed men at work', in Fryer, D. and Ullah, P. *Unemployed People: Social and Psychological Perspectives* (1987)

Jennings, H. *Brynmawr: a Study of a Distressed Area* (1934)

John, A. (ed.) *Unequal Opportunities: Women's Employment in England 1800–1918* (Oxford, 1986)

Jones, D. Caradog (ed.) *Social Survey of Merseyside*, 3 vols (1934)

Jones, H. *Health and Society in Twentieth Century Britain* (1994)

Jones, S. G. *Workers at Play: a Social and Economic History of Leisure 1918–39* (1986)

Keating, P. (ed.) *Into Unknown England* (1976)

Kelvin, P. and Jarrett, J. *Unemployment: Its Social-Psychological Effects* (Cambridge, 1985)

Knowles, K. and Hill, T. P. 'The Structure of Engineering Earnings', *Bulletin of the Oxford University Institute of Statistics*, 16, 9 & 10 (1954)

Knowles, K. and Robertson, D. 'Wages of Skilled and Unskilled Workers, 1880–1950', *The Bulletin of the Oxford University Institute of Statistics* (1951)

Lambert, R. *Nutrition in Britain 1950–60*. Occasional papers on social administration No. 6 (1964)

Lewis, J. 'Restructuring Women's Experience of Home and Family', in Lewis, J. (ed.) *Labour and Love: Women's Experience of Home and Family, 1850–1940* (Oxford, 1986)

Lewis, J. 'Social Facts, Social Theory and Social Change: the Ideas of Booth in Relation to those of Beatrice Webb, Octavia Hill and Helen Bosanquet', in Englander, D. and O'Day, R. (eds) *Retrieved Riches: Social Investigation in Britain 1840–1914* (Aldershot, 1995)

Lewis, J. *Women in England 1870–1950* (Brighton, 1984)

Liberal Christian League *How the Destitute Live* (1912)

Lindsay, D. E. *Report upon the Study of the Diet of the Labouring Classes in the City of Glasgow, 1911–12* (Glasgow, 1913)

Lindsey, C. A. and Lindsey C. L. 'Booth, Rowntree and Llewelyn-Smith: a Reassessment of Interwar Poverty', *Economic History Review* (1993)

Liverpool University *The Cost of Living of Representative Working-Class Families* (University Press, Liverpool, 1941)

Llewelyn-Smith, H. *et al. The New Survey of London Life and Labour*: Vol. VI *Survey of Social Conditions (2) Western Area* (1935)

Llewelyn-Smith, H. *et al. The New Survey of London Life and Labour*: Vol. III *Survey of Social Conditions (1) Eastern Area* (1932)

Loudon, I. *Death in Childbirth* (Oxford, 1992)

Lowe, R. *Adjusting to Democracy: the Role of the Ministry of Labour in British Politics 1916–39* (Oxford, 1986)

Lowe, R. *The Welfare State in Britain since 1945* (1993)

Mackenzie, W. A. 'Changes in the Standard of Living in the United Kingdom, 1860–1914', *Economica*, No. 3 (1921)

McKeown, T. *The Modern Rise of Population* (1976)

McKibbin, R. 'The Social Psychology of Unemployment in Interwar Britain', in Waller, P. J. (ed.) *Politics and Social Change in Modern Britain* (Oxford, 1987)

Macnicol, J. 'The Evacuation of School Children', in Smith, H. L. (ed.) *War and Social Change* (Manchester, 1986)

Mann, P. H. 'Life in an Agricultural Village in England', *Sociological Papers* (1904)

Marr, T. R. *Housing Conditions in Manchester and Salford* (1904)

Marsh, C. 'Unemployment in Britain', in Gallie, D. (ed.) *Employment in Britain* (Oxford, 1988)

Mass Observation *Evacuation* (University of Sussex, 1987)

Mayhew, H. *London Labour and London Poor*, 3 vols (London, 1851–2) and 4 vols (London, 1861–2)

Mearns, A. 'The Bitter Cry of Outcast London', in Keating, P. (ed.) *Into Unknown England* (1976)

M'Gongile, G. C. M. and Kirby, J. *Poverty and Public Health* (1936)

Middlemass, K. *Politics in Industrial Society* (1979)

Miller, D. S. 'Nutritional Surveys', in Oddy, D. J. and Miller, D. S. (eds) *The Making of the Modern British Diet* (1976)

Ministry of Food, *The Urban Working-Class Household Diet 1940–49* (1951)

Ministry of Health, *Final Report of the Departmental Committee on Maternal Mortality and Morbidity* (1932)

Ministry of Labour Gazette, 'Enquiry into Working Class Family Budgets' (October 1937)

Minority Report of the Poor Law Commission, Part I, Summary and Conclusions (1909)

Morgan, K. O. *The People's Peace* (Oxford, 1990)

Munro Kerr, J. M. *Maternal Mortality and Morbidity: a Study of their Problems* (Edinburgh, 1933)

National Research Council, *Recommended Dietary Allowances* (1980)

Neild, W. 'Comparative Statement of the Income and Expenditure of Certain Families of the Working-Classes in Manchester and Dukfield, in the Years 1836 and 1841', *Journal of the Statistical Society*, IV (1841)

Newman, G. *Infant Mortality: a Social Problem* (1906)

Nicholson, J. L. 'Employment and National Income during the War', *Bulletin of the Oxford Institute of Statistics*, 7, 4 (1945)

O'Day, A. *The Edwardian Age* (1979)

Oddy, D. J. 'Working-Class Diets in Late Nineteenth-Century Britain', *Economic History Review* (1970)

Oddy, D. J. and Miller, D. S. (eds) *The Making of the Modern British Diet* (1976)

Owen, A. D. K. *A Survey of the Standard of Living in Sheffield* (Sheffield, 1933)

Pamuk, E. R. 'Social Class Inequality in Mortality from 1921–1971 in England and Wales', *Population Studies* (1985)

Parker, H. M. D. *Manpower* (HMSO, 1957)

Paton, D. N. and Findlay, L. *Poverty, Nutrition and Growth*. Medical Research Council Special Report, No. 101 (1926)

Paton, N., Dunlop, J. C. and Inglis, E. *On the Dietaries of the Labouring Classes of the City of Edinburgh* (Edinburgh, 1901)

Pember Reeves, M. *Round About a Pound a Week* (Virago, 1979)

Piachaud, D. 'Poverty in Britain 1899 to 1983', *Journal of Social Policy*, 17 (1988)

Pilgrim Trust *Men without Work* (Cambridge, 1938)

Pollard, S. 'Real Earnings in Sheffield, 1851–1914', *Yorkshire Bulletin of Economic and Social Research*, 9 (1957)

Pollard, S. 'Wages and Earnings in the Sheffield Trades, 1851–1914', *Yorkshire Bulletin of Economic and Social Research*, 6 (1954)

Potsan, M. M. *British War Production* (HMSO, 1952)

Prais, S. J. and Houthakker, H. S. *The Analysis of Family Budget* (Cambridge, 1971)

Rathbone, E. *How the Casual Labourer Lives* Report of the Liverpool Joint Research Committee on Domestic Conditions and Expenditure of the Families of Certain Liverpool Labourers (Liverpool, 1909)

Rein, M. 'Problems in the Definition and Measurement of Poverty', in Townsend, P. (ed.) *The Concept of Poverty* (Essex, 1970)

Roberts, E. *Women's Work, 1840–1940* (Cambridge, 1995)

Roberts, E. 'Working-Class Standards of Living in Barrow and Lancaster, 1890–1914', *Economic History Review* (1977)

Roberts, E. 'Working-Class Standards of Living in Three Lancashire Towns, 1890–1914', *International Review of Social History* (1982)

Roberts, R. *The Classic Slum* (Manchester, 1971)

Robertson, D. J. *The Economics of Wages and the Distribution of Income* (1961)

Robertson, D. J. *Factory Wage Structures and National Agreements* (Cambridge, 1960)

Rottier, G. 'The Evolution of Wage Differentials: a Study of British Data', in Dunlop, J. T. (ed.) *The Theory of Wage Determination* (1966)

Routh, G. *Occupation and Pay in Great Britain, 1906–79* (1980)

Rowbotham, S. *Hidden from History* (1973)

Rowntree, B. S. *The Human Needs of Labour* (revised 1937)

Rowntree, B. S. *Poverty and Progress* (1941)

Rowntree, B. S. *Poverty: a Study in Town Life*, 4th edn (1902)

Rowntree, B. S. *The Responsibility of Women Workers for Dependants* (Oxford, 1921)

Rowntree, B. S. and Kendall, M. *How the Labourer Lives: a Study of the Rural Labour Problem* (1913)

Rowntree, B. S. and Lasker, B. *Unemployment: a Social Study* (1911)

Rowntree, B. S. and Lavers, G. R. *Poverty and the Welfare State* (1951)

Royal Commission on the Distribution of Income and Wealth, Report No. 1 (Diamond Report) (1975) Cmd 6171

Schulz, T. 'The Cost of Inexpensive Nutrition before and after the War', *Bulletin of the Oxford Institute of Statistics* (1952)

Schulz, T. 'Family Expenditure in 1949' (Part I and Part II), *Bulletin of the Oxford Institute of Statistics* (1951)

Schulz, T. '"Human Needs" Cost of Living for a Single Person', *Bulletin of the Oxford Institute of Statistics*, 5, 9 (1943)

Schulz, T. '"Human Needs" Cost of Living for a Single Person', *Bulletin of the Oxford Institute of Statistics*, 12, 6 (1950)

Schulz, T. 'Human Needs Diets from 1936 to 1949', *Bulletin of the Oxford Institute of Statistics*, 11 (1949)

Schultz, T. 'Income, Family Structure and Food Expenditure before and after the War', *Bulletin of the Oxford Institute of Statistics*, 24 (1962)

Schultz, T. 'The Means of Subsistence', *Bulletin of the Oxford Institute of Statistics* (1955)

Schulz, T. 'Working-class Food Consumption', *Bulletin of the Oxford Institute of Statistics*, 14, 2 (1952)

Searle, G. R. 'Critics of Edwardian Society: the Case of the Radical Right', in O'Day, Alan (ed.) *The Edwardian Age* (1979)

Seers, D. 'The Cost of Living, 1938–48', *Bulletin of the Oxford Institute of Statistics*, 11, 4 (1949)

Seers, D. 'The Increase in Working Class Cost of Living since before the War', *Bulletin of the Oxford Institute of Statistics*, 10, 4 (1948)

Seers, Dudley, *The Levelling of Incomes since 1938* (Oxford University Institute of Statistics, n/d)

Sells, D. *British Wage Boards* (Brookings Institution, 1939)

Sen, A. 'Issues in the Measurement of Poverty', *Scandinavian Journal of Economics*, 81 (1979)

Sen, A. *Poverty and Famines* (1981)

Sheldon, J. H. *The Social Medicine of Old Age* (Nuffield Foundation, 1949)

Showler, B. and Sinfield, A. (eds) *The Workless State: Studies in Unemployment* (Oxford, 1981)

Singer, H. W. 'Unemployment and Health', Pilgrim Trust Unemployment interim paper No. 4, Cambridge (Pilgrim Trust, 1937)

Skidelsky, R. *Politicians and the Slump* (1969)

Smith, C. *Britain's Food Supplies in Peace and War* (1940)

Smith, H. L. (ed.) *War and Social Change* (Manchester, 1986)

Smith, R. *Unemployment and Health* (Oxford, 1987)

Snowden, P. *The Living Wage* (1912)

Spring Rice, M. *Working Class Wives* (Penguin, 1939 and Virago, 1981)

Stern, J. 'The Relationship between Unemployment, Morbidity and Mortality in Britain', *Population Studies*, 37 (1983)

Summerfield, P. *Women Workers and the Second World War* (Manchester, 1984)

Thane, P. 'The Family Lives of Old People', in Johnson, P. and Thane, P. (eds) *Old Age from Antiquity to Post Modernity* (1998)

Thane, P. *The Foundation of the Welfare State*, 2nd edn (2000)

Thane, P. *Old Age in English History* (Oxford, 2000).

Thomas, M. 'Unemployment in Interwar Britain', in Eichengreen, B. and Hatton, T. J. (eds) *Interwar Unemployment in International Perspective* (Dordrecht, 1988)

Thomas, M. 'Wage Behaviour in Inter-War Britain: a Sceptical Enquiry', in Grantham, G. and Mackinnon, M. (eds) *Labour Market Evolution* (1997)

Tilly, L. and Scott, J. *Women, Work and the Family* (1978)

Titmuss, R. *Birth, Poverty and Wealth* (1943)

Titmuss, R. *Poverty and Population* (1938)

Titmuss, R. *Problems of Social Policy* (HMSO, 1950)

Tomlinson, J. *Employment Policy, The Crucial Years 1939–55* (Oxford, 1987)

Tout, H. *The Standard of Living in Bristol* (1937)

Townsend, P. (ed.) *The Concept of Poverty* (Essex, 1970)

Townsend, P. *Poverty in the United Kingdom* (1979)

Townsend, P. and Wedderburn, D. *The Aged and the Welfare State* (1970)

Treble, J. *Urban Poverty in Britain* (1979)

Truswell, A. S. 'Minimal Estimates of Needs and Recommended Intakes of Nutrients', in Yudkin, J. (ed.) *The Diet of Man: Needs and Wants* (1978)

Tunstall, J. *Old and Alone: a Sociological Study of Old People* (1966)

Urban Working Class Household Diet, 1940–49 (HMSO, 1951)

Veit-Wilson, J. 'Condemned to Deprivation? Beveridge's Responsibility for the Invisibility of Poverty?', in Hills, J., Ditch, J. and Glennerster, H. *Beveridge and Social Security* (Oxford, 1994)

Veit-Wilson, J. 'Muddle or Mendacity? The Beveridge Committee and the Poverty Line', *Journal of Social Policy*, 21, 3 (1992)

Veit-Wilson, J. 'Paradigms of Poverty: a Rehabilitation of B. S. Rowntree', in Englander, D. and O'Day, R. (eds) *Retrieved Riches: Social Investigation in Britain 1840–1914* (Aldershot, 1995)

Vincent, D. *Poor Citizens* (1991)

Wagstaff, A. 'Time Series Analysis of the Relationship between Unemployment and Mortality: a Survey of Econometric Critiques and Replications of Brenner's Studies', *Social Science Medicine*, 21, 9 (1985)

Warr, P. *Work, Unemployment and Mental Health* (Oxford, 1987)

Webster, C. 'Healthy or Hungry Thirties?', *History Workshop Journal* (1982)

Whiteside, N. 'Counting the Cost: Sickness and Disability among Working People in an Era of Industrial Recession, 1920–39', *Economic History Review* (1987)

Wilkinson, E. *The Town That Was Murdered* (1939)

Wilkinson, R. 'Class Mortality Differentials, Income Distribution and Trends in Poverty 1921–81', *Journal of Social Policy*, 18, 3 (1988)

Williams, K. *From Pauperism to Poverty* (1981)

Williamson, J. G. *Did British Capitalism Breed Inequality?* (1985)

Williamson, J. G. 'The Structure of Pay in Britain, 1710–1911', *Research in Economic History*, 7 (1982)

Winter, J. M. 'Aspects of the Impact of the First World War on Infant Mortality in Britain', *Journal of European Economic History* (1982)

Winter, J. M. 'The Decline of Mortality in Britain, 1870–1950', in Barker, T. and Drake, M. (eds) *Population and Society in Britain 1850–1980* (1982)

Winter, J. M. *The Great War and the British People* (1985)

Winter, J. M. 'The Impact of the First World War on Civilian Health in Britain', *Economic History Review*, 20 (1977)

Winter, J. M. 'Infant Mortality, Maternal Mortality and Public Health in Britain in the 1930s', *Journal of European Economic History*, 8

Winter, J. M. 'Public Health and the Political Economy of War, 1914–18', *History Workshop*, 26 (1988)

Wood, G. H. 'Real Wages and the Standard of Comfort since 1850', *Journal of the Royal Statistical Society* (1909)

Woolf, B. 'Studies on Infant Mortality, Part II. Social Aetiology of Stillbirths and Infant Deaths in County Boroughs of England and Wales', *British Journal of Social Medicine* (1974)

World Health Organisation *Energy and Protein Requirements*. Report of the Joint Expert Committee of the Food and Agriculture Organisation of the United Nations and the World Health Organisation *ad hoc* committee, Technical Report series, No. 522 (1973)

Wright, J. F. 'Real Wage Resistance: Eighty Years of the British Cost of Living', *Oxford Economic Papers*, 36 (November 1984) Supplement

Zweiniger-Bargielowska, Ina *Austerity in Britain* (Oxford, 2000)

INDEX